Dec 1999

"Happy ... "

Love

xxx

CW01635087

Blackthorn Press

Published by Blackthorn Press
Blackthorn Press, Blackthorn House,
Middleton Rd, Pickering,
York YO18 8AL, UK.

First Published 1999

Copyright [] Blackthorn Press 1999.

ISBN 0 9535072 1 1

The publishers would like to record their thanks to J M Dent & Co and to Gospatric Home for permission to republish this book. Our thanks also to the Trustees of the Beck Isle Museum in Pickering for allowing us use of the photographs in the final chapter.

EVOLUTION OF AN ENGLISH TOWN: PICKERING.

by

Gordon Home & John Rushton

This volume is one of a limited edition of 500.

It is Number (Two hundred and fifty-eight -258-) of 500.

John Rushton

John Rushton

B P

Blackthorn Press

THE EVOLUTION
OF AN
ENGLISH TOWN

NOTE

The cover of this volume bears a representation of the arms of the Duchy of Lancaster, Pickering belonging to that royal property. The shield is in proper colours, and on each side of the arms a halbert is represented. It is drawn from one of those formerly carried by two freeholders of Duchy land when the proclamation was read at the opening of markets.

All rights reserved

Hall Garth, Pickering.

The EVOLUTION of an ENGLISH TOWN

Being the story of the ancient town of PICKERING in Yorkshire from Prehistoric times up to the year of our Lord Nineteen Hundred & 5

BY

GORDON HOME

LONDON: J. M. DENT & CO:
Aldine House W.C. 1905
NEW YORK: E. P. DUTTON & CO:

To

ALL THOSE WHO HAVE
GIVEN THEIR GENEROUS HELP
IN THE COMPILATION
OF THIS BOOK

Preface

When I learned from Alan Avery, the proprietor of the Blackthorn Press, that he was proposing to reprint my late father's book, "The Evolution of an English Town", I was more than delighted. My father, who was born in 1878, wrote the story of the ancient town of Pickering when he was only 26 years of age and I understand that it is considered to be a gem of its type. It was one of the earliest of the fifty books of a topographical or historical nature that he wrote during his long life and it was the first of a series of books on Yorkshire, York and York Minster which made him, at the time, probably the most prolific author of books on the County then living.

My father died thirty years ago this year at the good age of 91 and he published his last book, "Cyprus, Then and Now" when he was 80. His writings thus spanned 60 years.

His great love of Yorkshire was passed on to my twin sister and I when early in the war, having leased our home in West Surrey to the army, we moved into rooms first at the Lettered Board, later at Low Kingthorpe Farm, then a charming farmhouse in the village of Middleton before moving to Whitby. During the school holidays my father and mother introduced us to the North Riding of Yorkshire and a very happy time it was for us as we picnicked in Newtondale and explored all the remarkable countryside with many a history lesson from my father to increase our knowledge and understanding of the topography and history of this wonderful part of Yorkshire.

In his original preface my father paid tribute to the help that he received from Dr John L. Kirk, the founder of the Kirk Museum in York now known as the Castle Museum. My father and Dr Kirk became close friends and indeed Dr and Mrs Kirk travelled the early motor roads of France together in 1908 with my father and a year or two later he wrote his first book on the motor routes of France. Mrs Kirk was always urging her husband to slow down with frequent cries of "Ralentir" which my father recalled tried the patience of the two males in the party not a little!

If we do not understand history and appreciate all that surrounds us we will never really understand life and I sincerely hope that this timeless work will give enormous pleasure, not only to those who live in Pickering, but to those who have lived there in the past or have past associations with it.

Gospatric Home

PREFACE

THE original suggestion that I should undertake this task came from the Vicar of Pickering, and it is due to his co-operation and to the great help received from Dr John L. Kirk that this history has attained its present form. But beyond this I have had most valuable assistance from so many people in Pickering and the villages round about, that to mention them all would almost entail reprinting the local directory. I would therefore ask all those people who so kindly put themselves to great trouble and who gave up much time in order to help me, to consider that they have contributed very materially towards the compilation of this record.

Beyond those who live in the neighbourhood of Pickering, I am particularly indebted to Mr Richard Blakeborough for his kind help and the use of his invaluable collection of Yorkshire folklore. Mr Blakeborough was keen on collecting the old stories of hobs, wraithes and witches just long enough ago to be able to tap the memories of many old people who are no longer with us, and thus his collection is now of great value. Nearly all the folklore stories I am able to give, are those saved from oblivion in this way.

I have also had much help from Mr J. Romilly

Allen and from Mr T. M. Fallow of Coatham, who very generously gave his aid in deciphering some of the older records of Pickering.

To Professor Percy F. Kendall who so kindly gave me permission to reproduce his map showing the Vale of Pickering during the Glacial Epoch, as well as other valuable help, I am also greatly indebted; and I have to thank Professor W. Boyd Dawkins for his kindness in reading some of the proofs, and for giving valuable suggestions.

GORDON HOME.

EPSOM, *May* 1905.

CONTENTS

CHAPTER XIII

CHAPTER XIV

THE PURPOSE OF THE FOOTNOTES

Having always considered footnotes an objectionable feature, I have resorted to them solely for reference purposes. Therefore, the reader who does not wish to look up my authorities need not take the slightest notice of the references to the footnotes, which in no case contain additional facts, but merely indications of the sources of information.

LIST OF ILLUSTRATIONS

INTRODUCTION

EVERY preface in olden time was wont to begin with the address "Lectori Benevolo"—the indulgence of the reader being thereby invoked and, it was hoped, assured. In that the writer of this at least would have his share, even though neither subject, nor author, that he introduces, may stand in need of such a shield.

Local histories are yearly becoming more numerous. In few places is there more justification for one than here.

I. The beauty of the scenery is not well known. This book should do something to vindicate its character. There is no need on this point to go back to the time of George III.'s conversation at the levée with Mrs Pickering's grandfather. "I suppose you are going back to Yorkshire, Mr Stanhope? A very ugly country, Yorkshire." This was too much for my grandfather—(the story is told in her own words)—"We always consider Yorkshire a very picturesque country." "What, what, what," said the King, "a coalpit a picturesque object! what, what, what, Yorkshire coalpits picturesque! Yorkshire a picturesque country!"[1] Only within the last few months one of us had a letter refusing to consider a vacant post: the reason given being that this was a colliery district. There is no pit to be found for miles. Many can, and do, walk, cycle, or motor through the Vale. Others, who are unable to come and see for themselves, will, with the help of Mr Home, be in a better position to appreciate at its true worth the charm of the haughs and the changing views of the distant Wolds, and of the russet brown or purple expanse of the upland moors.

II. The stranger on a visit, no less the historian or antiquary, has till now often been puzzled for a clue, and ignorant where to turn for authentic data, would he attempt to weave for himself a connected idea of the incidents of the past and their bearing on the present. There has been no lack of material buried in ancient records, or preserved in the common oral traditions of the folk: but hitherto no coherent account that has been published. Speaking for ourselves, we are glad the task of dealing with the "raffled hank" of timeworn customs and obscure traditions as well as the more easily ascertained facts of history is falling to the author's practised pen. For the future, at any rate, there should be less difficulty in understanding the manner of life and method of rule with which past and present generations belonging to the Town of Pickering have been content to dwell.

[1] "Memoirs of Anna M. W. Pickering."

III. "Foreigners"[1] are sometimes at a loss to understand the peculiar spirit of those who in York, for instance, are known as "Moor-enders." This spirit shows itself in different ways; but perhaps in nothing so much as the intense attachment of the townsmen to their birthplace. This local patriotism is no whit behind that to be found in Spain—"seldom indeed a Spaniard says he is a Spaniard, but speaks of himself as being from Seville, Cadiz, or some forgotten town in La Mancha, of which he speaks with pride, referring to it as "mi tierra."[2] Our readers will learn there is some reason for this attachment; and may, like some of us, who tho' born elsewhere claim adoption as citizens, fall under the witchery of its spell.

May the venture to compass these ends succeed, to use an old saying, "ez sartin ez t' thorn-bush."[3]

E. W. D.

THE VICARAGE, PICKERING.
25th September 1904.

[1] C. R. L. Fletcher in his "History of England" tells us that townsmen of the thirteenth century were wont to brand their brethren in all the neighbouring towns as "foreigners." Those we call foreigners, they called aliens. The expression itself was made use of not long ago at a meeting of the Urban Council.

[2] R. B. Cunninghame Graham, "Hernando de Soto."

[3] It used to be the custom for the parson to collect the tithe by placing a branch of thorn in every tenth stook; he choosing the stooks and sending his cart along for them. R. Blakeborough, "Yorkshire Humour and Customs."

THE EVOLUTION
OF AN
ENGLISH TOWN

CHAPTER I

Concerning those which follow

"Brother," quod he, "where is now youre dwellyng,
Another day if that I sholde you seche?"
This yeman hym answerde, in softe speche:
"Brother," quod he, "fer in the north contree,
Where as I hope som tyme I shal thee see."

The Friar's Tale. *Chaucer.*

IN the North Riding of Yorkshire, there is a town of such antiquity that its beginnings are lost far away in the mists of those times of which no written records exist. What this town was originally called, it is impossible to say, but since the days of William the Norman (a pleasanter sounding name than "the Conqueror,") it has been consistently known as Pickering, although there has always been a tendency to spell the name with y's and to abandon the c, thus producing the curious-looking result of *Pykeryng*; its sound, however was the same.

In his Chronicles, John Stow states on the authority of "divers writers" that Pickering was built in the year 270 B.C., but I am inclined to think that the earliest settlements on the site or in the neighbourhood of the present town must have been originated at an infinitely earlier period.

But despite its undisputed antiquity there are many

even in Yorkshire who have never heard of the town, and in the south of England it is difficult to find anyone who is aware that such a place exists. At Rennes during the great military trial there was a Frenchman who asked "Who is Dreyfus?" and we were surprised at such ignorance of a name that had been on the lips of all France for years, but yet we discover ourselves to be astonishingly lacking in the knowledge of our own little island and find ourselves asking "why should anyone trouble to write a book about a town of which so few have even heard?" But it is often in the out-of-the-way places that historical treasures are preserved, and it is mainly for this reason and the fact that the successive periods of growth are so well demonstrated there, that the ancient town of Pickering has been selected to illustrate the evolution of an English town.

I have endeavoured to produce a complete series of pictures commencing with the Ice Age and finishing at the dawn of the twentieth century. In the earlier chapters only a rough outline is possible, but as we come down the centuries and the records become more numerous and varied, fuller details can be added to the pictures of each age, and we may witness how much or how little the great series of dynastic, constitutional, religious and social changes effected a district that is typical of many others in the remoter parts of England.

Built on sloping ground that rises gently from the rich, level pastures of the Vale of Pickering, the town has a picturesque and pleasant site. At the top of the market-place where the ground becomes much

Pickering from the North-West.

steeper stands the church, its grey bulk dominating every view. From all over the Vale one can see the tall spire, and from due east or west it has a surprising way of peeping over the hill tops. It has even been suggested that the tower and spire have been a landmark for a very long time, owing to the fact that where the hills and formation of the ground do not obstruct the view, or make road-making difficult, the roads make straight for the spire.

With few exceptions the walls of the houses are of the same weather-beaten limestone as the church and the castle, but seen from above the whole town is transformed into a blaze of red, the curved tiles of the locality retaining their brilliant hue for an indefinite period. Only a very few thatched roofs remain to-day, but the older folks remember when most of the houses were covered in that picturesque fashion.

Pickering has thus lost its original uniform greyness, relieved here and there by whitewash, and presents strong contrasts of colour against the green meadows and the masses of trees that crown the hill where the castle stands. The ruins, now battered and ivy-mantled, are dignified and picturesque and still sufficiently complete to convey a clear impression of the former character of the fortress, three of the towers at angles of the outer walls having still an imposing aspect. The grassy mounds and shattered walls of the interior would, however, be scarcely recognisable to the shade of Richard II. if he were ever to visit the scene of his imprisonment.

Since the time of Henry VIII. when Leland described the castle, whole towers and all the interior buildings except the chapel have disappeared. The chief disasters probably happened before the Civil War, although we are told, by one or two eighteenth century writers, as an instance of the destruction that was wrought, that after the Parliamentary forces had occupied the place and "breached the walls," great quantities of papers and parchments were scattered about Castle-gate, the children being attracted to pick them up, many of them bearing gilt letters. During the century which has just closed, more damage was done to the buildings and in a short time all the wooden floors in the towers completely disappeared.

Stories are told of the Parliamentary troops being quartered in Pickering church, and, if this were true, we have every reason to bless the coats of whitewash which probably hid the wall-paintings from their view. The series of fifteenth century pictures that now cover both walls of the nave would have proved so very distasteful to the puritan soldiery that it is impossible to believe that they could have tolerated their existence, especially when we find it recorded that the font was smashed and the large prayer-book torn to pieces at that time.

Pickering church has a fascination for the antiquary, and does not fail to impress even the most casual person who wanders into the churchyard and enters the spacious porch. The solemn massiveness of the Norman nave, the unusual effect of the coloured paintings above the arches, and the carved stone effigies of

Rosamund Tower, Pickering Castle.

knights whose names are almost forgotten, carry one away from the familiar impressions of a present-day Yorkshire town, and almost suggest that one is living in mediæval times. One can wander, too, on the moors a few miles to the north and see heather stretching away to the most distant horizon and feel that there, also, are scenes which have been identically the same for many centuries. The men of the Neolithic and Bronze Ages may have swept their eyes over landscapes so similar that they would find the moorlands quite as they knew them, although they would miss the dense forests of the valleys and the lower levels.

The cottages in the villages are, many of them, of great age, and most of them have been the silent witnesses of innumerable superstitious rites and customs. When one thoroughly realises the degrading character of the beliefs that so powerfully swayed the lives of the villagers and moorland-folk of this district, as late as the first twenty years of the nineteenth century, one can only rejoice that influences arose sufficiently powerful to destroy them. Along with the revolting practises, however, it is extremely unfortunate to have to record the disappearance of many picturesque, and in themselves, entirely harmless customs. The roots of the great mass of superstitions have their beginnings so far away from the present time, that to embrace them all necessitates an exploration of all the centuries that lie between us and the pre-historic ages, and in the pages that follow, some of these connections with the past may be discovered.

CHAPTER II

The Forest and Vale of Pickering in Palæolithic and Pre-Glacial Times.

The Palæolithic or Old Stone Age preceded and succeeded the Great Glacial Epochs in the Glacialid.

IN that distant period of the history of the human race when man was still so primitive in his habits that traces of his handiwork are exceedingly difficult to discover, the forest and Vale of Pickering seem to have been without human inhabitants. Remains of this Old Stone Age have been found in many parts of England, but they are all south of a line drawn from Lincoln to Derbyshire and North Wales. In the caves at Cresswell Craggs in Derbyshire notable Palæolithic discoveries were made, but for some reason these savage hordes seem to have come no further north than that spot. We know, however, that many animals belonging to the pre-glacial period struggled for their existence in the neighbourhood of Pickering.

It was during the summer of 1821 that the famous cave at Kirkdale was discovered, and the bones of twenty-two different species of animals were brought to light. Careful examination showed that the cave had for a long time been the haunt of hyænas of the Pleistocene Period, a geological division of time, which embraces in its latter part the age of Palæolithic man. The spotted hyæna that is now to be found only in

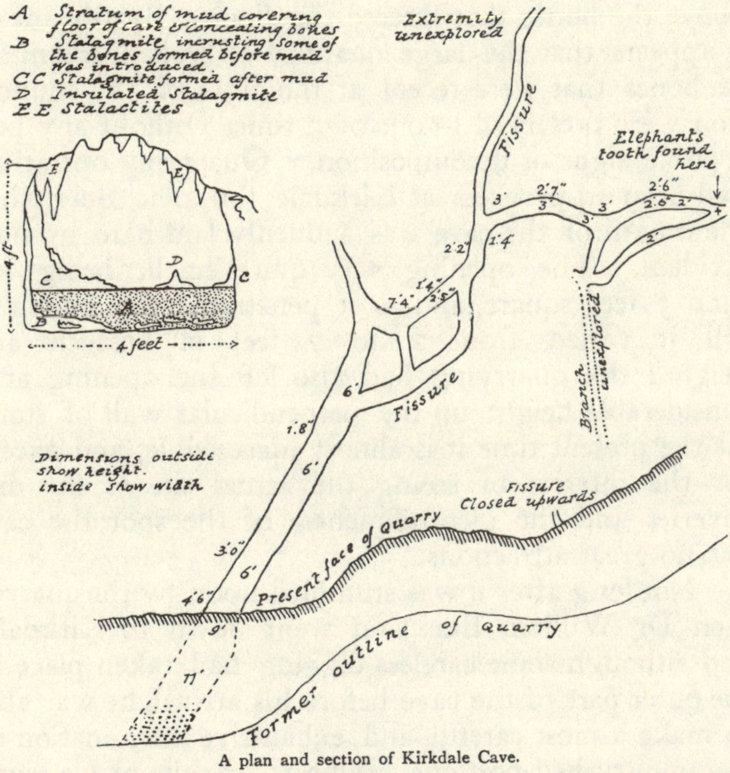

A plan and section of Kirkdale Cave.

Africa, south of the Sahara,[1] was then inhabiting the forests of Yorkshire and preying on animals now either extinct or only living in tropical climates. The waters of Lake Pickering seem to have risen to a sufficiently

[1] Dawkins, W. Boyd. "Early man in Britain," p. 103.

high level at one period to drive out the occupants of the cave and to have remained static for long enough to allow the accumulation of about a foot of alluvium above the bones that littered the floor. By this means it appears that the large quantity of broken fragments of bones that were recent at the time of the inundation were preserved to our own times without any perceptible signs of decomposition. Quarrying operations had been in progress at Kirkdale for some time when the mouth of the cave was suddenly laid bare by pure accident. The opening was quite small, being less than 5 feet square, and as it penetrated the limestone hill it varied from 2 to 7 feet in breadth and height; the quarrying had also left the opening at a considerable height up the perpendicular wall of stone. At the present time it is almost inaccessible, and except for the interest of seeing the actual site of the discoveries and the picturesqueness of the spot the cave has no great attractions.

Not long after it was stumbled upon by the quarrymen Dr William Buckland went down to Kirkdale, and although some careless digging had taken place in the outer part of the cave before his arrival, he was able to make a most careful and exhaustive examination of the undisturbed portions, giving the results of his work in a paper read before the Royal Society in 1822.[1] Besides the remains of many hyænas there were teeth or bones of such large animals as the elephant,

[1] Buckland, The Rev. Wm. "Account of an assemblage of fossil teeth and bones . . . at Kirkdale."

rhinoceros, hippopotamus, horse, tiger, bear, urus (Bos primi-genius) an unknown animal of the size of a wolf, and three species of deer. The smaller animals included the rabbit, water-rat, mouse, raven, pigeon, lark and a small type of duck. Everything was broken into small pieces so that no single skull was found entire and it was, of course, impossible to obtain anything like a complete skeleton. From the fact that the bones of the hyænas themselves had suffered the same treatment as the rest we may infer that these ferocious lovers of putrid flesh were in the habit of devouring those of their own species that died a natural death, or that possibly under pressure of hunger were inclined to kill and eat the weak or diseased members of the pack. From other evidences in the cave it is plain that its occupants were extremely fond of bones after the fashion of the South African hyæna.

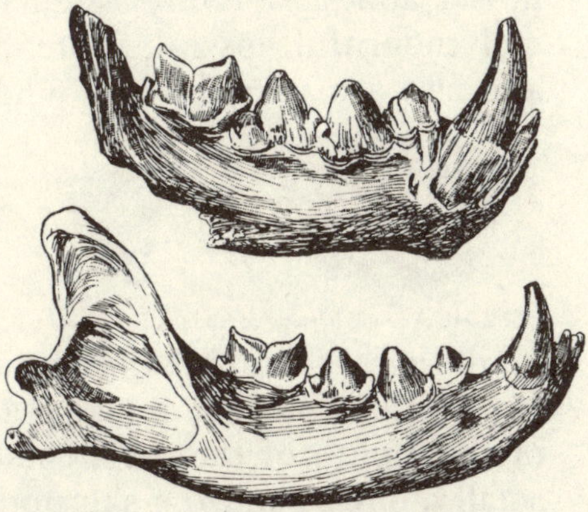

Jaws of Kirkdale (above) and Modern Hyæna (below). The Kirkdale Hyænas were evidently much more powerful than the modern ones.

Although the existing species have jaws of huge strength and these prehistoric hyænas were probably stronger still, it is quite improbable that they ever attacked such large animals as elephants; and the fact that the teeth found in the cave were of very young specimens seems to suggest that the hyænas now and then found the carcase of a young elephant that had died, and dragged it piecemeal to their cave. The same would possibly apply to some of the other large animals, for hyænas, unless in great extremes of hunger never attack a living animal. They have a loud and mournful howl, beginning low and ending high, and also a maniacal laugh when excited.

Teeth of young Elephants found at Kirkdale.

It might be suggested that the bones had accumulated in the den through dead bodies of animals being floated in during the inundation by the waters of the lake, but in that case the remains, owing to the narrowness of the mouth of the cave, could only have belonged to small animals, and the skeletons would have been more or less complete, and there are also evidences on many of the bones of their having been broken by teeth precisely similar to those of the hyæna.

We see therefore that in this remote age Britain enjoyed a climate which encouraged the existence of animals now to be found only in tropical regions, that herds of mammoths or straight-tusked elephants smashed their way through primæval forests and that the hippopotamus and the woolly or small-nosed rhinoceros frequented the moist country at the margin of the lake. Packs of wolves howled at night and terrorised their prey, and in winter other animals from northern parts would come as far south as Yorkshire.

In fact it seems that the northern and southern groups of animals in Pleistocene times appeared in this part of England at different seasons of the year and the hyænas of Kirkdale would, in the opinion of Professor Boyd Dawkins, prey upon the reindeer at one time of the year and the hippopotamus at another.

Following this period came a time of intense cold, but the conditions were not so severe as during the Great Glacial times.

Canine tooth or tusk of a Kirkdale bear (Ursus spelæus)

CHAPTER III

The Vale of Pickering in the Lesser Ice Age

LONG before even the earliest players took up their parts in the great Drama of Human Life which has been progressing for so long in this portion of England, great changes came about in the aspect of the stage. These transformations date from the period of Arctic cold, which caused ice of enormous thickness to form over the whole of north-western Europe.

Throughout this momentous age in the history of Yorkshire, as far as we can tell, the flaming sunsets that dyed the ice and snow with crimson were reflected in no human eyes. In those far-off times, when the sun was younger and his majesty more imposing than at the present day, we may imagine a herd of reindeer or a solitary bear standing upon some ice-covered height and staring wonderingly at the blood-red globe as it neared the horizon. The tremendous silence that brooded over the face of the land was seldom broken save by the roar of the torrents, the reverberating boom of splitting ice, or the whistling and shrieking of the wind.

The evidences in favour of this glacial period are too apparent to allow of any contradiction; but although geologists agree as to its existence, they do not find it easy to absolutely determine its date or its causes.

Croll's theory of the eccentricity of the Earth's orbit [1] as the chief factor in the great changes of the Earth's climate has now been to a great extent abandoned, and the approximate date of the Glacial Epoch of between 240,000 and 80,000 years ago is thus correspondingly discredited by many geologists. Professor Kendall inclines to the belief that not more than 25,000 years have elapsed since the departure of the ice from Yorkshire, the freshness of all the traces of glaciation being incompatible with a long period of post-glacial time.

The superficial alterations in the appearance of these parts of Yorkshire were brought about by the huge glaciers which, at that time, choked up most of the valleys and spread themselves over the watersheds of the land.

In the warmer seasons of the year, when the Arctic cold relaxed to some extent, fierce torrents would rush down every available depression, sweeping along great quantities of detritus and boulders sawn off and carried sometimes for great distances by the slow-moving glaciers. The grinding, tearing and cannonading of these streams cut out courses for themselves wherever they went. In some cases the stream would occupy an existing hollow or old water-course, deepening and widening it, but in many instances where the ice blocked a valley the water would form

[1] "Climate and Time." James Croll, 1889.

lakes along the edge of the glacier, and overflowing across a succession of hill shoulders, would cut deep notches on the rocky slopes.

Owing to the careful work of Mr C. E. Fox-Strangways and of Professor Percy F. Kendall, we are able to tell, almost down to details, what took place in the Vale of Pickering and on the adjacent hills during this period.

In the map reproduced here we can see the limits of the ice during the period of its greatest extension. The great ice-sheet of the North Sea had jammed itself along the Yorkshire coast, covering the lower hills with glaciers, thus preventing the natural drainage of the ice-free country inland. The Derwent carrying off the water from some of these hills found its outlet gradually blocked by the advancing lobe of a glacier, and the water having accumulated into a lake (named after Hackness in the map), overflowed along the edge of the ice into the broad alluvial plain now called the Vale of Pickering. Up to a considerable height, probably about 200 feet, the drainage of the Derwent and the other streams flowing into the Vale was imprisoned, and thus Pickering Lake was formed.

The boulder clay at the seaward end of the Vale seems to have been capped by ice of a thickness of nearly 100 feet which efficiently contained the waters of the lake until they overflowed through a depression among the hills to the south of Malton. If the waters escaped by any other outlet to the west near Gilling and Coxwold, it can scarcely have been more than a

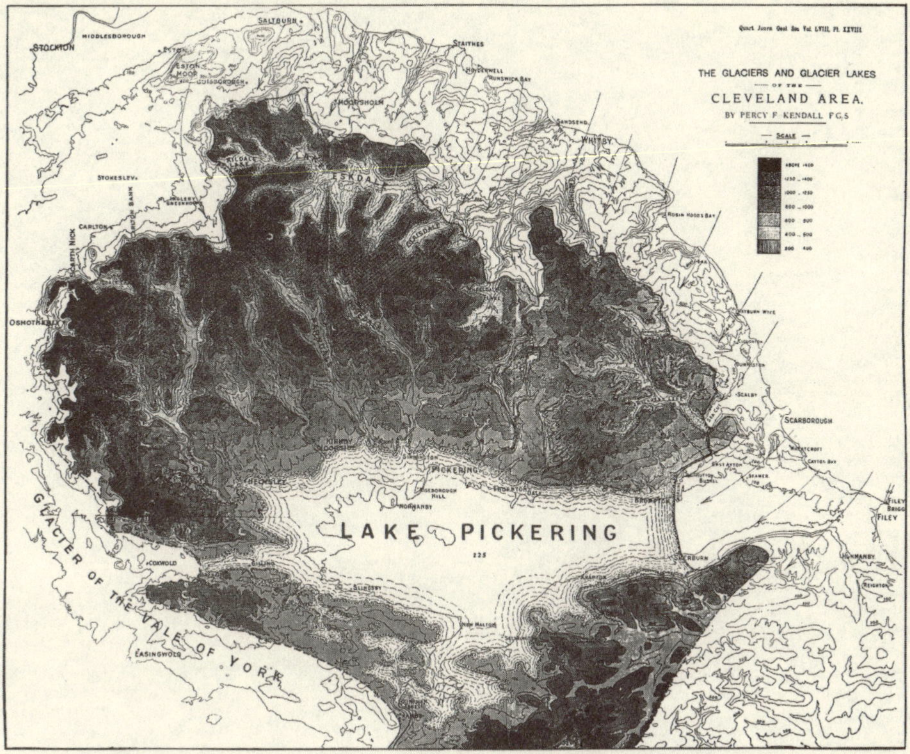

A Map of North-Eastern Yorkshire showing Lake Pickering during the maximum extension of the ice. The area covered by ice is left unshaded. The arrows show the direction of the glacier movements. (Reproduced from the *Quarterly Journal of the Geological Society*. by permission of Professor Percy F. Kendall.)

temporary affair compared to the overflow that produced the gorge at Kirkham Abbey, as the Gilling Gap was itself closed by the great glacier descending the Vale of York. The overflow of the lake by this route, south of Malton, must have worn a channel down to a lower level than 130 feet O.D. before the ice retreated from the seaward end of the Vale, otherwise the escape would have taken place over the low hills blocking the valley in that direction and the normal course of the drainage of the country would have been resumed. The southern overflow evidently dug its way through the hills fast enough to maintain that outlet, and at the present time the narrow gorge at Kirkham Abbey is only 50 feet above sea level, and the hills through which the Derwent passes at this point are from 200 to 225 feet high.

As the waters of the lake gradually drained away, the Vale was left in a marshy state until the rivers gradually formed channels for themselves. In recent times drainage canals have been cut and the streams embanked, so that there is little to remind one of the existence of the lake save for the hamlet still known as The Marishes. The name is quite obviously a corruption of marshes, for this form is still in use in these parts, but it is interesting to know that Milton spelt the word in the same way as the name of this village, and in Ezekiel xlvii. 11 we find: "But the miry places thereof, and the marishes thereof, shall not be healed." The ease with which a lake could again be formed in the Vale was demonstrated in October 1903 after the phenomenally wet summer and autumn of that year, by a flood that covered the fields for miles and in several places half submerged the hedges and washed away the corn stooks.

The evidence in favour of the existence of Lake Pickering is so ample that, according to Professor Kendall, it may be placed "among the well-established facts of glacial geology."[1]

We have thus an accredited explanation for the extraordinary behaviour of the river Derwent and its tributaries, including practically the whole of the drainage south of the Esk, which instead of taking the obviously simple and direct course to the sea, flow in the opposite direction to the slope of the rocks and the grain of the country. After passing through the ravine at Kirkham Abbey the stream eventually mingles with the Ouse, and thus finds its way to the Humber.

The splendid cañon to the north of Pickering, known as Newton Dale, with its precipitous sides rising to a height of 300 or even 400 feet, must have assumed its present proportions principally during the glacial period when it formed an overflow valley from a lake held up by ice in the neighbourhood of Fen Bogs and Eller Beck. This great gorge is tenanted at the present time by Pickering Beck, an exceedingly small stream, which now carries off all the surface drainage and must therefore be only remotely related to its great precursor that carved this enormous trench out of the limestone tableland. Compared to the torrential rushes of water carrying along

[1] *Quarterly Journal of the Geological Society*, vol. lviii. part 3, No. 231, p. 501.

A DIAGRAMMATIC VIEW OF NEWTON DALE DURING THE LESSER ICE AGE.

The overflow of the glacier dammed lakes at the head of the dale came down Newton Dale and poured into Lake Pickering.

huge quantities of gravel and boulders that must have flowed from the lake at the upper end, Newton Dale can almost be considered a dry and abandoned valley.

At Fen Bogs, where there is a great depth of peat, Professor Kendall has discovered that if it were cleared out, "the channel through the watershed would appear as a clean cut, 75 feet deep." The results of the gouging operations of this glacier stream are further in evidence where the valley enters the Vale of Pickering, for at that point a great delta was formed. This fan-shaped accumulation of bouldery gravel is marked in the geological survey maps as covering a space of about two square miles south of Pickering, but the deposit is probably much larger, for Dr Thornton Comber states that the gravel extends all the way to Riseborough and is found about 6 feet below the surface, everywhere digging has taken place in that direction. The delta is partly composed of rounded stones about 2 feet in diameter. These generally belong to the hard gritstone of the moors through which Newton Dale has been carved. Dr Comber also mentioned the discovery of a whinstone from the great Cleveland Dyke, composed of basaltic rock, that traverses the hills near Egton and Sleights Moor, two miles above the intake of Newton Dale at Fen Bogs.

The existence of this gravel as far towards the west as Riseborough, suggests that the delta is really of much greater magnitude than that indicated in the survey map. It has also been proved that Newton

Dale ceased its functions as a lake overflow, through the retreat of the ice-sheet above Eskdale long before the Glacial Period terminated, and this would suggest an explanation for the layer of Warp (an alluvial

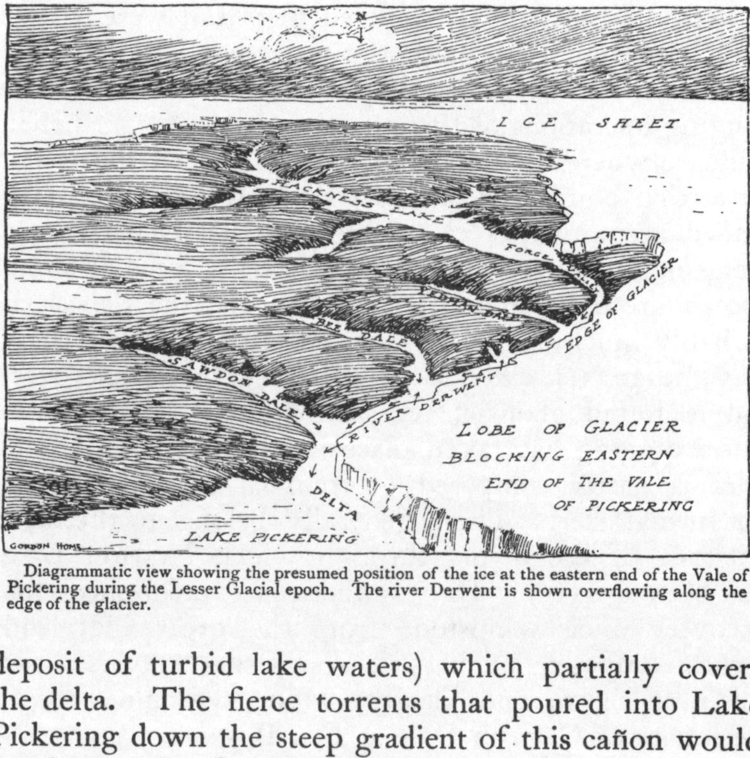

Diagrammatic view showing the presumed position of the ice at the eastern end of the Vale of Pickering during the Lesser Glacial epoch. The river Derwent is shown overflowing along the edge of the glacier.

deposit of turbid lake waters) which partially covers the delta. The fierce torrents that poured into Lake Pickering down the steep gradient of this cañon would require an exit of equal proportions, and it seems reasonable to suppose that the gorge at Kirkham Abbey was chiefly worn at the same time as Newton Dale.

Another delta was formed by the upper course of

the Derwent to which I have already alluded. In this instance, the water flowed along the edge of the ice and cut out a shelf on the hill slopes near Hutton Buscel, and the detritus was carried to the front of the glacier. This deposit terminates in a crescent-shape and now forms the slightly elevated ground upon which Wykeham Abbey stands. The Norse word Wyke or Vik means a creek or bay, and the fact that such a name was given to this spot would suggest that the Vale was more than marshy in Danish times, and perhaps it even contained enough water to float shallow draught boats. Flotmanby is another suggestive name occurring at the eastern corner of the lake about four miles from Filey. In modern Danish *flotman* means a waterman or ferryman, and as there is, and was then, no river near Flotmanby, there is ground for believing that the Danes who settled at this spot found it necessary to ferry across the corner of the lake. Before the Glacial Period, the Vale of Pickering was beyond doubt from 100-150 feet deeper at the seaward end than at the present time, and even as far up the Valley as Malton the rock floor beneath the deposit of Kimeridge clay is below the level of the sea.

CHAPTER IV

The Early Inhabitants of the Forest and Vale of Pickering

Almighty wisdom made the land
Subject to man's disturbing hand,
And left it all for him to fill
With marks of his ambitious will. . . .

Urgent and masterful ashore,
Man dreams and plans,
And more and more,
As ages slip away, Earth shows
How need by satisfaction grows,
And more and more its patient face
Mirrors the driving human race.

Edward Sandford Martin.

THE NEOLITHIC OR NEW STONE AGE
Succeeded the Old Stone Age and overlapped the Bronze Age.

THE BRONZE AGE
Succeeded the New Stone Age and overlapped the Early Iron Age.

THE EARLY IRON AGE
Succeeded the Bronze Age and continued in Britain until the Roman Invasion in B.C. 54.

(*All these periods overlapped.*)

THE Palæolithic men had reached England when it was part of the continent of Europe, but after the lesser Glacial Period had driven the hairy savages southwards a slow earth movement produced what is now the English Channel and Britain was isolated. Gradually the cold relaxed and vegetation once more became luxuriant, great forests appeared and England was again joined to the continent. Possibly the more genial climate which began to prevail in this country and the northward movement of the reindeer brought the first Neolithic men into England, and it has been suggested that some of these earlier tribes whose implements have been discovered in White Park Bay, County Antrim and the MacArthur Cave, near Oban, form a link between the Palæolithic and Neolithic people.

The culture of the New Stone Age was a huge advance upon that of the earlier races, although it is more than probable that the higher development existed in different parts of the world simultaneously with the lower, the more primitive people becoming influenced by the more advanced. A wave of great progress came with the Iberians of Spain who spread across France and reached Britain by means of boats at a time when it was probably once more an island.

Armed with bows and arrows and carefully finished stone axes and spears, clothed in skins and wearing ornaments of curious coloured stones or pieces of bone threaded on thin leathern cords, these Iberians or Neolithic men gradually spread all over the British Islands. They evidently liked the hills overlooking the fresh waters of Lake Pickering for their remains have been found there in considerable quantities.

The hills on all sides of the Vale are studded

with barrows from which great quantities of burial urns and skeletons have been exhumed, and wherever the land is under cultivation the plough exposes flint arrow and spear-heads and stone axes.

Many of the numerous finds of this nature have disappeared in small private collections and out of the many barrows that have been explored only in a certain number of instances have any accurate records been taken. It is thus a somewhat difficult task to discover how much or how little of the plunder of the burial mounds belongs to the Neolithic and how much to the Bronze and later ages. The Neolithic people buried in long barrows which are by no means common in Yorkshire, but many of the round ones that have been thoroughly examined reveal no traces of metal, stone implements only being found in them.[1] In Mr Thomas Bateman's book, entitled "Ten Years' Diggings," there are details of two long barrows, sixty-three circular ones, and many others that had been already disturbed, which were systematically opened by Mr James Ruddock of Pickering. The fine collection of urns and other relics are, Mr Bateman states, in his own possession, and are preserved at Lomberdale; but this was in 1861, and I have no knowledge of their subsequent fate.

One of the few long barrows near Pickering, of which Canon Greenwell gives a detailed account, is situated near the Scamridge Dykes—a series of remarkable mounds and ditches running for miles along the hills

[1] Greenwell, William. "British Barrows," p. 483.

north of Ebberston. It is highly interesting in connection with the origin of these extensive entrenchments to quote Canon Greenwell's opinion. He describes

The Scamridge Dykes above Troutsdale.

them as "forming part of a great system of fortification, apparently intended to protect from an invading body advancing from the east, and presenting many features in common with the wold entrenchments on the opposite side of the river Derwent. . . ." "The adjoining moor," he says, "is thickly sprinkled with round barrows, all of which have, at some time or other, been opened, with what results I know not;

while cultivation has, within the last few years (1877), destroyed a large number, the very sites of which can now only with great difficulty be distinguished. On the surface of the ground flint implements are most abundant, and there is probably no place in England which has produced more arrow-points, scrapers, rubbers, and other stone articles, than the country in the neighbourhood of the Scamridge Dykes." The doubts as to the antiquity of the Dykes that have been raised need scarcely any stronger refutation, if I may venture an opinion, than that they exist in a piece of country so thickly strewn with implements of the Stone Age. These entrenchments thus seem to point unerringly to the warfare of the early inhabitants of Yorkshire, and there can be little doubt that the Dykes were the scene of great intertribal struggles if the loss of such infinite quantities of weapons is to be adequately accounted for.

The size and construction of the Scamridge Dykes vary from a series of eight or ten parallel ditches and mounds deep enough and high enough to completely hide a man on horseback, to a single ditch and mound barely a foot above and below the ground level. The positions of the Dykes can be seen on the sketch map accompanying this book, but neither an examination of the map nor of the entrenchments themselves gives much clue as to their purpose. They do not keep always to the hill-tops and in places they appear to run into the valleys at right angles to the chief line. Overlooking Troutsdale, to the east of Scamridge farm, where the ground is covered with heather the excavations seem to have retained their original size, for at that point the parallel lines of entrenchments are deepest and most numerous. In various places the farmers have levelled cart tracks across the obstructions and in others they have been almost obliterated by ploughing, but as a rule, where cultivation touches them, the trenches have come to be boundaries for the fields.

The Neolithic people were only beginning to emerge from a state of absolute savagery, and it is possible that even at this time they were still cannibals. The evidence in support of this theory has been obtained from the condition of the bones found in long barrows, for, in many instances, they are discovered in such a dislocated and broken state, that there can be little doubt that the flesh was removed before burial. The long barrow at Scamridge is a good example of this, for the remains of at least fourteen bodies were laid in no order but with the component bones broken, scattered, and lying in the most confused manner. Half a jaw was lying on part of a thigh-bone and a piece of a skull among the bones of a foot, while other parts of what appeared to belong to the same skull were found some distance apart. Canon Greenwell, who describes this barrow with great detail, also mentions that this disarrangement was not due to any disturbance of the barrow after its erection, but, on the contrary, there were most certain indications that the bones had been originally deposited exactly as they were found. He also points out that this condition of things is obviously inconsistent with the idea that the bodies had been buried with the flesh still upon them, and goes on to say that "it appeared to Dr Thurnam that there were in these broken and scattered fragments of skulls and disconnected bones the relics of barbarous feasts, held at the time of the interment, when slaves, captives, or even wives were slain and eaten." But although this argument appeared to Canon Greenwell to have some weight, he is inclined to think that the broken condition of the bones may have been due to the pressure of the mound above them after they had been partially burnt with the fires which were lit at one end of the barrow and so arranged that the heat was drawn through the interior.

As the centuries passed the Neolithic people progressed in many directions. They improved their methods of making their weapons until they were able to produce axe-heads so perfectly ground and polished and with such a keen cutting edge that it would be impossible to make anything better. These celts like the arrow-heads were always fitted into cleft handles or shafts of wood, and it was probably at a later period that the stone hammer, pierced with a hole, made its appearance. Spinning and weaving in some extremely primitive fashion were evolved, so that the people were not entirely clothed in skins. They cultivated wheat to a small extent and kept herds of goats and horned sheep. The pottery they made was crude and almost entirely without ornament. The skeletons of this period show that although they led a

Flint arrow head of unusual shape.

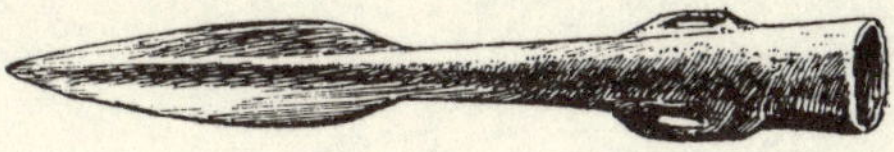

Bronze spear head.

Bronze celt found at Kirby Moorside.

Flint arrow head found at Yeddingham (*half size*).

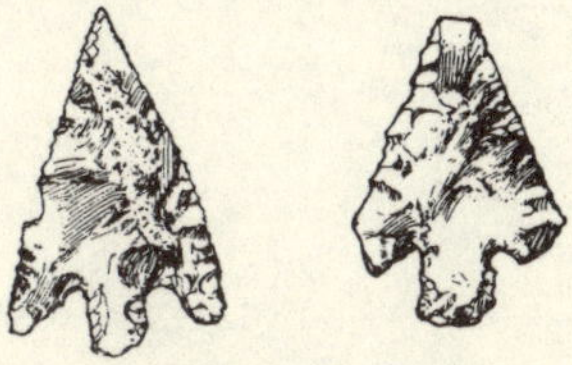

Flint arrow heads found at Moorcock and Wrelton (*half size*).

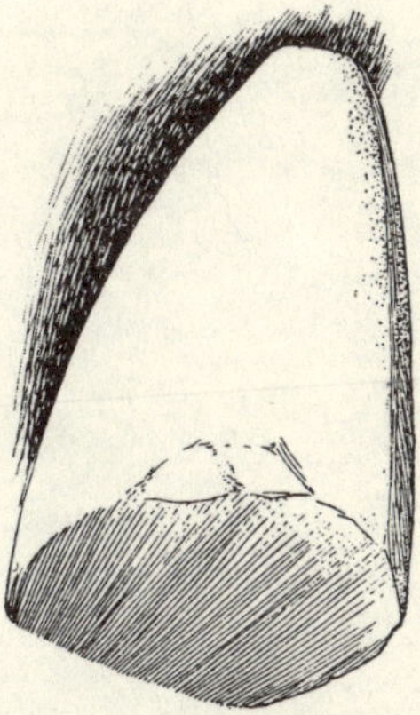

Highly polished celt of a bluish-white stone found at Scamridge.

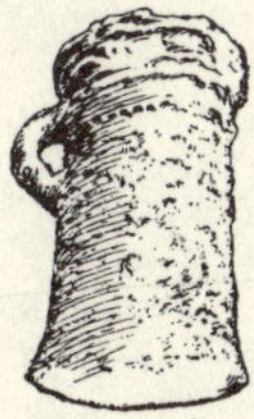

Bronze celt found at Scamridge.

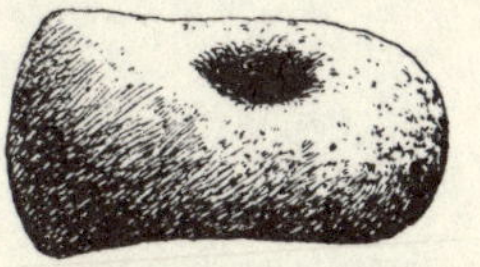

Stone hammer found at Cawthorne.

A flint knife, $4\frac{1}{8}$ inches long.

PRE-HISTORIC WEAPONS IN THE MUSEUM AT PICKERING.

life of great activity, probably as hunters, they were rather short in stature, averaging, it is thought by Dr Garson, less than 5 feet 6½ inches. Their jaws were not prognathous as in negroes, and their brow ridges were not nearly so prominent as in the men of the Old Stone Age, and thus their facial expression must have been mild.

Leaf-shaped arrow head found by Dr J. L. Kirk.

A most interesting discovery of lake-dwellings was made in 1893 by Mr James M. Mitchelson of Pickering, but although the relics brought to light are numerous, no one has yet been able to make any definite statement as to the period to which they belong. The Costa Beck, a stream flowing from the huge spring at Keld Head, on the west side of Pickering, was being cleaned out for drainage purposes at a spot a little over two miles from the town, when several pieces of rude pottery were thrown on to the bank. These excited Mr Mitchelson's interest and at another occasion his examination revealed more pottery and mixed up with the fragments were the bones of animals. Some piles forming two parallel rows about 4 feet apart were also discovered crossing the stream at right angles to its course.

The diagram given here shows the position of the piles as far as they were revealed in one of the excavations and it also shows their presumed continuation, but no reliance can be placed on anything but those actually dug out and indicated with a solid black spot. The piles were made of oak, birch and alder, with very rough pointed ends, and they measured from 6 to 10 inches in diameter. Three other rows cross the Costa in the same neighbourhood separated by a few hundred yards and as they lie at right angles to the stream which there forms a concave bend, they appear to converge upon one point. This would be what may roughly be termed an island between the Costa and a large drain where water in ancient times probably accumulated or flowed.

There can therefore be little doubt that the island was the home of prehistoric lake-dwellers who constructed their homes on rude platforms raised above the water or marshy ground by means of piles after the fashion of the numerous discoveries in Switzerland, and the present habits of the natives of many islands in the Pacific. Among the quantities of skulls and bones of animals, pottery and human skeletons, no traces of metal were brought to light and the coarse jars and broken urns were, with one exception, entirely devoid of ornamentation. The ground that was removed before the chief discoveries were made, consisted of about 8 or 10 inches of cultivated soil, below which came about 2 feet 6 inches of stiff blue clay, and then about 6 feet of peat resting on the Kimmeridge clay that formed the bottom of Lake Pickering. Most of the relics were found resting on the clay so they must have remained there for a sufficient time to have allowed these thick deposits to have formed, and it is possible that they may be associated with some of the Neolithic people who took to this mode of living

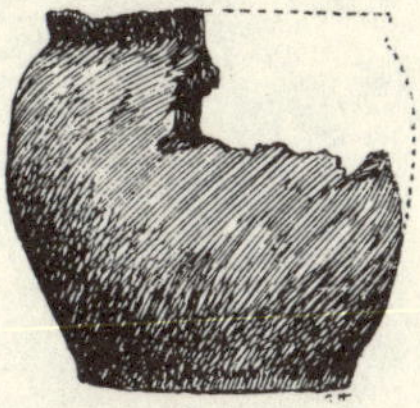

A vase of black earthenware.

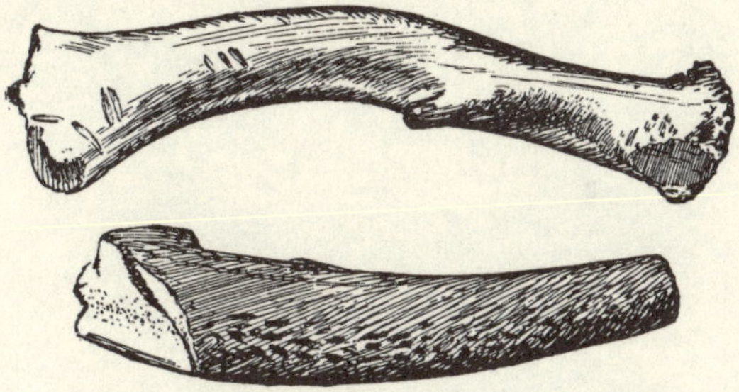

Two pieces of horn, one showing attempts to cut with some instrument. The lower piece has been neatly cut at both ends.

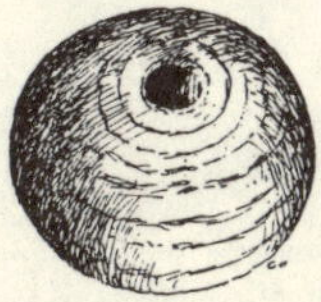

A whorl stone for weaving.

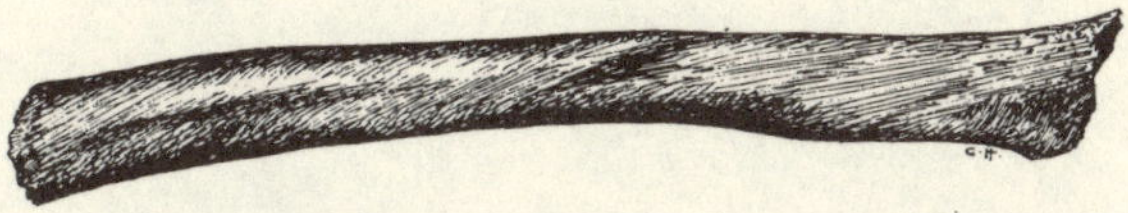

A human femur (thigh bone). The ends show signs of having been gnawed by wolves.

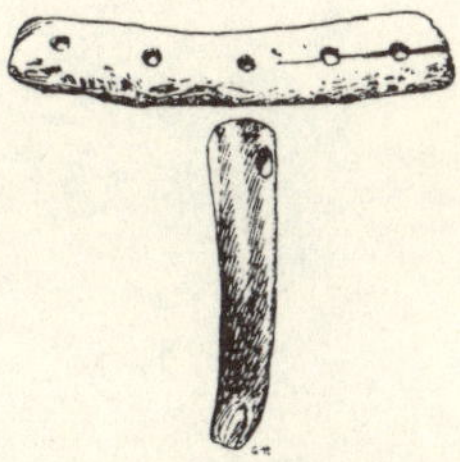

Ornaments made from deer's horn, found with the skeleton of a woman.

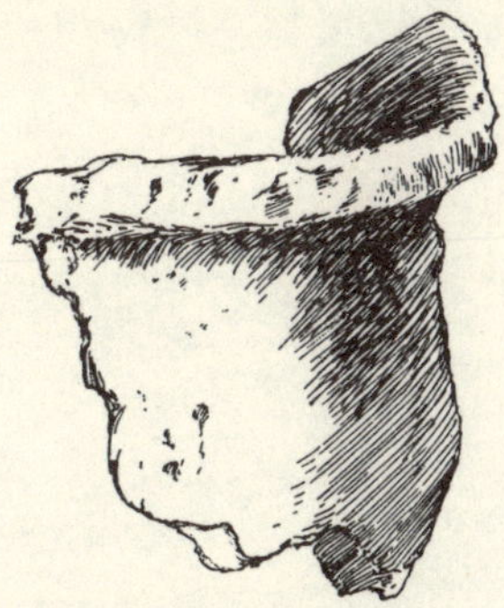

Fragment of a large earthenware jar or urn.

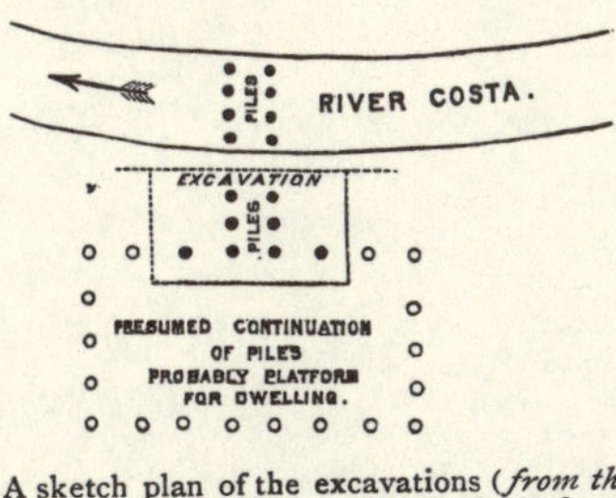

A sketch plan of the excavations (*from the Proceedings of the Yorkshire Geological and Polytechnic Society*.

DETAILS OF THE DISCOVERIES IN THE LAKE DWELLINGS.

when the Celtic invaders with their bronze weapons were steadily driving them northwards or reducing them to a state of slavery. A complete account of the discoveries was in 1898 read by Captain Cecil Duncombe at a meeting of the members of the Anthropological Institute and in the discussion which followed,[1] Mr C. H. Reid gave it as his opinion that the pottery probably belonged to a period not much earlier than the Roman occupation. Against this idea we have a most interesting statement made on another occasion by Professor Boyd Dawkins concerning one of the human bones; on examining the femur illustrated here he said that it could only have belonged to an individual possessing prehensile toes, and he also pointed out that the ends of this bone show signs of having been gnawed by dogs or similar animals. Captain Duncombe, who was to some extent quoting Professor Boyd Dawkins, said that the bones were "apparently those of a very small race." The complete skeleton of a young woman was found with the exception of the skull. "Though an adult," he says, "she could not, judging from the thigh-bones, have exceeded 4 feet 6 inches in height, and the owner of the longest thigh-bone would not have exceeded 5 feet. Though the bones are those of a people of short stature they are remarkable for their very prominent ridges for the attachment of the muscles, such as are quite unknown at the present day in England. They denote a race

[1] *Journal of the Anthropological Institute*, New Series (1899), vol. i. p. 150.

inured to hard toil, or one leading a life of constant activity." On the breast bone of the woman were found the two ornaments illustrated. They were made from the tines of a red deer's horn.

Another interesting discovery was the evidence of different attempts to cut some pieces of deer's horn. The shallow grooves were probably made by rubbing with a rib bone or some other sharp edge and sand and water. A small black vase unornamented but in perfect condition was dug up near the remains of the young woman. There were numerous skulls of the prehistoric ox or bos longifrons and also of the straight-horned sheep. A piece of the antlers of a great palmated deer now extinct tends to place the discoveries at an early time, but until more evidence is forthcoming the period to which these lake-dwellers belong must remain uncertain.

A list of the bones discovered includes the following:—

Human (of at least four individuals).
Deer (of three species).
Horse (a small variety), numerous.
Ox (Bos longifrons), numerous.
Sheep (straight-horned), numerous.
Goat (one skull).
Pig (both wild and domesticated).
Wolf.
Fox.
Otter.

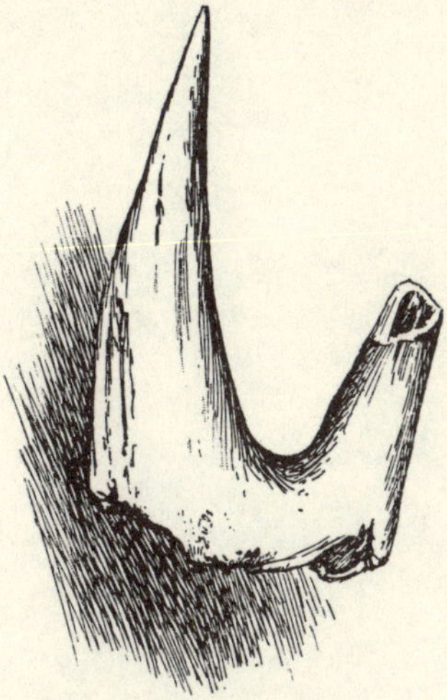

Part of the horns of a Great Palmated Deer.

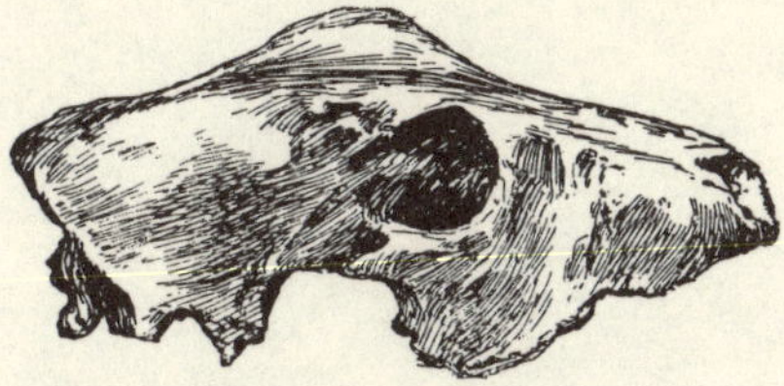

The skull of a Wolf.

Part of the skull of a Straight-horned Sheep.

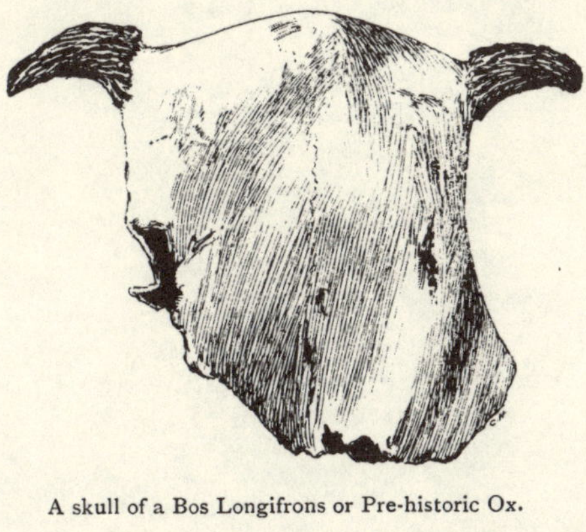

A skull of a Bos Longifrons or Pre-historic Ox.

Some examples of remains of Pre-historic Animals discovered in the Lake Dwellings by the river Costa.

Beaver (one skull).
Voles (of different kinds).
Birds.

The introduction of metal into Britain was due to the successive waves of Celtic Aryans who by means of their bronze weapons were able to overcome the Neolithic people. The Brythons or Britons, one of these Celtic peoples, seem to have succeeded in occupying the whole of England. They buried their dead in the round barrows which are to be found in most parts of the country but are particularly numerous on the hills immediately surrounding Pickering and on the wolds to the south of the Vale.

Some of the round barrows, as already mentioned, contain no traces of metal but in a number of those near Pickering have been found bronze Celts and spear-heads accompanied by beautifully finished weapons of stone. There can be no doubt, therefore, that the use of metal crept in slowly, and that stone, horn and bone continued to be used for many centuries after its introduction.

The Celtic people were possessed of a civilisation infinitely more advanced than that of the Neolithic or Iberian races. They were the ancestors of the "Ancient Britons" who offered such a stout resistance to the Roman legions under Julius Cæsar.

Not only are there innumerable barrows or burial mounds constructed by this early race on the hills above the Vale, but on Beacon Hill, the slight eminence just to the west of Pickering Castle, at Cawthorne and also at

Cropton, there are evidences of what may be their fortifications, while the plough is continually bringing to light more relics of the period. A fine collection of these have been brought together and are to be seen in Mr T. Mitchelson's private museum near Pickering Church. Two large cases contain a most remarkable series of burial urns, incense cups and food vessels all found in barrows in the neighbourhood. The urns are generally ornamented with bands of diagonal or crossed markings and other designs as well as with the impressions of twisted pieces of hide or grasses. The bases are usually very small for the size of the urns, after the fashion of those in Canon Greenwell's examples in the British Museum. In that collection may be seen several cinerary urns, incense cups and food vessels from Hutton Buscel, Ganton, Slingsby, Egton and other places in the vicinity of Pickering. They belong to the same period as those in Mr Mitchelson's museum and are, on account of the simplicity and comparative rarity of the bronze implements that have been discovered with them, considered to belong to the earliest bronze period, that is, to the time of the first Celtic invasions. Many of the objects in Mr Mitchelson's museum are not labelled with the place of their origin, the manuscript catalogue made some years ago having been lost ; but with a few exceptions the entire collection comes from barrows situated in the neighbourhood, having been brought together by Mr Thomas Kendall more than fifty years ago.

A complete skeleton in a stone cist is now lying in a glass case in the museum. It was discovered acci-

A Complete Skeleton in a Stone Cist belonging to the Early Bronze Age.

It was discovered by a farmer in a field between Appleton-le-Moor and Spaunton, and is now in the Museum at Pickering. [*Copyright reserved by Dr J. L. Kirk.*

dentally by a farmer between Appleton-le-Moor and Spaunton. He had decided to remove a huge stone that had been an obstacle when ploughing, and in doing so found that he had removed the top stone of a cist belonging to the early Bronze Age. The man has a round or brachycephalic skull with the prominent brow-ridges and powerful jaws of the Celtic people, and his right arm was arranged so that the hand was beneath the skull. By his left hand was the food vessel that is now placed on the left side of the skull, and at his feet are a number of small bronze studs or rivets.

These Bronze Age men seem to have had a very general belief in the spirit world, for the dead warrior was buried with his weapons as well as food, so that he might be sustained while he hunted in the other world with the spirit of his favourite axe or spear. The museum contains examples of socketed bronze celts and spear heads, as well as an infinite variety of arrow-heads, flint knives, stone hammers and celts, and also coloured beads and other ornaments.

Thus we find that in these early days mankind teemed in this part of Yorkshire. From all points around the shallow lake the smoke of fires ascended into the sky, patches of cultivation appeared among the trees, and villages, consisting of collections of primitive wooden huts, probably surrounded by a stockade, would have been discernible.

A closer examination of one of these early British villages would have discovered the people clothed in woven materials, for an example of cloth of the period was discovered by Canon Greenwell in this locality and is now to be seen in the British Museum. The grinding of corn in the stone querns, so frequently found near Pickering, would have been in progress; fair-haired children with blue eyes would be helping the older folk in preparing food, dressing skins, making

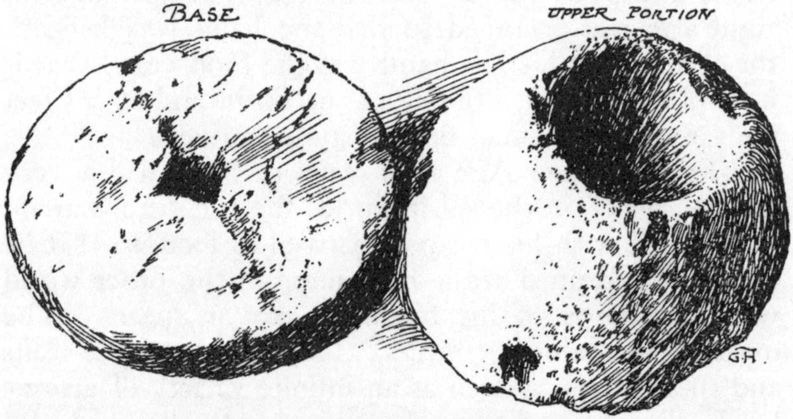

A Quern, now in the Pickering Museum.

bows and arrows, and the innumerable employments that the advancing civilisation demanded.

It is at this period that we reach the confines of history, records of an extremely unreliable character it is true, but strangely enough there are references by very early writers to the founding of Pickering. That the place should be mentioned at all in these fabulous writings is an interesting fact and gives Pickering an importance in those distant centuries which is surprising. John Stow in his "Summarie of Englyshe Chronicles," published in 1565, gives the following fanciful story of the father of the founder of Pickering.

> "Morindus, the bastard son of Danius, began to reigne in Britain: he (as our Chronicles saye) fought with a kynge, who came out of Germanye, and arrived here, and slew hym with all his power. Moreover (as they write) of the Irishe seas in his tyme, came foorthe a wonderfull monster: whiche destroyed muche people. Wherof the king hearyng would of his valiaunt courage, needes fyght with it: by whō he was cleane devoured, whē he had reigned viii. yeres." B.C. 311

His two youngest sons were Vigenius and Peredurus, and of them Stow writes:—

> "Vigenius and Peredurus, after the takyng of their brother [Elidurus, the former King] reigned together. vii. yeres. Vigenius thā died, and Peredurus reygned after alone. ii. yeares. He buylded the towne of Pyckeryng after the opinion of divers writers." B.C. 270

Raphael Holinshed, who was a contemporary of Stow and used many of his sources of information, gives the following account of the same period[1]:—

> "Vigenius and Peredurus, the yoongest sonnes

[1] Holinshed, Raphael; "Chronicles of England, Scotland and Ireland," p. 461.

D

of Morindus, and brethren to Elidurus, began to reigne jointlie as kings of Britaine, in the year of the world 3701, after the building of Rome 485. . . . These two brethren in the English chronicles are named Higanius and Petitur, who (as Gal. Mon. [Geoffrey of Monmouth] testifieth) divided the realme betwixt them, so that all the land from Humber westward fell to Vigenius or Higanius, the other part beyond Humber northward Peredure held. But other affirme, that Peredurus onelie reigned, and held his brother Elidurus in prison by his owne consent, for somuch as he was not willing to governe.

"But Gal. Mon. saith, that Vigenius died after he had reigned 7 yeares, and then Peredurus seized all the land into his owne rule, and governed it with such sobrietie and wisedome, that he was praised above all his brethren, so that Elidurus was quite forgotten of the Britains. But others write that he was a verie tyrant, and used himselfe verie cruellie towards the lords of his land, whereupon they rebelled and slue him. But whether
Caxton. by violent hand, or by naturall sicknesse, he finallie departed this life, after the consent of most writers, when he had reigned eight yeares, leaving no issue behind him to succeed in the governance
Eth. Bur. of the Kingdome. He builded the towne of Pikering, where his bodie was buried."

Whatever memorial was raised to this legendary

Burial Urns and Other Vessels in Pickering Museum.

They were found in barrows in the following places, reading from left to right, top row :—(1) Blansby Park (containing bones and ashes) ; (2) Cawthorne (3) Hutton Buscelmoor ; (4) Cockmoor Hall Warren ; (5) Snainton Moor ; (6) Raindale, " No Man's Land." Lower Row :—(1) Blansby Park ; (2) below Ebberston ; (3) Newton Towers, near Helmsley ; (4) Fylingdales (a food vessel) : (5) Cawthorne (contains ashes.)

[Copyright reserved by Dr John L. Kirk.

king of the Brigantes, has totally disappeared. It may have been a mighty barrow surrounded with great stones and containing the golden ornaments worn by Peredurus, but if it existed outside the imaginations of the Chroniclers it would probably have been plundered and obliterated during the Roman occupation or by marauding Angles or Danes.

Mr Bateman tells us that in 1853, two Celtic coins in billon or mixed metal of the peculiar rough type apparently characteristic of and confined to the coinage of the Brigantes, were found by quarrymen engaged in baring the rock near Pickering.

There may have been two British fortresses at Pickering at this time, one on the site of the present castle and one the hill on the opposite side of the Pickering Beck, where, as already mentioned, the circular ditches and mounds indicate the existence of some primitive stockaded stronghold.

At Cawthorne, a few miles to the north, there are British enclosures adjoining the Roman camps; and at Cropton, on the west side of the village and in a most commanding position, a circular hill-top shows palpable evidences of having been fortified.

Of the megalithic remains or "Bride Stones," as they are generally termed in Yorkshire, it is difficult to say anything with certainty. Professor Windle, in his list of those existing in the county,[1] mentions among others—

[1] Windle, Bertram, C.A., "Remains of the Pre-historic Age in England," pp. 203-4.

1. "The Bride Stones" near Grosmont (Circle).
2. "The Bride Stones," Sleights Moor (Circle).
3. Simon Houe, near Goathland Station.
4. "The Standing Stones" (three upright stones), $1\frac{3}{4}$ miles S.-W. of Robin Hood's Bay, on Fylingdales Moor.

CHAPTER V

How the Roman Occupation of Britain affected the Forest and Vale of Pickering

B.C. 55 to A.D. 418

THE landings of Julius Cæsar, in 55 and 54 B.C., and the conflicts between his legions and the southern tribes of Britain, were little more, in the results obtained, than a reconnaissance in force, and Yorkshire did not feel the effect of the Roman invasion until nearly a century after the first historic landing.

The real invasion of Britain began in A.D. 43, when the Emperor Claudius sent Aulus Plautius across the Channel with four legions; and after seven years of fighting the Romans, taking advantage of the inter-tribal feuds of the Britons, had reduced the southern half of England to submission.

Plautius was succeeded by Ostorius Scapula in A.D. 50, and from Tacitus[1] we learn that he "found affairs in a troubled state, the enemy making irruptions into the territories of our allies, with so much the more insolence as they supposed that a new general, with an army unknown to him, and now that the

[1] Tacitus, the Oxford Translation, revised 1854, vol. I, book xii. pp. 288-90.

winter had set in, would not dare to make head against them." Scapula, however, vigorously proceeded with the work of subjugation, and having overcome the Iceni of East Anglia and the Fen Country, he was forcing his way westwards into Wales when he heard of trouble brewing in the North. "He had approached near the sea which washes the coast of Ireland," says Tacitus, "when commotions, begun amongst the Brigantes, obliged the general to return thither." The Brigantes were the powerful and extremely fierce tribe occupying Yorkshire, Durham, Cumberland, and Westmorland, and among them were the people whose remains are so much in evidence near Pickering. They had probably been under tribute to the Romans, and their struggle against the invaders in this instance does not appear to have been well organised, for we are told that when the Romans arrived in their country, they "soon returned to their homes, a few who raised the revolt having been slain, and the rest pardoned." We also know that in A.D. 71 Petilius Cerealis attacked the Brigantes and subdued a great part of their country; and as the Romans gradually brought the tribe completely under their control, they established the camps and constructed the roads of which we find so many evidences to-day. The inhabitants of the hills surrounding the Vale of Pickering were overawed by a great military station at Cawthorne on a road running north and south from that spot. It may have been the Delgovicia mentioned in the first Antonine Iter., and in that case Malton would have been Derventione,

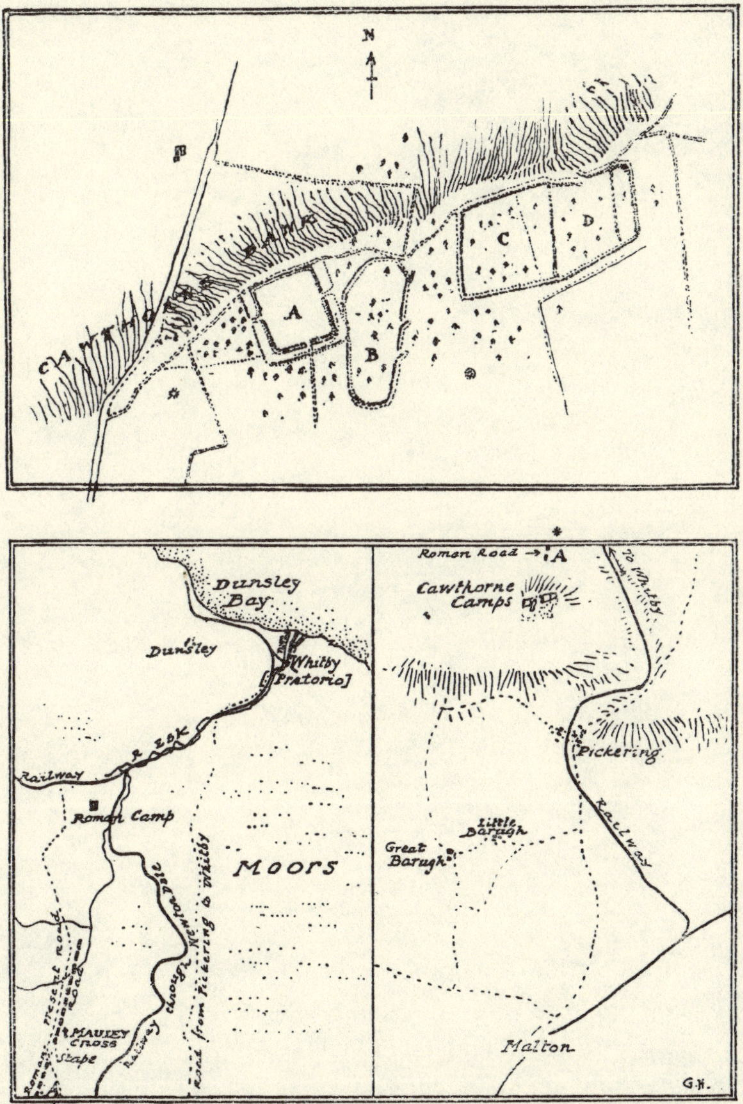

A Sketch Map of the Roman Road from Malton to the Coast, and a Plan of the Camps on the Road at Cawthorne.
(From the Ordnance Survey.)

and Whitby, or some spot in Dunsley Bay, would have been Prætorio, but at the present time there is not sufficient data for fixing these names with any certainty. It has also been supposed by General Roy [1] that Cawthorne was occupied by the famous 9th legion after they had left Scotland, owing to the similarity of construction between the most westerly camp at Cawthorne and the one at Dealgin Ross in Strathern, where the 9th legion were supposed to have had their narrow escape from defeat by the Caledonians during Agricola's sixth campaign. But this also is somewhat a matter of speculation.

Coming to the firmer ground of the actual remains of the Roman roads and camps, we find that traces of a well-constructed road, locally known as Wade's Causeway, have been discovered at various points on a line drawn from Malton to Cawthorne and Whitby. Some of these sections of the road have disappeared since Francis Drake described them in 1736,[2] and at the present time the work of destruction continues at intervals when a farmer, converting a few more acres of heather into potatoes, has the ill-luck to strike the roadway.

In the month of January this year (1905), I examined a piece of ground newly taken under cultivation at Stape. It was about half a mile north of the little inn and just to the west of Mauley Cross. The stones

[1] Roy, Major Gen. William: "The Military Antiquities of the Romans in Britain," 1793, Plate xi.

[2] Drake, Francis: "Eboracum," p. 36.

were all thrown out of their original positions and a pile of them had been taken outside the turf wall for road-mending and to finish the walls against the gate posts, but the broad track of the roadway, composed of large odd-shaped stones, averaging about a foot in width, was still strikingly in evidence—a mottled band passing straight through the chocolate-coloured soil.

All who have described the road state that on each side of the causeway where it remains undisturbed there is a line of stones placed on their edges in order to keep the stones in place, but in this instance the stones were too much disturbed to observe their original formation. Among the furrows I discovered quantities of flint-flakes, indicating the manufacture of stone implements on this site, no flints being naturally found in the neighbourhood.

The road went through the most perfectly constructed of the three square camps at Cawthorne from west to east, cutting through one corner of the adjacent oval camp. It then seems to have passed down the slack a little to the north-east, and crossing the stream below (probably in Roman times by a wooden bridge) it takes a fairly straight course for the little hamlet of Stape just mentioned. The slope from the camps is extremely steep, and in 1817, when Dr Young wrote his "History of Whitby," he tells us that there were no traces of the road at that point. Going back to 1736, however, we find that Drake, in his "History of York" published in that year, says, "At the foot of the hill began the road or causeway, very plain"; he also tells us that he first heard of the road, with the camp upon it, from Mr Thomas Robinson of Pickering—"a gentleman well versed in this kind of learning." Drake, enthusiastically describing his examination of the road, says, " I had not gone a hundred paces on it, but I met with a *mile stone* of the *grit kind*, a sort not known in this country. It was placed in the midst of the causeway, but so miserably worn, either by sheep or cattle rubbing against it, or the weather, that I missed of the inscription, which, I own, I ran with great eagerness to find. The causeway is just twelve foot broad, paved with a flint pebble [probably very hard limestone], some of them very large, and in many places it is as firm as it was the first day, a thing the more strange in that not only the distance of time may be considered, but the total neglect of repairs and the boggy rotten moors it goes over. In some places the *agger* is above three foot raised from the surface. The country people curse it often for being almost wholly hid in the ling, it frequently overturns their carts laden with turf as they happen to drive across it. It was a great pleasure to me to trace this wonderful road, especially when I soon found out that it pointed to the bay aforesaid. I lost it sometimes by the interposition of valleys, rivulets, or the exceeding great quantity of ling growing on these moors. I had then nothing to do but observe the line, and riding crossways, my horse's feet, through the ling, informed me when I was upon it. In short, I traced it several miles, and could have been pleased to have gone on with it to the seaside, but my time would not allow me. However, I prevailed upon Mr Robinson to send his servant, and a very intelligent person of *Pickering* along with him, and they not only made it fairly out to *Dunsley*, but brought me a sketch of the country it went through with them. From which I have pricked it out in the map, as the reader will find at the end of this account."

I have examined Drake's map but find that he has simply ruled two perfectly straight parallel lines between Cawthorne and Dunsley, so that except for the fact that Mr Robinson's servant and the intelligent Pickeronian found that the road did go to Dunsley we have no information as to its exact position. Young, however, describes its course past Stape and Mauley Cross over Wheeldale and Grain Becks to July or Julian Park. In the foundation of a wall round an enclosure at that point he mentions the discovery of an inscribed Roman stone of which a somewhat crude woodcut is given in his "History of Whitby." The inscription appears to be ILVIVILVX, and Young read it as LE. VI. VI. L. VEX, or in full LEGIONIS SEXTÆ VICTRICIS QUINQUAGINTA VEXILLARII, meaning, "Fifty vexillary soldiers of the sixth legion, the Victorious." This rendering of the abbreviations may be inaccurate, and some of the letters before and after those visible when the stone was discovered may have been obliterated, but Dr Young thought that the inscription was probably complete. On Lease Rigg beyond July Park the road cuts through another Roman camp of similar dimensions to the western one at Cawthorne. In the map reproduced here a much clearer idea of the course of the road can be had than by any description. I have marked the position of the road to the south of Cawthorne as passing through Barugh, where Drake discovered it in 1736. "From the camp" (Cawthorne), he writes, "the road disappears towards York, the *agger* being either sunk or removed by the country people for their buildings. But taking the line, as exactly as I could, for the city, I went down the hill to *Thornton-Risebrow*, and had some information from a clergyman of a kind of a camp at a village called vulgarly BARF; but corruptly, no doubt, from BURGH. Going to this place, I was agreeably surprised to fall upon my long lost road again; and here plainly appeared also a small intrenchment on it; from whence, as I have elsewhere hinted, the *Saxon* name *Burgh* might come. The road is discernible enough, in places, to *Newsam-Bridge* over the river *Rye;* not far from which is a *mile-stone* of *grit* yet standing. On the other side of the river the *Stratum*, or part of it, appears very plain, being composed of large blue pebble, some of a tun weight; and directs us to a village called *Aimanderby*. *Barton on the Street*, and *Appleton on the Street*, lye a little on the side of the road." Drake then proceeds to speculate as to the likelihood of the road still making a bee-line for York, or whether it diverged towards Malton, then no doubt a Roman station; but as his ideas are unimportant in comparison with his discoveries, we will leave him to return to the camps at Cawthorne. The hill they occupy forms part of a bold escarpment running east and west between Newton upon Rawcliff and Cropton, having somewhat the appearance of an inland coast-line. On the north side of the camps the hill is precipitous, and there can be little doubt that the position must, in Roman times, have been one of the strongest in the neighbourhood. This is not so apparent to-day as it would be owing to the dense growth of larch and fir planted by Mr James Mitchelson's father about forty years ago. There are, however, peeps among the trees which reveal a view of the great purple undulations of the heathery plateau to the north, and the square camp marked A on the plan is entirely free from trees although completely shut in by the surrounding plantation. In the summer it is an exceedingly difficult matter to follow the ditches and mounds forming the outline of the camps, for besides the closely planted trees the bracken grows waist high. The *vallum* surrounding each enclosure is still of formidable height, and in camp A is double with a double fosse of considerable depth. Camps C and D are both rectangular, but C, the largest of the four, is stronger and more regular in shape than D, and it may have been that D was the camp of the auxiliaries attached to the legion or part of a legion quartered there. The five outer gates of C and D are protected by overlapping earthworks, the opening being diagonal to the face of the camp, but the opening between these two enclosures is undefended. Camp B may have been for cattle or it may have been another camp of auxiliaries, for unlike the other three it is oval and might even have been a British encampment used by the Romans when they selected this commanding site as their headquarters for the district.

To fix the origin of a camp by its formation is very uncertain work and no reliance can be placed on statements based on such evidence; but Camp A bears the stamp of Roman work unmistakably, and the fact that the Roman road cuts right through its east and west gates seems a sufficiently conclusive proof. It is also an interesting fact that between forty and fifty years ago Mr T. Kendall of Pickering discovered the remains of a chariot in a barrow on the west side of Camp A. Fragments of a wooden pole 11 feet long, and of four spokes, could be traced as well as the complete iron tyres of both wheels, and portions of a hub. These remains, together with small pieces of bronze harness fittings, are now carefully arranged in a glass case in Mr Mitchelson's museum at Pickering.

There is a mill just to the south of Pickering known as Vivers Mill, and near Cawthorne there is a farm where Roman foundations have been discovered, known as Bibo House. Both these names have a curiously Roman flavour, but as to their origin I can say nothing.

The three or four plans of these camps that have been published are all inaccurate; the first, in Drake's "Eboracum," being the greatest offender. General Roy has shown camps B and C in the wrong positions in regard to A, and even Dr Young, who himself notices these mistakes, is obliged to point out that the woodcut that is jammed sideways on one of his pages is not quite correct in regard to camp C (marked A on his plan), although otherwise it is fairly accurate.

A small square camp is just visible in a field to the east of Cawthorne; there is an oval one on Levisham Moor, and others square and oval dotted over the moors in different directions, but they are of uncertain origin. There can be little doubt that subsidiary camps and entrenchments would have been established by the Romans in a country where the inhabitants were as fierce and warlike as these Brigantes, but whether the dominant power utilised British fortresses or whether they always built square camps is a matter on which it is impossible to dogmatise.

A number of Roman articles were dug up when the cutting for the railway to Sinnington was being made, and the discoveries at this point are particularly interesting as the site is in an almost direct line between Cawthorne and Barugh.

We are possessed, however, of sufficient evidence to gain a considerable idea of Pickering during the four hundred years of the Roman occupation. We have seen that the invaders constructed a great road on their usual plan, going as straight as the nature of the country allowed from their station at Malton to the sea near or at Whitby; that on this road they built large camps where some hundreds, possibly thousands of troops were permanently stationed, although the icy-cold blasts from the north-east may have induced them to occupy more protected spots in winter. Roman chariots, squads of foot soldiers, and mounted men would have been a common sight on the road, and to the sullen natives the bronze eagle would gradually have become as familiar as their own totem-posts. Gradually we know that the British chiefs and their sons and daughters became demoralised by the sensual pleasures of the new civilisation and thus the invaders secured themselves in their new possessions in a far more efficacious manner than by force of arms.

The Britons remained under the yoke of Rome until A.D. 418, when the Anglo-Saxon Chronicle tells us that " This year the Romans collected all the hoards of gold that were in Britain ; and some they hid in the earth, so that no man afterwards might find them, and some they carried away with them into Gaul," and in A.D. 435 we find the record that " This year the Goths sacked the city of Rome and never since have the Romans reigned in Britain." The Brigantes were thus once more free to work out their own destiny, but the decay of their military prowess which had taken place during the Roman occupation made them an easy prey to the daring Saxon pirates who, even before the Romans finally left England, are believed to have established themselves in scattered bodies on some parts of the coast. The incursions of these warlike peoples belong to the Saxon era described in the next chapter.

CHAPTER VI

The Forest and Vale in Saxon Times

A.D. 418 to 1066

THERE seems little doubt that the British re-remained a barbarous people throughout the four centuries of their contact with Roman influences, for had they progressed in this period they would have understood in some measure the great system by which the Imperial power had held the island with a few legions and a small class of residential officials. Having failed to absorb the new military methods, when left to themselves, there was no unifying idea among the Britons, and they seem to have merely reverted to some form of their old tribal organisation. The British cities constituted themselves into a group of independent states generally at war with one another, but sometimes united under the pressure of some external danger. Under such circumstances they would select some chieftain whose period of ascendency could be measured only by the continuance of the danger.

From Bede's writings we find that the Scots from the west and the Picts from the north continually harassed the Britons despite occasional help from Rome, and despite the wall they built across the north of

England. In these straits the British invited help from the Angles and Saxons, who soon engaged the northern tribesmen and defeated them. The feebleness of the Britons having become well known among the continental peoples, the Angles, Saxons and Jutes began to steadily swarm across the North Sea in powerful, armed bands. Having for a time assisted the Britons they began to seek excuses for quarrels, and gradually the Britons with brief periods of success were beaten and dispossessed of their lands until they were driven into the western parts of the island. The Angles occupied most of northern England, including the kingdom of Northumbria, of which Yorkshire formed a large part. These fierce Anglo-Saxon people, with an intermixing of Danish blood, a few centuries later were the ancestors of a great part of the present population of the county. Sidonius Apollinaris, a Bishop of Gaul, who wrote in the fifth century, says, "We have not a more cruel and more dangerous enemy than the Saxons: they overcome all who have the courage to oppose them; they surprise all who are so imprudent as not to be prepared for their attack. When they pursue they infallibly overtake; when they are pursued their escape is certain. They despise danger; they are inured to shipwreck; they are eager to purchase booty with the peril of their lives. Tempests, which to others are so dreadful, to them are subjects of joy; the storm is their protection when they are pressed by the enemy, and a cover for their operations when they meditate an attack. Before they quit their own shores, they devote to the altars of their gods the tenth part of the principal captives; and when they are on the point of returning, the lots are cast with an affectation of equity, and the impious vow is fulfilled."

Gradually these invaders settled down in Britain, which soon ceased to be called Britain, and assumed the name Angle-land or England. In A.D. 547 Ida founded the kingdom of Northumbria, one of the divisions forming the Saxon Heptarchy, and among the villages and families that owed allegiance to him were those of the neighbourhood of Pickering. The first fortifications by the Anglo-Saxons were known as *buhrs* or *burgs*. Some of them were no doubt Roman or British camps adapted to their own needs, but generally these earth works were required as the fortified home of some lord and his household, and there can be little doubt that in most instances new entrenchments were made, large enough to afford a refuge for the tenants as well as their flocks and herds.

Pickering itself must have been an Anglo-Saxon village of some importance, and the artificial mound on which the keep of the castle now stands would probably have been raised during this period if it had not been constructed at a much earlier date. It would have palisades defending the top of the mound, and similar defences inside the entrenchments that formed the basecourt. These may have occupied the position of the present dry moat that defends the castle on two of its three sides. If Pickering had been

THE TOWER OF MIDDLETON CHURCH NEAR PICKERING.

The lower portion, owing to the quoins which somewhat resemble the "long and short" work of the Saxons, has been thought to be of pre-Norman date. The blocked doorway appearing in the drawing has every appearance of Saxon workmanship.

founded by the Anglo-Saxons we should have expected a name ending with "ton," "ham," "thorpe," or "borough," but its remarkable position at the mouth of Newton Dale may have led them to choose a name which may possibly mean an opening by the "ings" or wet lands. It is, however, impossible at the present time to discover the correct derivation of the name. It probably has nothing whatever to do with the superficial "pike" and "ring," and the suggestion that it means "The Maiden's Ring" from the Scandinavian "pika," a maiden, and "hringr," a circle or ring, may be equally incorrect. The settlements in the neighbourhood must have occupied the margin of the marshes in close proximity to one another, and most of them from the suffix "ton" would appear to have been the "tuns" or fortified villages named after the family who founded them. Thus we find between Pickering and Scarborough at the present time a string of eleven villages bearing the names Thornton, Wilton, Allerston, Ebberston, Snainton, Brompton, Ruston, Hutton (Buscel of Norman origin), Sawdon, Ayton and Irton. In the west and south there are Middleton, Cropton, Wrelton, Sinnington, Appleton, Nawton, Salton, Marton, Edston or Edstone, Habton, (Kirby) Misperton, Ryton, Rillington, and many others. Other Anglo-Saxon settlements indicating someone's ham or home would appear to have been made at Levisham, Yedingham and Lastingham. Riseborough seems to suggest the existence of some Anglo-Saxon fortress on that very suitable elevation in the Vale of Pickering. Barugh, a little to the south, can scarcely be anything else than a corruption of "buhr" or "burg," for the Anglian invaders, if they found the small Roman camp that appears to have been established on that slight eminence in the vale would have probably found it a most convenient site for one of their own fortifications. Names ending with "thorpe," such as Kingthorpe, near Pickering, also indicate an Anglo-Saxon origin. Traces of the "by" or "byr," a single dwelling or single farm of the Danes, are to be found thickly dotted over this part of England, but in the immediate neighbourhood of Pickering there are only Blansby, Dalby, Farmanby, Aislaby, Roxby, and Normanby. To the east near Scarborough there are Osgodby, Killerby, Willerby, Flotmanby, and Hunmanby, so that it would appear that the strong community of Anglo-Saxon villages along the margin of the vale kept the Danish settlers at a distance.

Goathland, which was often spelt Gothland, has a most suggestive sound, and the family names of Scoby and Scoresby seem to be of Danish origin. The "gate" of the streets of Pickering is a modification of the Danish "gade," meaning a "way," for the town was never walled. The influence of the Danes on the speech of this part of Yorkshire seems to me apparent in the slight sing-song modulation so similar to that of the present day people of Denmark.

In A.D. 597 Augustine commenced his missionary work among the Saxons, and King Ethelbert of Kent was baptised on June the 2nd of that year. Twenty-seven years later Edwin, the powerful king of Northumbria, married Ethelburga, daughter of Ethelbert. When she accompanied her husband to his northern kingdom she took with her Paulinus, who was ordained bishop of the Northumbrians. "King Aldwin, therefore," Bede tells us,[1] "together with all the nobles of his nation, and very many of the common people, received the faith and washing of sacred regeneration, in the eleventh year of his reign, which is the year of the Lord's incarnation, 627, and about the year 180 from the coming of the Angles into Britain. Moreover, he was baptised at York, on the holy day of Easter, the day before the Ides of April, in the church of the holy apostle Peter, which he himself built of wood in that place with expeditious labour, while he was being catechised and prepared in order to receive baptism." The Northumbrians from this time forward were at least a nominally Christian people, and the seventh century certainly witnessed the destruction of many of the idols and their shrines that had hitherto formed the centre for the religious rites of the Anglo-Saxons. Woden or Odin, Thor and the other deities did not lose their adherents in a day, and Bede records the relapses into idolatry of Northumbria as well as the other parts of England. There can be no doubt that fairies and elves entered largely into the mythology of the Anglo-Saxons, and the firmness of the beliefs in beings of that

[1] Bede's "Ecclesiastical History of the English Nation," translated by Gidley, Rev. L., 1870, p. 152.

nature can be easily understood when we realise that it required no fewer than twelve centuries of Christianity to finally destroy them among the people of Yorkshire. In Chapter XI. we see something of the form the beliefs and superstitions had assumed at the time of their disappearance.

In the seventh century most of the churches erected in Yorkshire were probably of wood, but the example of King Edwin at York, who quickly replaced the timber structure with a larger one of stone, must soon have made itself felt in the country. Nothing, however, in the form of buildings or inscribed stones for which we have any evidence for placing at such an early date remains in the neighbourhood of Pickering, although there are numerous crosses and traces of the masonry that may be termed Saxon or Pre-Conquest.

The founding of a monastery at Lastingham is described by Bede, and with the particulars he gives we can place the date between the years 653 and 655. Bishop Cedd was requested by King Oidilward, who held rule in the parts of Deira, "to accept some possession of land of him to build a monastery to which the king himself [Æthelwald] also might frequently come to pray to the Lord, and to hear the Word, and in which he might be buried when he died." Further on we are told that Cedd "assenting to the king's wishes, chose for himself a place to build a monastery among lofty and remote mountains, in which there appeared to have been more lurking places of robbers and dens of wild beasts than habitations of men."

The early font in the Chapel of Ease at Levisham, that was serving until recently as a cattle trough in a farmyard.

THE BROKEN CROSS by the ruins of WYKEHAM ABBEY. Scarcely any traces of carving are visible.

A carved cross built into the wall of the tower (interior) of Middleton Church. The head is hidden in the angle of the wall.

This account is of extreme interest, being the only contemporary description of this part of Yorkshire known to us. "Moreover," says Bede, "the man of God, studying first by prayers and fastings to purge the place he had received for a monastery from its former filth of crimes, and so to lay in it the foundations of the monastery, requested of the king that he would give him during the whole ensuing time of Lent leave and licence to abide there for the sake of prayer; on all which days, with the exception of Sunday, protracting his fast to evening according to custom, he did not even then take anything except a very little bread and one hen's egg, with a little milk and water. For he said this was the custom of those of whom he had learnt the rule of regular discipline, first to consecrate to the Lord by prayers and fastings the places newly received for building a monastery or a church. And when ten days of the quadragesimal fast were yet remaining, there came one to summon him to the king. But he, in order that the religious work might not be intermitted on account of the king's affairs, desired his presbyter Cynibill, who was also his brother, to complete the pious undertaking. The latter willingly assented; and the duty of fasting and prayer having been fulfilled, he built there a monastery which is now called Læstingaeu [Lastingham], and instituted rules there, according to the customs of the monks of Lindisfarne, where he had been educated. And when for many years he [Cedd] had administered the episcopate in the aforesaid province, and also had taken charge of this monastery, over which he set superiors, it happened that coming to this same monastery at a time of mortality, he was attacked by bodily infirmity and died. At first, indeed, he was buried outside, but in process of time a church was

SAXON SUNDIAL AT KIRKDALE.
(*From a rubbing by Mr J. Romilly Allen, F.S.A.*)

built of stone in the same monastery, in honour of the blessed mother of God, and in that church his body was laid on the right side of the altar." Cedd's death took place in 664, and Ceadda or Chad, one of his brothers, succeeded him as he had desired.

Nothing remains of the buildings of this early monastery, and what happened to them, and what caused their disappearance, is purely a matter of conjecture. We can only surmise that they were destroyed during the Danish invasions of the ninth century.

At Kirkdale church, which is situated close to the cave already described, there was discovered about the year 1771 a sundial bearing the longest known inscription of the Anglo-Saxon period. The discoverer was the Rev. William Dade, rector of Barmston, in the East Riding, and a letter of great length, on the stone, from the pen of Mr J. C. Brooke, F.S.A. of the Herald's College, was read at the Society of Antiquaries in 1777.

The sundial, without any gnomon, occupies the central portion of the stone, which is about 7 feet in length, and the inscription is closely packed in the spaces on either side.

It reads as follows, the lines in brackets having the contractions expanded:—

\+ ORM · GAMAL · SVNA · BOHTE · SCS̄
[+ ORM · GAMAL · SUNA · BOHTE · SANCTUS]

GREGORIVS · MINSTER · ĐONNE HIT
[GREGORIUS · MINSTER · THONNE HIT]

PES ÆL TOBROCAN · ⁊ TOFALAN · ⁊ HE
[WES ÆL TOBROCAN · & TOFALAN · & HE]

HIT IET · MACAN · NEPAN · FROM GRVNDE
[HIT LET · MACAN · NEWAN · FROM GRUNDE]

XPE : ⁊ SCS GREGORIVS · IN EADPARD
[CHRISTE : & SANCTUS GREGORIUS · IN EADWARD]

DAGVM CN̄G ⁊ N TOSTI DAGVM EORL +
[DAGUM CYNING & IN TOSTI DAGUM EORL +]

Completed under the dial.

\+ ⁊ HAPARĐ ME PROHTE · ⁊ BRAND PR̄S
[+ & HAWARTH ME WROHTE · & BRAND {PRÆPOSITUS / PRESBYTERS}]

The modern rendering is generally accepted as: "Orm, the son of Gamal, bought St Gregory's minster (or church) when it was all broken and fallen, and caused it to be made anew from the ground for Christ and St Gregory in the days of King Edward, and in the days of Earl Tosti, and Hawarth wrought me and Brand the Prior, (priest or priests)."

Along the top of the dial and round the perimeter the inscription reads:—

+ P IS	IS	DÆGES	SOL MERCA
THIS	IS	DAY'S	SUNMARKER
	ÆT	ILCVM	TIDE
	AT	EACH	TIDE OR HOUR.

It is interesting to know that the antiquaries of a century or more ago rendered this simple sentence as: "This is a draught exhibiting the time of day, while the sun is passing to and from the winter-solstice." They also made a great muddle of the words: "& HE HIT LET MACAN NEWAN," their rendering being "CHEHITLE AND MAN NEWAN," the translation being supposed to read: "Chehitle and others renewed it, etc." With Mr Brooke's paper is given a large steel engraving of the stone, but it is curiously inaccurate in many details. At Edstone church there is another sundial over the south doorway as at Kirkdale, and there is every reason to believe that it belongs to the same period. The inscription above the dial reads:—

OROLOGI VIATORUM.

On the left side is the following:—

LOTHAN ME WROHTE A.

From the drawing given here the inscription is palpably incomplete, as though the writer had been suddenly stopped in his work. Nothing is known of Lothan beyond the making of this sundial, so that the fixing of the date can only be by comparative reasoning. At Kirkdale, on the other hand, we know that Tosti,

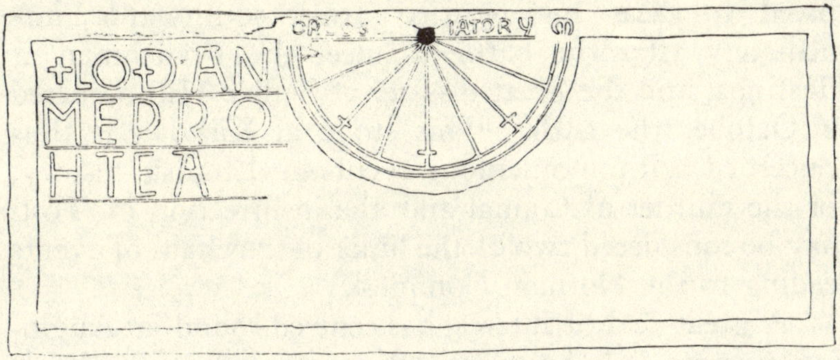

SAXON SUNDIAL AT EDSTONE.
(From a rubbing by Mr J. Romilly Allen, F.S.A.)

Harold's brother, became Earl of Northumbria in 1055, we know also that the Northumbrians rose against Tosti's misgovernment and his many crimes, among which must be placed the murder of the Gamal mentioned in the inscription, and that in 1065 Tosti was outlawed, his house-carles killed, and his treasures seized. After this we also know that Tosti was defeated by the Earls Edwin and Morcar, and having fled to Scotland, submitted himself to Harold Hardrada, King of Norway, who had arrived in the Tyne with his fleet early in

September 1066, that they then sailed southwards, and having sacked Scarborough defeated Edwin and Morcar at Fulford near York only eight days before the landing of William the Norman at Pevensey. Harold having made forced marches reached York on September the 24th, and defeated his brother and the Norwegian king, both being slain in the battle which was fought at Stamford Bridge on the Derwent. Harold was forced to take his wearied army southwards immediately after the battle to meet the Frenchmen at Hastings, and the great disaster of Senlac Hill occurred on October the 14th. This stone at Kirkdale is thus concerned with momentous events in English history, for the murder of Gamal and the insurrection of Tosti may be considered two of the links in the chain of events leading to the Norman Conquest.

A great deal of interest has centred round an Anglo-Saxon cross-slab built into the west wall of Kirkdale church. At the time of its discovery the late Rev. Daniel H. Haigh[1] tells us that a runic inscription spelling *Kununc Oithilwalde*, meaning "to King Æthelwald," was quite legible. This would seem to indicate that the founder of Lastingham monastery was buried at Kirkdale, or that the site of Bede's, "Læstingaeu" was at Kirkdale if the stone has not been moved from its original position.

The inscription has now perished, but Bishop Browne tells us[2] that when he had photographs taken

[1] *Yorkshire Archæological Journal*, v. 134.

[2] Browne, Rt. Rev. G. F.: "The Conversion of the Heptarchy," p. 151.

Fragment of a stone cross in Pickering Church.

A curious figure on the shaft of a pre-Norman cross in the north aisle of Middleton Church.

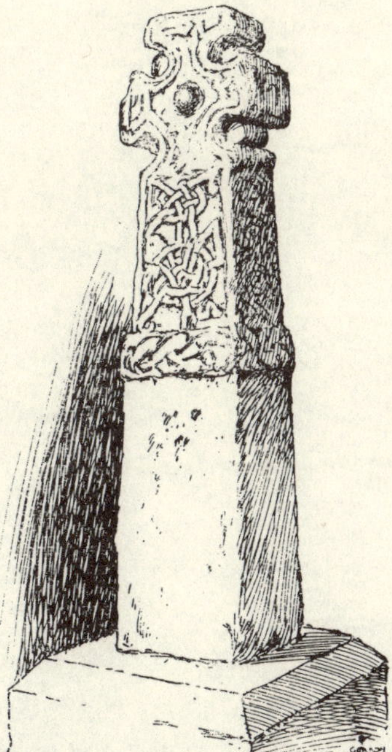

A pre-Norman cross in Middleton Church.

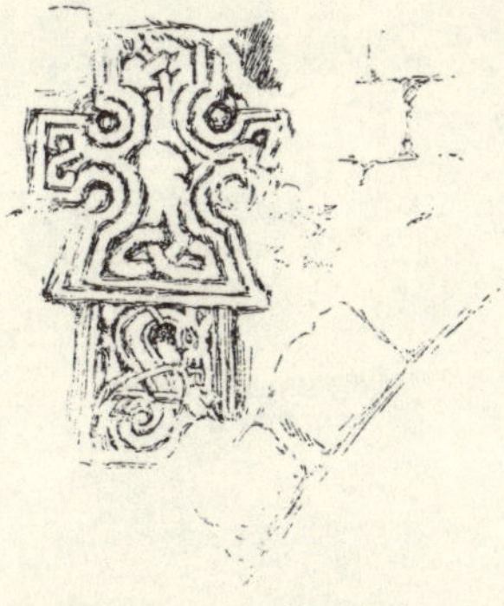

The richly carved head of a pre-Norman cross in the south wall of the nave of Ellerburne Church.

SAXON OR PRE-NORMAN REMAINS AT AND NEAR PICKERING.

of the stone in 1886 "there was only one rune left, the 'Oi' of the king's name." "I have seen, however," he says, "the drawing made of the letters when the stone was found, and many of them were still legible when the Rev. Daniel Haigh worked at the stone." There seems little doubt that this most valuable inscription might have been preserved if the stone had been kept from the action of the air and weather.

There are several other pre-Norman sculptured stones at Kirkdale. They are generally built into the walls on the exterior, and are not very apparent unless carefully looked for. In the vestry some fragments of stone bearing interlaced ornament are preserved.

Not only at Kirkdale are these pre-Norman stones built into walls that appear to belong to a date prior to the Conquest, but also at Middleton there is a fine cross forming part of the fabric of the church tower. The west doorway now blocked up is generally considered to be of Saxon work, but the quoins of the tower, though bearing much resemblance to the pure "long and short" work that may be seen at Bradford-on-Avon, are composed of stones that are almost equal in height.

The Rev. Reginald Caley has suggested that the original Saxon tower of Brompton church may have been incorporated into the present structure whose walls are of unusual thickness, the stone work in some places showing characteristics of pre-Norman workmanship. At Ellerburne the curious spiral ornaments of the responds of the chancel arch have also been attributed to pre-Norman times, but in this case and possibly at Middleton also, the Saxon features may have appeared in Norman buildings owing to the employ-

CROSS SLAB INSERTED IN WEST WALL OF KIRKDALE CHURCH.

The runes which gave rise to the belief that this was the gravestone of King Æthelwald have perished.

SLAB WITH INTERLACED ORNAMENT AT KIRKDALE CHURCH.

(*Both crosses are from the Associated Architectural Societies' Reports.*)

ment of Saxon workmen, who did not necessarily for several years entirely abandon their own methods, despite the fact that they might be working under Norman masters. There is a very roughly hewn font in the little chapel of Ease, in the village of Levisham. It bears a cross and a rope ornamentation, and may possibly be of pre-Norman origin, although it was being used as a cattle trough in a neighbouring farm-yard before the restoration in 1884. The parish church of Levisham, standing alone in the valley below the village, has a very narrow and unadorned chancel arch. This may possibly belong to Saxon or very early Norman times, but Mr Joseph Morris [1] has pointed out that a similar one occurs at Scawton, which is known to have been built in 1146, and the evidence of a Saxon stone built into the south-east corner of the chancel of Levisham church supports my belief in the later date. On the south wall of the chancel of Lockton church I have seen a roughly shaped oblong stone bearing in one corner the markings of a very rude sundial, and I find that there is another on the wall of a cottage in the same village.[2] I am unable to give its position, but from a drawing I have examined, it appears to be of more careful workmanship than the one built into the church wall. At Sinnington church another of these very crude sundials has been discovered, and what may be part of a similar one is high up on the east wall of the chancel of Ellerburne church. At Kirby Moorside a fine cross with interlaced work is built into the porch of the vicarage. At Wykeham there is a very plain cross of uncertain age, and Ellerburne, Lastingham, Sinnington,

[1] Morris, J. E.: "The North Riding of Yorkshire," p. 33.

[2] Illustrated, facing p. 209, "Associated Architectural Societies' Reports," vol. xii. 1873.

Kirkdale, Kirby Misperton, and Middleton are all rich in carved crosses and incised slabs. Pickering church only possesses one fragment of stone work that we may safely attribute to a date prior to the Conquest. It seems to be part of the shaft or of an arm of a cross, and bears one of the usual types of dragon as well as knot or interlaced ornament. The font, which has been thought by some to be of Saxon origin, seems to be formed from

Two Crossheads at Sinnington Church.
The one on the left shows a Crucifixion.

part of the inverted base of a pillar, and though composed of old material, probably dates in its present form of a font from as recent a period as the restoration of Charles II., the original font having been destroyed in Puritan times (Chapter X.). It would appear that when it was decided to build a large Norman church at Pickering the desire to put up a building that would be a great advance on the previous structure—for we cannot suppose that Pickering was without a church in Saxon times—led to the destruction of every trace of the earlier building.

Hinderwell mentions a curious legend in connection with the cave in a small conical hill at Ebberston, that has since been destroyed. The country people called it Ilfrid's Hole, the tradition being that a Saxon king of that name took shelter there when wounded after a battle. An inscription that was formerly placed above the cave said: "Alfrid, King of Northumberland, was wounded in a bloody battle near this place, and was removed to Little Driffield, where he lies buried; hard by his entrenchments may be seen." The roughly built stone hut with a domed roof that now crowns the hill is within twenty yards of the site of the cave, and was built by Sir Charles Hotham in 1790 to preserve the memory of this legendary king.

In the period that lay between the conversion of Northumbria to Christianity in 627, and the ravages of Dane and Northman in the ninth and tenth centuries, we know by the traces that survive that the Saxons built a church in each of their villages, and that they placed beautifully sculptured crosses above the graves of their dead. The churches were small and quite simple in plan, generally consisting of a nave and chancel, with perhaps a tower at the west end. Owing to the importance of Pickering the Saxon church may have been a little in advance of the rest, and its tower may have been ornamented as much as that of Earl's Barton, but we are entering the dangerous realms of conjecture, and must be reconciled to that one fragment of a pre-Norman cross that is now carefully preserved in the south aisle of the present building.

CHAPTER VII

The Forest and Vale in Norman Times

A.D. 1066–1154

IN the early years of the reign of William I., when the northern counties rose against his rule, the Pickering district seems to have required more drastic treatment than any other. In 1069 the Conqueror spent the winter in the north of England, and William of Malmesbury describes how "he ordered the towns and fields of the whole district to be laid waste; the fruits and grain to be destroyed by fire or by water . . . thus the resources of a once flourishing province were cut off, by fire, slaughter, and devastation; the ground for more than sixty miles, totally uncultivated and unproductive, remains bare to the present day." This is believed to have been written about 1135, and would give us grounds for believing that the desolation continued for over sixty years. A vivid light is thrown on the destruction wrought at Pickering by the record in the Domesday Book, which is as follows:—

"In *Picheringa* there are to be taxed thirty-seven carucates of land, which twenty ploughs may till. Morcar held this for one manor, with its berewicks

Bartune (Barton), *Neuuctune* (Newton), *Blandebi* (Blandsby) and Estorp (Easthorp). It is now the king's. There is therein one plough and twenty villanes with six ploughs; meadow half a mile long and as much broad: but all the wood which belongs to the manor is sixteen miles long and four broad. This manor in the time of King Edward was valued at fourscore and eight pounds; now at twenty shillings and four-pence."[1]

This remarkable depreciation from £88 to £1 and 4d. need not be, as Bawdwen thought, a mistake in the original, but an ample proof of the vengeance of the Conqueror. All the lands belonging to the powerful Saxon Earls Edwin and Morcar seem to have suffered much the same fate.

The Domesday account also mentions that

"To this manor belongs the soke of these lands, viz.: *Brunton* (Brompton), *Odulfesmare* ( ), *Edbriztune* (Ebberston), *Alnestune* (Allerston), *Wiltune* (Wilton), *Farmanesbi* (Farmanby), *Rozebi* (Roxby), *Chinetorp* (Kinthorp), *Chilnesmares* ( ), *Aschilesmares* ( ), *Maxudesmares* ( ), *Snechintune* (Snainton), *Chigogemers* ( ), *Elreburne* (Ellerburne), *Torentune* (Thornton), *Leuccen* (Levisham), *Middeletun* (Middleton) and *Bartune* (Barton). In the whole there are fifty carucates to be taxed, which twenty-seven ploughs may till. There are now only ten villanes, having two ploughs: the

1 "Dom Boc," the Yorkshire Domesday. The Rev. Wm. Bawdwen, 1809, p. 11

rest is waste; yet there are twenty acres of meadow. The whole length is sixteen miles and the breadth four."

The unrecognisable names all end in mare, mares or mers, suggesting that they were all on the marshes and Bawdwen is probably incorrect in calling *Loctemares*—Low-moors. Associated with each place the Domesday record gives the names of the former landowners.

I give them in tabular form:—

Manor in Domesday	Modern Name	Held by
Bruntune	Brompton	Ulf
Truzstal	Troutsdale	Archil
Alurestan	Allerston	Gospatric
Loctemares	Low-moors or marshes	Archil
Torentun	Thornton-le-dale	Torbrand, Gospatric and Tor
Elreburne	Ellerburne	Gospatric
Dalbi	Dalby	,,
Chetelestorp	Kettlethorp	,,
Lochetun	Lockton	Ulchil
Aslachesbi	Aislaby	Gospatric
Wereltun	Wrelton	,,
Caltorne	Cawthorne	,,
Croptune	Cropton	,,
Abbetune	Habton	Ulf and Cnut
Ritun	Ryton	Canute
Berg.	Barugh	Ligulf
Berg	,,	Esbern
Wellebrune	Welburn	Grim
Normanebi	Normanby	Gamel
Bragebi	Brawby	Ulf
Chirchebi	(?) Kirby Moorside	Torbrant
Chirchebi	(?) Kirkdale	Gamel
Lestingeham	Lastingham	,,
Spantun	Spaunton	,,

Manor in Domesday	Modern Name	Held by
Dalbi	Dalby	Gamel
Sevenicton	(?) Sinnington	Torbrand
Hotun	Hutton-le-hole or Hutton Buscel	Torbrant
Atun	Ayton	Gamel
Micheledestun	Great Edstone	,,
Parva Edestun	Little Edstone	Torbrant
Mispeton, now Kirby Misperton	Belonging to Chirchebi	

The number of ploughs, of oxgangs and carucates, and of villanes and bordars in each manor is given in Domesday, but to give each extract in full would take up much space and would be a little wearisome.

We know that the impoverished country was, like the rest of England, given by the Conqueror to his followers. The village of Hutton Buscel obtains its name from the Buscel family which came over to England with William the Norman. Hinderwell, quoting[1] from some unnamed source, tells us that "Reginald Buscel (whose father came over with the Conqueror) married Alice, the sister of William, Abbot of Whitby, and at the time of his marriage, gave the church of Hotun, which his father had built, to the monastery of Whitby." This was before the year 1154, and the lower part of the tower of the present church of Hutton Buscel, being of Norman date, may belong to that early building.

On Vivers Hill to the east of the village of Kirby Moorside there are indications among the trees of what is believed to have been the castle of the Stutevilles.

[1] Thomas Hinderwell: "History of Scarborough," p. 331.

Robert de Stuteville is said to have come over with the Conqueror, and to have received land at Kirby Moorside as a reward for his services.

The country having received the full fury of William's wrath very slowly recovered its prosperity under Norman rulers. On the slope of the hills all the way from Scarborough to Helmsley, castles began to make their appearance, and sturdy Norman churches were built in nearly every village.

The great Norman keep of Scarborough Castle with its shattered side still frowns above the holiday crowds of that famous seaside resort, but of the other strongholds of the district built in this castle-building age it is not easy to speak with certainty. But the evidences of Norman work are fairly plain at Pickering Castle, and there seems little doubt that a fortress of some strength was built at this important point to overawe the inhabitants. Mr G.T. Clark in his "Mediæval Military Architecture"[1] says that he considers Pickering Castle to represent "one great type of Anglo-Norman fortress —that is, a castle of Norman masonry upon an English earthwork, for the present walls, if not Norman, are unquestionably laid on Norman lines." He thinks that the earthworks would be taken possession of and fortified either late in the eleventh or early in the twelfth century, and that the keep, the chief part of the curtain walls, and the Norman door near the northwest corner are remains of this building. The gateways

[1] George T. Clark: "Mediæval Military Architecture in England," p. 372.

THE SOUTH SIDE OF THE NAVE OF PICKERING CHURCH.

The arches on the north side are of much simpler Norman work. The nearest painting shows the story of the legendary St Katherine of Alexandria. [*The Copyright is reserved by Dr John L. Kirk.*

may be Norman or they may belong to the time of Richard II. (1377-99), but Mr Clark inclines to the earlier date. It is possible that the Norman doorway just mentioned may have been an entrance to one of the towers mentioned by Leland but now completely lost sight of. The architrave has a beaded angle ornamented with pointed arches repeated, and if it is of late Norman date it is the only part of the castle which Mr Clark considers to be "distinctly referable to that period."

There is no doubt at all that the arcades of the present nave of Pickering church were built at this time, and the lower part of the tower is also of Norman date. The north arcade is earlier than that on the south side, having perfectly plain semi-circular arches and massive columns with fluted capitals. On the south the piers are much more ornate, the contrast being very plainly seen in the photograph reproduced here.

To have necessitated such a spacious church at this time, Pickering must have been a populous town; possibly it grew on account of the safety afforded by the castle, and it seems to indicate the importance of the place in the time of the Norman kings.

One of the most complete little Norman churches in Yorkshire is to be seen at Salton, a village about six miles south-west of Pickering. It appears to have been built at the beginning of the twelfth century, and afterwards to have suffered from fire, parts of the walls by their redness showing traces of having been burnt.

A very thorough restoration has given the building a

The South Doorway of the Norman Church of Salton.

It is ornamented with very curious double beak-heads. In the upper corners are given two of the curious corbels on the south side of the nave.

rather new aspect, but this does not detract from the interest of the church. The chancel arch is richly ornamented with two patterns of zig-zag work, the south door of the nave has a peculiar decoration of double beak-heads, and though some of the early

Curious Ornament in the Norman Chancel Arch at Ellerburne.

The crude carving suggests Saxon work, and it was possibly the production of Saxon masons under Norman supervision.

windows have been replaced by lancets, a few of the Norman slits remain. Middleton church has already been mentioned as containing what appears to be a Saxon doorway in the tower. This may have been saved from an earlier building together with the lower part of the tower, but if it did not come into existence before the conquest the tower and nave were built in early Norman times. The south arcade probably belongs to the latest phase of Transitional Norman architecture, if not the commencement of the early English period. Running along the west and north walls of the north aisle is a stone bench, an unusual feature even in Norman churches.

Ellerburne church has some very interesting Norman work in the chancel arch. The ornament is so crude that it would seem as though very primitive Saxon workmen had been working under Norman influence, for, while the masonry is plainly of the Norman period, the ornament appears to belong to an earlier time. There must have been a church at Normanby at this period, for the south door of the present building is Norman. Sinnington church also belongs to this time. The Norman chancel arch was taken down many years ago, but the stones having been preserved in the church it was found possible to replace them in their original position at the Restoration in 1904. There are remains of three doorways including the blocked one at the west end. The south doorway is Transitional Norman, and is supposed to have been added about 1180. The porch and present chancel belong to the thirteenth century, but during the Restoration some interesting relics of the earlier Norman chancel were discovered in the walls of the fabric that replaced it. A small stone coffin containing human remains with several wild boars' tusks and a silver wire ring was found in the nave.

THE TRANSITIONAL NORMAN CRYPT UNDER THE CHANCEL OF LASTINGHAM CHURCH.
It is a complete little underground church, having nave, apse, and aisles.

Lastingham church as it now stands is only part of the original Transitional Norman church, for there are evidences that the nave extended to the west of the present tower which was added in the fifteenth century. It appears that the western part of the nave was destroyed or injured not many years after its erection, and that the eastern part was repaired in early English times. The chancel with its vaulted roof and circular apse, and the crypt beneath, are of the same date as the original nave, and though the capitals of the low columns in the crypt might be thought to be of earlier work, expert opinion places them at the same Transitional Norman date. The crypt has a nave, apse and aisles, and is therefore a complete little underground church. Semi-circular arches between the pillars support the plain vaulting only a few feet above one's head, and the darkness is such that it requires a little time to be able to see the foliage and interlaced arches of the capitals surmounting the squat columns.

At Brompton the Perpendicular church contains evidences of the building of this period that once existed there, in the shape of four Norman capitals, two of them built into the east wall of the south aisle and two in the jambs of the chancel arch. In the massive walls of the lower part of the tower there may also be remains of the Norman building.

At the adjoining village of Snainton the old church was taken down in 1835, but the Norman stones of the south doorway of the nave have been re-erected, and now form an arch in an adjoining wall. The font of the same period having been found in a garden, was replaced in the church on a new base in 1893. In Edstone church the Norman font, with a simple arcade pattern running round the circular base, is still to be seen, and at Levisham the very plain chancel arch mentioned in the preceding chapter is also of Norman work. Allerston church has some pieces of zig-zag ornament built into the north wall, and Ebberston church has a slit window on the north side of the chancel, and the south door built in Norman times. The nave arcade at Ebberston may belong to the Transitional Norman period and the font also.

The Norman font at Edstone.

Most of the churches in the neighbourhood of Pickering are, therefore, seen to have either been built in the Norman age or to possess fragments of the buildings that were put up in that period. The difficulty of preventing the churches from being too cold was met in some degree by having no windows on the north side as at Sinnington, and those windows that faced the other cardinal points were sufficiently small to keep out the extremes of temperature.

The written records belonging to the Norman period of the history of Pickering seem to have largely disappeared, so that with the exception of the Domesday Book, and a few stray references to people or places in this locality, we are largely dependent on the buildings that have survived those tempestuous years.

Pickering appears to have been a royal possession during the whole of this time, and it is quite probable that the Norman kings hunted in the forest and lodged with their Courts in the castle, for a writ issued by Henry I. is dated at Pickering.

CHAPTER VIII

The Forest and Vale in the Time of the Plantagenets

A.D. 1154 to 1485

THE story of these three centuries is told to a most remarkable extent in the numerous records of the Duchy of Lancaster relating to the maintenance of the royal Forest of Pickering. They throw a clear light on many aspects of life at Pickering, and by picking out some of the more picturesque incidents recorded we may see to what extent the severe forest laws kept in check the poaching element in the neighbourhood. We can also discover some incidents in connection with the visits of some of the English kings to the royal forest of Pickering, as well as matters relating to the repair of the castle.

In the Parliament of 1295, in Edward I.'s reign, Pickering, for the first and only occasion, sent representatives to the national assembly. The parliamentary return states [1] that the persons returned on that occasion were

Robertus Turcock
Robertus Turcock,

but whether this is a mistake by the recorder or

[1] G. R. Park, "The Parliamentary Representation of Yorkshire, 1886," pp. 266 and 283.

whether two men of the same name were returned is uncertain.

Among the High Sheriffs of Yorkshire in the fourteenth and fifteenth centuries were

1390	Richard II.	Jacobus de Pykering.
1394	„	„ „
1398	„	„ „
1432	Henry VI.	Sir Richard de Pykering.
1450	„	Sir James de Pykering knt.

In 1311 Johannes de Cropton was one of the members for Scarborough in Edward II.'s Parliament of that year.

Pickering was held as royal property by William the Conqueror, and with a few short intervals it has remained crown property until the present day. It is therefore no matter for surprise to find that several of the Plantagenet kings came to hunt in the forest. It appears to have been a royal possession in the time of Henry I., and also in February 1201, when King John visited the castle,[1] for a charter granted by him to the nuns of Wykeham is dated at Pickering. In 1248 William Lord d'Acre was made keeper of the castle, but towards the close of his reign Henry III. (1216-1272) gave the castle, manor, and forest of Pickering to his son Edmund Crouchback, and from him the property has descended through the Lancastrian branch of the royal family, so that it now forms part of the possessions of the Duchy of Lancaster.

[1] Young's "History of Whitby," vol. ii. p. 733.

From other records we find that King John was also at Pickering for at least a day in August 1208 and in March 1210.

In 1261 Pickering Castle was held against Henry III. by Hugh le Bigod, and some of the wardrobe accounts of the reign of Edward II. have reference to a visit to Pickering. The place must have had painful memories for the king in connection with the capture of his favourite Piers Gaveston at Scarborough Castle in 1312. This visit was, however, separated from that fateful event by eleven years.

"3 August 1323, at Pickering. Paid to William Hunt, the King's huntsman, by way of gift at the direction of Harsike—£1; to Agnes, wife of Roger de Mar, porter of the chamber, gift—10s.: to Guillot de la Pittere, groom of the Queen's chamber, gift—£1; to Dighton Wawayn, valet of Robert Wawayn, carrying letters from his master to the king, gift—2s. To John, son of Ibote of Pickering, who followed the king a whole day when he hunted the stag in Pickering chase, gift by order—10s.; to Walter de Seamer, Mariner, keeper of the ship called the Magdalen, of which Cook atte Wose was master, a gift, the money being given to John Harsike to give him —£1.

"23 August, at Egginton, on Blakey Moor. Paid to Sir Roger de Felton, Knight of the King's Chamber, for his ransom at the time when he was taken by the Scots at Rievaulx in company with the Earl of Richmond, in October, 1322, a gift by the hands of John Harsike, who delivered the money to Sir Roger in the King's presence. £100.

"To Edmund Dorney, the King's palfreyman, who always followed the King when he hunted—£1.

"31 August, at Glascowollehouse. Paid to Ernest, running footman of Sir Robert del Idle, who carried letters to the King, a gift 6s. 8d.; to Dan Thomas de Broghton, monk of Rievaulx, to buy him a coat, a gift—10s."

The entries show that the king journeyed to Whorlton Castle to stay with Nicholas de Meynell. He seems to have gone by way of Lockton and Spaunton Moor, and appears to have stayed a night at Danby. The accounts mention an amount paid on September 1st to certain foresters' servants who set the king's nets to take roe-deer in Whorlton Park, and we also discover that the day's sport was varied by the singing of Alice the red-haired and Alice de Whorlton, who gave "Simon de Montfort" and other songs before the king, and received a gift of 4s.

The poor of Pickering profited by the royal visits. Here are two items in the accounts.

"26 September [1323] at Skipton. Paid, by order of the King, to Lorchon Sewer alms distributed by the King at Pickering—3d."

In 1334 Edward III. was more generous than his predecessor, for we find "26 May. Alms—to Sir Walter de London, King's Almoner, for food for 100 poor on the feast of Corpus Christi at Pickering, at the hands of his clerk Henry—12s. 6d."

During the hunting in the forest a hound was lost and recovered as follows:—

"June, (at Beverley), given to Robert de Bridgegate, leading to the King a hound lost at Pickering, a gift the same day 6s. 8d."

The reference to the Scottish raid as far south as Rievaulx Abbey touches an event of great interest. In 1322 the Scots, led by Robert Bruce, had entered England and plundered many places, including the splendid Cistercian monastery just mentioned, and the following record shows that the Vale of Pickering purchased immunity for 300 marks.

"John Topcliffe Rector of Semer Wm. Wyern & John Wickham with others of Pickering with the assent of the whole community, on Tuesday 13th Oct. 1322 purchased from Robert Bruce through the Earl of Moray for 300 marks, to be paid at Berwick, half at Candlemas next & the other half at Trinity next, the immunity of the Vale of Pickering from the River Seven on the west to the sea on the east. Further they say that Nich^s Haldane, Wm. Hastings and John Manneser, at the request of the men of the whole community, surrendered at Rievaulx to Robert Bruce on Saturday the 17th of Oct. following, to sojourn as hostages in Scotland until the 300 marks were paid. Further they say that the 300 marks are still unpaid, for afterwards the men of the community refused payment and once for all. Further they said that the said Nicholas William and John are still in prison in Scotland, and all the men and all townships, manors, hamlets, lands and tenements of the said Vale within the bounds aforesaid were preserved from all damage and injury whatsoever through the above-mentioned ransom."

From the Chronicle of John Hardyng we find that Richard II. was imprisoned at Pickering before being taken to Knaresborough, and finally to Pontefract. The lines in his quaint verse must have been written between 1436 and 1465.

> "The Kyng the[n] sent Kyng Richard to Ledis,
> There to be kepte surely in previtee,
> Fro the[n]s after to Pykeryng we[n]t he nedes,
> And to Knauesburgh after led was he,
> But to Pountfrete last where he did die."[1]

There seems little doubt that the story of the murder of the king at Pontefract Castle by Sir Piers Exton is untrue, but "nothing is certainly known of the time, place, or manner of his death."

The records of the Coucher Book contain a mass of interesting and often entertaining information concerning the illicit removals of oak trees from the forest, hunting and killing the royal deer and other animals, as well as many other offences.

At the forest Eyre, a sort of assizes, held at Pickering in 1334 to deal with a great accumulated mass of infringements on the rights of the forest, the first case is against Sir John de Melsa, Lord of Levisham, who was, according to the jury, "in the habit of employing men to make and burn charcoal out of browsewood

[1] The Chronicle of John Hardyng, edited by Henry Ellis, 1812, p. 356.

and dry sticks in his woods at Levisham, which are now within the bounds of the forest, and he exposes the charcoal for sale, injuring the lord and annoying the deer, by what right they know not. Sir John is summoned, appears, and pleads that he and his ancestors and the tenants of the Manor of Levisham have from ancient time taken the browsewood and dry sticks in the said woods and burnt them into charcoal, and afterwards exposed them for sale, and given them away at pleasure as part of his and their manorial rights. He asks that the officers of the forest may try the question. As it clearly appears to the Court by the answer of Sir John that he is making a claim to take a profit in the forest which he did not claim on the first day of the Eyre, as the custom is, and as proclamation was made, judgment is given that the liberty be seized into the Lord's hands, and Sir John is to answer for its value in the meantime. Afterwards Sir John appears, and prays that he may be allowed to pay a composition for making his claim, and a composition of 6s. 8d. is fixed. Surety, Richard de Naulton. The jury also present that a bridge called Friar Bridge, beyond the Costa, across which people are wont to pass on horseback and on foot going from Pickering to Malton, is in such bad repair that people cannot pass over, but have to make a divergence of about a mile and a half in the forest, treading down and injuring the pasturage of the deer. The Abbot of Rievaulx and all Abbots of that place are bound to repair it. He is summoned, appears, and does not deny that he and they are bound to repair it, but he says that the bridge is not in such bad repair that people cannot pass over it as they are wont and ought to do without doing harm to any one. He asks that an inquiry may be made by the officers of the forest. An inquiry is directed. The foresters, verderers, and regarders, sworn and charged, say on their oaths, that after the summons for the Eyre was issued, the bridge was in such bad repair that people being unable to pass over it made a divergence into the forest, annoying the Lord's deer and treading down their pasturage. Afterwards the Abbot repaired it so that it requires nothing further, and people can quite well pass over it. Therefore as to the present repair of the bridge the Abbot is acquitted, but he is to be amerced because he did not repair it before.

"The jury also present that the present Prior of Bridlington erected a sheepfold at Newland in the forest, 100 feet long and 12 feet broad, injuring thereby the Lord's deer, notwithstanding that on another occasion at the last Eyre of the Justices the sheepfold was ordered to be taken down. By what right they know not. The Prior appears and prays to be allowed to compound with the Lord, and that he and his successors may rent the sheepfold in perpetuity, inasmuch as it no longer injures the deer. Since the foresters, verderers, and regarders prove that it is so the Prior is permitted to compound by the payment of 13s. 4d. (surety Ralph de Morton), and he is likewise given a grant for ever of the sheepfold at a

SOME OF THE WALL PAINTINGS ON THE SOUTH SIDE OF THE NAVE OF PICKERING CHURCH.

The upper left-hand corner shows what is apparently the funeral of the Virgin Mary with the miserable Prince astride the coffin. On the long strip and on the two spandrels are scenes from the Death and Resurrection of Our Lord.

* The last of the seven acts of corporal mercy is shown here.

[*Copyright reserved by Dr John L. Kirk.*

yearly rent of 6d. at Michaelmas. The Prior is to hold it for ever quit of regard. The jury also present that the bridge and road of Pul within the forest, which are common highways for carriages, carts, drifts, and packsaddles are in such bad repair that none can pass over them. The Prior of the Hospital of St John, by reason of his tenure of lands which formerly belonged to the Knights Templars, and the Prioress of Yedingham, are bound to repair and maintain them. They are summoned. The Prioress appears in person, the Prior by his attorney, Walter de Trusseley. The Prioress says that neither she nor any of her predecessors ever from ancient time repaired or ought to repair it, because she says that the Prior, by reason of his tenure of the lands which belonged to the Templars, is bound to repair and maintain the bridge and road as often as need requires, in the same way that the Templars, before the abolition of their Order, from ancient time, by reason of their tenure of their lands at Foulbridge, which the Prior now holds, repaired and maintained the bridge and road. She asks that an inquiry may be directed." The Prior, by his attorney, denies most of the charges seriatim, but the judgment of the Court is that "the Prior be distrained to compel him to repair and make good the bridge and road to the east, and is to be amerced because he has not done it sooner, and the Prioress is to be acquitted because the road to the west of the bridge is not at present out of repair."

This is a typical example of the manner of recording these quarrels over responsibilities and delinquencies in connection with the forest, each side seeming to deny in detail most of the charges brought forward. Most of the cases relating to the stealing of oaks and brushwood and to poaching matters generally are compounded for.

The following is a case of officers of the forest making themselves a nuisance with the local people. "The jury also present that whereas John de Monmouth has 20^{s} [? a year], a toft and two oxgangs of land, with the appurtenances in Pickering, John Scot 30^{s} a year, and William Courtman 5^{s} at the Earl's expense for being fosterers in the West Ward [of Pickering Forest], yet they surcharge all the inhabitants with their living and that of their servants, annoying the country. They are summoned, appear, and compound. . . . The jury also present that Richard Cockard of Helmsley, John de Harlay, and William Gower, forester, of Scalby, Langdale, and Fullwood, under colour of their office, collect sheaves in autumn and wool and keep servants on board in the country. They are summoned, appear, and make composition. . . ." "The jury also present that John de Shirburn drew the timber of a house in Pickering within the forest of Shirburn without the forest, and John Beal of West Heslerton drew the timber of a barn in Pickering within the boundery of the forest to West Heslerton without the forest, and John de Shirburn and Thomas Bret likewise drew the timber of a house at Pickering within the boundaries of the forest to Shirburn without the forest, injuring the Earl and contrary to the assize of the forest. They are summoned, appear, and each makes composition."

"Henry the Fowler, of Barugh, Adam the Fowler, of Ayton, William Hare and William Fox, catch birds in the forest by means of birdlime-nets and other contrivances." The Clergy were frequently involved in the taking of timber from the forest. "Robert de Hampton, Rector of Middleton, took at different times three green oaks below Cropton Castle, and on a third occasion took there a green oak, without the demesne, without livery of the foresters or warrant.—

"In mercy:—

"The Abbot of Whitby took a green oak in Goathland within the demesne, value 3^d, and was let out on bail. He has not surrendered and does not appear to judgment with his bail, and he is responsible for the value and a fine of 3^s. Afterwards it appears that his bail are dead, so proceedings against them are stayed.

"Eldred of Ellerburne, deceased, carried off a green oak within the demesne, value 7^d. His successor, Edmund de Hastings, is responsible for its value, a fine of 7^d and also 7^d, the value of vert likewise taken in the Hay.

"Hugh, Vicar of Ebberston, deceased, took a green oak without the demesne without livery of the foresters or warrant; John, son of Geoffrey, and John de la Chymyne, his executors, are responsible.—

"The Lady Beatrice of Farmanby, deceased, took a green oak without the demesne, without livery of the foresters or warrant. Her successor, William Hastings, is responsible.

"The Rector of Brompton, deceased, felled two green oaks without the demesne, without livery of foresters or warrant. The same persons responsible.

"The Preceptor of Foulbridge felled and carried away four green oaks in fence month. The Prior of the Hospital of St John is responsible.

"The Prioress of Wykeham claims for herself and her tenants in Wykeham and Ruston to receive and take housebote and hedgebote in the woods of North Cave heads and Barley, according to the assize of the forest, and common of pasture for all animals except goats in the same woods and the wastes and moors adjoining, that is to say, northwards from Yarlesike. . . . The Justices consider that before allowing her claims an inqury should be made as to how the Prioress and her predecessors have exercised their rights."

"Sir John de Meaux claims to have housebote and hedgebote for himself, his men and tenants of Levisham in his woods of Levisham, in accordance with the assize of the forest, and reasonable estovers of turves in his demesnes of Levisham, for himself, his men and his tenants, and ironstone and a smelting-place in his woods of Levisham, paying to the Earl an annual rent of 2s and æries of falcons, merlins and sparrow-hawk, and whatever honey is found in his woods at Levisham, and he claims to have a woodward in such woods. He is ready to prove that all these rights having been exercised by himself and his ancestors from ancient time, the housebote and hedgebote being appurtenant to his free tenement in Levisham, and brousewood and dry wood being taken to feed his furnaces. An inquiry is directed, and it is found that Sir John and his ancestors have from ancient time enjoyed the rights so claimed without interruption. Judgment is given in accordance with the verdict."

"Ralph de Bulmer claims to have a free park at Thornton Riseborough, and to keep hounds to hunt there. He claims that King John by deed granted to one Alan de Winton, then holder of the park, and his heirs, liberty to inclose and make a free park, and to keep his hounds to hunt there; by virtue whereof Alan, whose estate he now holds, exercised the rights. He says that Edward II. inspected the grant of John, and granted to Ralph, that he and his heirs might hold the park with its appurtenances as Alan held it, without let or hindrance on the part of the King or his Justices, Escheators, Sheriffs, or other bailiffs, or officers whatsoever.

"Thomas de Pickering and Margaret, his wife, claim to have a woodward to keep their demesne wood at Lockton, and that no one may lop branches therein or fell any tree without their consent, and that they may fell and give away at pleasure green trees and dry, and give and sell dry trees at pleasure without view of the foresters." In the following claim a mention is made of the "wildcat." "Thomas Wake of Liddell claims to have a free chase for fox, hare, wildcat, and badger, within the boundaries of his barony of Middleton, namely, from the place called Alda on the Costa to the standing stone above the Spital Myre of Pickering, etc."

"Hugh de Nevill is indicted, for that whilst he was bailiff of Pickering, under colour of his office, he arrested one Robert the Dyer, lately residing in Ebberston, bound his hands as if he were a felon, though he had not been indicted, and took from him a horse, harness, and other goods and chattels to the value of 20^{s}. Afterwards he entrusted him to the care of his servant to take to York, but when they reached Malton, the servant let his prisoner escape.

"Henry de Rippley, sub-bailiff of Pickering, fined for having seized goods and chattels of Sir Robert de Scarborough, at Ebberston, for which he was indicted and found guilty on his own confession, 3^{s} 4^{d}."

A case in which the poachers showed their total disregard for the officers of the forest is given as follows.

"Stephen son of Richard of Eskdale, Nicholas the Taylor of Whitby, and John de Moorsholm of Sneaton Thorpe, were indicted for having, on Wednesday 23rd March 1334, at Blakey Moor [near Saltersgate], within the forest, hunted with bows, arrows and greyhounds, and taken sixty-six harts and hinds, of which they cut off the heads of nine and fixed them upon stakes in the Moor."

"As regards those who caught hares and wandered in the forest with bows and arrows contrary to the assize of the forest, Mathilda de Bruys is accustomed to hunt and catch hares." She compounded for 5^s, Robert Bruce and John Perot being sureties.

The Coucher Book mentions that Henry I. issued a writ dated at Pickering. This would suggest that Pickering Castle was standing between 1100 and 1135, for the king would scarcely have visited the place unless he had had proper quarters for himself and his suite, and the castle alone could have afforded this. A record of 1347 mentions the pillory at Pickering, and suggests a lively scene that took place in the august presence of the Earl of Lancaster. "William de Kirkby and others conspired amongst themselves to indict John de Buckton, Hugh de Neville, John de Barton, and others for that they on Monday, 25th June 1347, took six harts in Pickering Forest and set up the head of one in the sight of the Earl of Lancaster upon the pillory in Pickering town, in consequence of which John de Buckton, Hugh de Neville and John de Barton were taken and imprisoned in Pickering Castle and suffered great loss of their goods. Afterwards, in the same town, William appeared in the King's Bench and asked to be allowed to compound for the offences presented against him, as well as those to which he had already pleaded as the rest. The request was granted, and he paid the fine entered in the rolls."

"The jurors of the several wappentakes of Yorkshire presented that David de Wigan and others on Wednesday, 11th July 1347, violently entered by night the house of Thomas, Vicar of Ebberston, seized him and led him to Pickering Castle until he compounded with them for £2, though," adds the record, "he had never been indicted for any offence" (!) This David de Wigan must have terrorised the neighbourhood at this time, for he and others scarcely a week later "seized Adam del Selley Bridge at Selley Bridge [near Marishes Road Station] and led him with them until he compounded with them for £4." On the same Tuesday they violently seized Robert de Sunley at Calvecote and led him to Pickering Castle until he paid £2. On the 30th July Thomas Oliver of Sawdon was taken in the same manner and detained for five days. After all this David was summoned and he pleaded guilty. By trustworthy witnesses, however, it was proved that he was penniless and had nothing wherewith to satisfy the king for his offences, and "having regard to the state of his health and condition he was let off." We wonder what the Vicar of Ebberston thought of this lenient treatment of such a Barabbas. Geoffrey de Wrightington, a late bailiff of Pickering, seems to have taken part in these offences, and he was also responsible for having seized Hugh de Neville in Pickering Church, and for having imprisoned him "in the depths of the gaol in iron fetters for seven weeks, though Hugh had never been indicted." John Scott of Pickering also spent nine weeks in prison at the pleasure of this desperate fellow. On the 30th August 1346 he took £4 by force from Henry de Acaster, the vicar of Pickering, when he was journeying between Coneysthorpe and Appleton le Street. His methods are well shown by the following. "Geoffrey also on Sunday, 17th

September 1346, seized Adam de Selley Bridge by force at Pickering and imprisoned him until he had compounded with him for 6 [? £], and when Adam paid the fine Geoffrey made him swear on the Book that he would tell no one how he came to pay the fine or to be imprisoned." After all this Geoffrey was let off with a fine when called to account three years later.

In the minister's accounts for 1322 appear the "wages of a forester to keep Pickering Forest, a door-keeper and a watchman in the castle, each 2^d^ a day for 34 weeks." There are references to thatch for the porter's lodge, the brewhouse, the kitchen, and small upper apartment within the castle. This thatching took a man three days with two women to help him all the time; the man received 9^d^ and the women 2^d^ each for the work.

The chaplain of the castle chapel received a yearly salary of £3; repairs by contract to the seven glass windows in the chapel cost 10d, and wine and lights 2s. Under the heading of Small Expenses comes "making 14 hurdles to lie on the draw bridge and other bridges to preserve them from the cart-wheels 1^s^; making a hedge round the fishpond, cutting and carrying boughs, wages of the hedger—4^s^ 6^d^; making a long cord of hemp 20 ells long weighing 6 stone of hemp for the Castle well—4^s^ 9^d^ ; burning after Feb. 2 old grass in Castle Ings that new grass may grow—8^d^ ; 8 men cutting holly, ivy and oak boughs in different parts of the forest for the deer in a time of snow and ice, 9 days at 2^d a day—12^s $2\frac{1}{2}^d$; wages of a man sent to the king [Edward II.] with a letter from the bailiff to acquaint the king with certain secrets by letters of privy seal, going, residing there and returning, 9 days at 3^d a day for food and wages —3^s 9^d."

In the Close Rolls of 1324, there is an order to "John de Kelvington, keeper of the Castle and honor of Pickering, to cause to be newly constructed a barbican before the Castle gate with a stone wall and a gate with a drawbridge in the same, and beyond the gate a new chamber, a new postern gate by the King's Tower and a roof to a chamber near the small hall; to cover with thin flags that roof and the roof of the small kitchen, to remove the old roof of the King's prison and to make an entirely new roof covered with lead, and to thoroughly point, both within and without, the walls of the castle and tower, and to clean out and enlarge the Castle ditch. All this to be done out of the issues of the honor as the King has enjoined him by word of mouth, and the expense incurred therein when duly proved will be allowed him in his accounts. Pickering, 10th August, 1323."

About the year 1314 there is an item in the accounts of eighty planks bought at Easingwold and carried to the castle and laid in the gangway leading from the chamber of the Countess to the chapel. The nails for this work cost 5s. 6d.

Soon after this comes the cost of the new hall in the castle. "Clearing, digging and levelling the place

The Devil's or Dyet Tower on the South-East side of Pickering Castle.
This is often called the Rosamund Tower, but the records call it the Dyet Tower.

within the castle where the bakehouse was burnt to build there a hall with a chamber 14^{s} 1$\frac{1}{2}^{d}$, building the stone wall of the hall and chamber, getting and carrying 400 cartloads of stone, digging and carrying soil for mortar, buying 27 quarters of lime—£5 19^{s} 11^{d}; contract for joiners' work, wages for those employed to saw planks and joists, 152 planks for doors and windows, 80 large spikes, 600 spike nails, 1000 broad headed nails and 20,000 tacks, 22 hinges for the doors, 28 hinges for the windows and 2600 laths with carriage for the same—£9 0^{s} 1$\frac{1}{2}^{d}$; roofing the buildings with thin flags by piece-work, collecting moss for the same [to stop up the crannies] plastering the floor of the upper room and several walls within the chamber, making a chimney piece of plaster of Paris (plastro parisiensi), together with the wages of the chaplain who was present at the building—£5 1^{s} 10$\frac{1}{2}^{d}$." A few years later came some more repairs to the castle: "a carpenter 4 days mending the wind battered roof of the old hall with old shingles 1^{s}, 300 nails for that purpose 9^{d}; a man 10 days roofing with tin the small kitchen, the garderobe at the corner of the kitchen, the cellar, outside the new hall, within the tower and porter's lodge—2^{s} 6^{d}." Hay and straw for the roofs was brought "from the Marsh to Pickering"; two men were employed to clean out the castle well which had been so blocked up as to become quite dry that year and another charge is for a new rope and for repairing the bucket of the well.

In 1326 there is a reference to the King's patent

writ, dated 7th December, by which the Castle was committed by Edward II. "to his beloved cousin Henry, Earl of Lancaster," and the keeper, John de Kilvington, was "to deliver the Castle and Honour to the Earl together with its military stores, victuals and other things."

From a small green-covered foolscap volume lent me by Mr Arthur Hill of Thorton-le-dale, I have taken the following description of the "Bounds of the Forest of Pickering, as far as the waters are concerned."

"From How Bridge along the Rye to where the Seven falls into the Rye, the whole length of the Seven.

"Wheeldale Beck to

"Mirke Esk to

"The Eske and along the Eske to where Lythe Beck falls into the Eske

"Where the Derwent springs and along the Derwent to where Tillabeck falls into the Derwent.

"Along Tillabeck to King's Bridge.

"Along the Harford to the Derwent.

"Along the Derwent to where the Rye falls into the Derwent.

"Along the Rye to Howe Bridge."

The records relating to Pickering are all so accessible since their publication by the North Riding Record Society that those who want to read more details of these picturesque mediæval days can do so with very little trouble, but from the extracts that I have made, a general idea of the class of information contained in the Duchy Records may be obtained.

One of the Wall Paintings in Pickering Church.

St Christopher, the patron saint of travellers with the Infant Christ on his shoulder. The saint is shown treading upon the serpent and grasping his staff, which is growing at the edge of the stream. [*The copyright is reserved by Dr John L. Kirk*

In this period many additions and alterations were made to Pickering church. The Transitional Norman tower was largely rebuilt, and the spire was added in the Decorated style of Gothic prevalent in the fourteenth century. Below the battlements of the tower there are shields, but the details have almost entirely weathered away. The reticulated windows of the church belong to the same period. They are very fine examples of the work of that time. The north aisle, the chancel, and probably the north window of the north transept also belong to this period, so that work of an extensive nature must have been progressing on the church as well as the castle at the same time. The walls of the nave and chancel appear to have been raised in the latter half of the fifteenth century, and this would be shortly before the remarkable series of wall paintings came into existence. The date of these pictures can be brought down to fairly narrow limits, for the arms carried by the four knights who are shown about to murder St Thomas à Becket belong to the years between 1450 and 1460, according to Mr J. G. Waller. The Rev. G. H. Lightfoot, a former vicar of Pickering, mentions[1] the discovery of traces of earlier paintings of superior execution when the present ones were being restored, but of these indications no sign is now visible.

When the church was re-opened after the restoration in 1879, the walls of the nave were covered with a thick coat of yellow wash, but there were many

[1] *Yorkshire Archæological Journal*, 1895.

living who remembered the accidental discovery of the strange pictures that were for a time exposed to the wondering gaze of the congregation. The distraction caused by this novelty led to the coat of yellow wash that undoubtedly did infinite harm to the paintings. At the subsequent restoration, which was carried out by degrees as the necessary funds were forthcoming, it was found that portions of some of the figures had perished, and it is a most regrettable fact that the restoration included the painting in of certain missing parts whose details could only be supplied by analogy. From Mr Lightfoot's description it seems that in the large picture of St George and the Dragon a considerable part of the St George's body was missing; that the representation of Herod's Feast and the lowest scene of the life of St Katherine of Alexandria were very badly damaged by the attachments of mural tablets. On the whole, however, the paintings when uncovered were in a good state of preservation, and the colours were more vivid than they were left after the re-touching by Mr Jewitt.

Taking the pictures along the north wall in order, the first is the huge representation of St George, then facing the porch entrance on a still larger scale is the figure of St Christopher, bearing on his left shoulder the infant Christ. This position, facing those who enter the church, is the usual one for St Christopher, for he was the patron-saint of travellers, and the size is in keeping with the tradition which speaks of the saint as standing twelve cubits high. He is shown using a

THE SEVEN CORPORAL ACTS OF MERCY.

They are, from left to right :—(1) Feeding the hungry (partly missing in photograph)*; (2) Giving drink to the thirsty ; (3) Compelling the stranger to come in ; (4) Clothing the naked ; (5) Visiting those in prison ; (6) Visiting the sick ; (7) Burying the dead.

* This appears in another photograph showing scenes from the life of our Lord.

THE MARTYRDOM OF ST EDMUND.

SOME OF THE WALL PAINTINGS IN PICKERING CHURCH.

[*The Copyright is reserved by Dr John L. Kirk.*

tree as his staff, and the Evil One is being trampled underfoot in the form of a serpent.

Adjoining St Christopher is the curious painting showing Herod's Feast, a very rare subject to be chosen for wall paintings. Although this picture has been so much restored the figures were very carefully traced out where only faint indications could be seen, so that it now presents the original work where it was not totally destroyed with considerable accuracy. It is really three scenes, although it appears as one. Herod's daughter is on the right performing a mediæval tumble dance before the king and queen and their two guests, and on the left St John the Baptist is shown, still kneeling, although his head lies on the pavement. Salome is holding the charger against her breast. In the central portion of the picture she appears carrying the head of St John in the dish. The picture above this shows the coronation of the Virgin Mary, and the wall of heaven is higher still.

The martyrdom of St Edmund in the next spandrel is a most realistic picture. The saint is tied to a tree and is pierced by fourteen arrows. The black-letter inscriptions read " Edmund Prync and martyr."

> " Heven blys to hes mede
> Hem sall have for hys gud ded "

Above this picture is the painting already mentioned of St Thomas à Becket being approached by the four knights who are about to murder him.

On the south side of the nave the chief part of the

wall is given up to the legend of St Katherine of Alexandria. She was said to be the daughter of Costus, King of Alexandria, and was married to a son of Constantine Chlorius, the Roman Governor of York.

The upper panel shows the temple of Serapis, and St Katherine endeavouring to convert the Emperor Maximin to Christianity. Further to the right she is shown entering the prison into which she was cast. The emperor, impressed both by her beauty and her arguments, endeavours with the help of several philosophers to persuade her to give up her belief in Christianity; they are, however, all converted by her, and soon after they are executed at the emperor's command. St Katherine is then stripped to the waist and beaten in the presence of the emperor, who is shown on the extreme right as well as the left of the second panel. After further imprisonment the saint is joined by the Empress Faustina, a new convert, who comforts the prisoner, and is shown joining with her in prayer.

Further on, the emperor is shown testing the saint's faith by the wheel, but two angels appear, and having broken the wheels the attendants are overthrown. The last scene, in which St Katherine is kneeling, is so much "restored" that its interest is very much impaired.

The long and narrow series of pictures over the arches represents the seven corporal acts of mercy, namely, feeding the hungry, giving drink to the thirsty, compelling a stranger to come in, clothing the naked, visiting those in prison, visiting the sick, and burying the dead. Continuing in the same line appear re-

THE MARTYRDOM OF ST THOMAS À BECKET.
The Four Knights are seen approaching the "Turbulent Priest."

HEROD'S FEAST.

It is composed of three pictures. On the right, Salome is performing a "Tumble" dance before Herod, his queen, and two guests, while St John the Baptist is holding up a warning hand: in the centre, Salome has the head of St John in a charger, and on the left the execution is shown.

SOME OF THE WALL PAINTINGS ON THE NORTH WALL OF THE NAVE OF PICKERING CHURCH.

[*The Copyright is reserved by Dr John L. Kirk.*

presentations of Christ in the Garden of Gethsemane, healing the ear of Malchus, Christ before Pilate, the scourging of our Lord, and then follow scenes of the Crucifixion, followed by the burial and resurrection. In the spandrel over the third pillar from the west the descent of Christ into Hades, represented by a great dragon's jaw, is shown. Adam holding an apple, and followed by Eve and many other spirits, is shown coming to meet our Lord. Between the clerestory windows there are three paintings which seem to belong to a series associated with the Virgin Mary. The first, which may represent the Assumption, has not been restored, and very little remains to be seen. The second, according to Mr Keyser, shows the burial, and on the coffin appears the Jewish Prince Belzeray, who is said to have interfered with the funeral by raising himself astride the coffin. The legend says that he became fixed to the pall, and only escaped after repentance and the united prayers of the apostles.

Of the third picture only a portion remains, the upper part being new plaster, but the figures of some of the apostles who are shown may have been standing by the deathbed of the Virgin. The coronation scene already mentioned on the north side of the nave would thus complete a series of four pictures.

Just by the lectern at the north-east corner of the nave is a recumbent effigy of a knight wearing armour of the period when chain-mail was being exchanged for plate armour. This was during the fourteenth century. The arms on the shield are those of Bruce, and belonging to this period there has been discovered a license to Sir William Bruce to have a chantry in Pickering Church. There can therefore be little doubt that this nameless effigy is that of Sir William Bruce. The deed is dated "Saturday, the feast of St John the Evangelist, 1337," and it states that a license was given

The Effigy of Sir William Bruce in Pickering Church.
The arms on the shield are drawn separately on the right.

in consideration of one messuage and two bovates of land in the village of Middleton near Pickering for a certain chaplain to celebrate Divine (mysteries) daily in the Church of St Peter, Pickering (the full dedication is to God, St Peter, and St Paul), for the souls of the masters, William and Robert of Pickering, Adam de Bruce and Mathilda his wife." The two beautifully

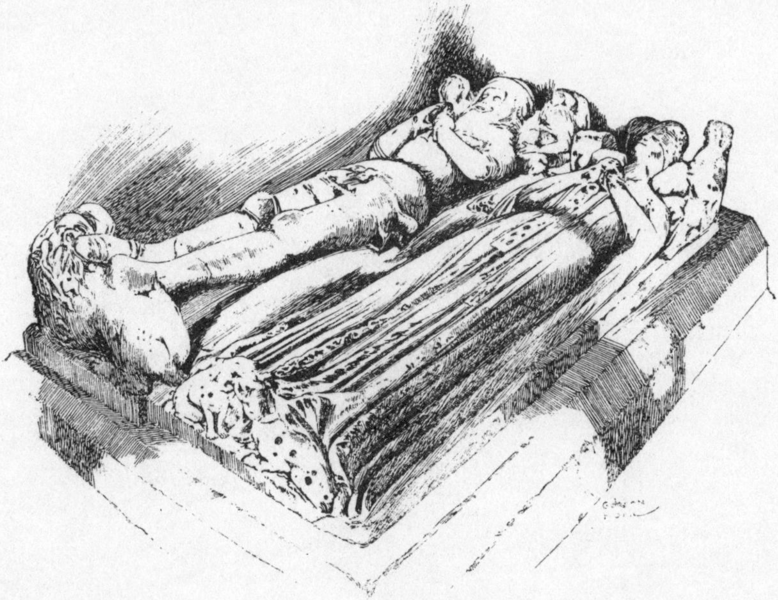

The richly carved Effigies in the Bruce Chapel of Pickering Church.
The man bears the arms of Rockcliffe on his surcoat. Both figures wear the collar of SS.

carved figures of a knight and his lady that lie in the Bruce Chapel are not Bruces for the surcoat of the man is adorned with the arms of the Rockcliffes—an heraldic chess-rook and three lions' heads. Both the knight and his lady wear the collar of SS, the origin of which is still wrapped in obscurity. Traces of gilding are visible in several places on the wings of the angels that support the heads of both figures, as well as in other parts of the carving where the detail is not obliterated. The date of these monuments is believed to have been either the end of the fourteenth or the very beginning of the fifteenth centuries. In the south-east corner of the north transept, almost hidden by deep shadows, there lies a truncated effigy of a man in armour of about the same period as that of Sir William Bruce, but there is nothing to identify these mutilated remains. The sedilia in the chancel seem to be coeval with that part of the church. They are ornamented with some curious carving and some heads, one of them, very much restored, representing apparently a bishop, priest, and deacon; the fourth head is a doubtful quantity.

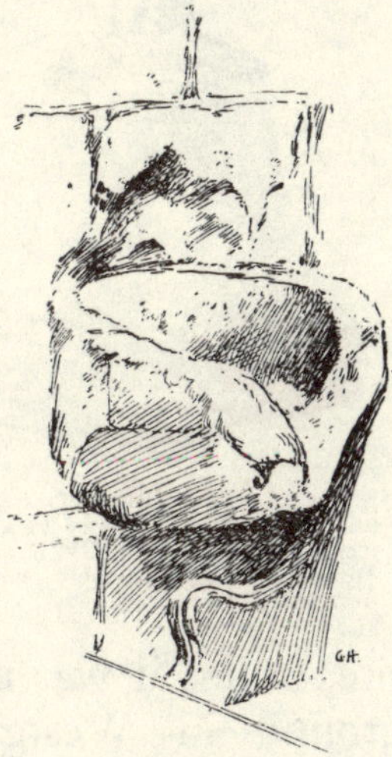

The holy-water stoup in Pickering Church.

Close to the sedilia is a piscina decorated in a similar manner.

Near the porch, in the usual position, is a holy-water stoup that has the front part of the basin broken off. This may possibly have happened at the same time as the smashing of the font in Puritan days mentioned in a later chapter. The curious little recess in the west wall of the Bruce Chapel might have been utilised for more than one purpose, but it is difficult to say whether it was for holding a lamp, whether it may at one time have been a low side window, or whether it was at any time used as an opening for a bell rope to be pulled from within.

THE SANCTUS BELL, formerly used by the Town Crier of Pickering. It bears the name "Vilyame Stokeslai," and probably dates from the fourteenth century.

A hospital of St Nicholas at Pickering is often mentioned among the records of this time, but I am unable to discover the site, unless it was near to where there was a burying-ground in Westgate. The castle chapel was also dedicated to St Nicholas, and some confusion may thus have arisen.

Up to about the year 1880 the town-crier of Pickering was using a small mediæval bell that has since been handed over to the authorities of the British Museum by the Registrar of the Duchy of Lancaster. The bell is engraved with four figures—a crucifix, St George and the Dragon, the Virgin and Child, and St John the Baptist, and round the haunch runs the inscription

"VILYAME STOKESLAI." As nothing at all is known of the history of the bell it is difficult to say much as to its origin, but it appears to belong to the fourteenth century, and *may* be associated with a William Stokesley of Whitby whose name appears at that date.

Much more could be written about this period from many standpoints, but from what has been given some of the salient facts of these centuries stand out clearly. It is plain that the people — rich and poor — drew largely upon the forest for free supplies of timber and venison, despite the severity of the laws. It also appears that the officers of the forest frequently abused their power to the damage and often at the expense of the personal security of the townsfolk and villagers. The importance of Pickering at this time is emphasised by many royal visits and to some extent by the sending of members to Parliament on one occasion. Much building at the church and castle took place in the period described, and it is quite possible that some of the oldest cottages with fork framework date from Plantagenet times, and that the fallen beams we see lying among the nettles of the ruined cottages were taken from the forest without payment or permission.

CHAPTER IX

The Forest and Vale in Tudor Times

A.D. 1485 to 1603

THE Wars of the Roses had allowed the royal possessions to fall into a state of great disorder, so that the Duchy of Lancaster records belonging to the early years of the reign of Henry VII. contain many references to the necessity for vigorously checking infringements on the forest that had been taking place. A patent dated 26th of October 1489,[1] says, "To our t[rusty] and w[elbeloved] Brian Sandford Stuard of our honnor of Pykeryng in our Countie of York and Constable of our Castle there and master Forster of our game within the said honnor and to al forsters and kepers within the same and in their absence to ther deputies ther and to every of them gretyng. Forasmuch as it is common unto our knowledge that our game of dere and warenne within our seid Honnor is gretly diminnisshed by excessive huntyng within the same and likely to be destroied, without restreynt in the same be had in that behalf, we desire the Replenisshyng of our seid game, not only for our singler pleasure but also for the disport of other our servantes and subgettes of Wirshipp in theis parties. And

1 "North Riding Records," vol. i., New Series, p. 123.

therfor we wol and straitly charge you all & every of you that from hensforth ye suffre no manner of personne or personnes of what estate degree or condicion soever he or they be, to have shot sute ne course at any of our game within our seid Honnor duryng the space of iij years next ensuyng after the date herof, without special warraunt undre our seale of oure seid Duchie and if any personne or personnes presume or attempt in any wise the breche of this our special restreinte and commandment, we eftsounes wol and straitly charge you al and every of you, that without delai ye certifie us of theire name or names so offendyng, to thentent that we maye provide for their lawful punycion in that

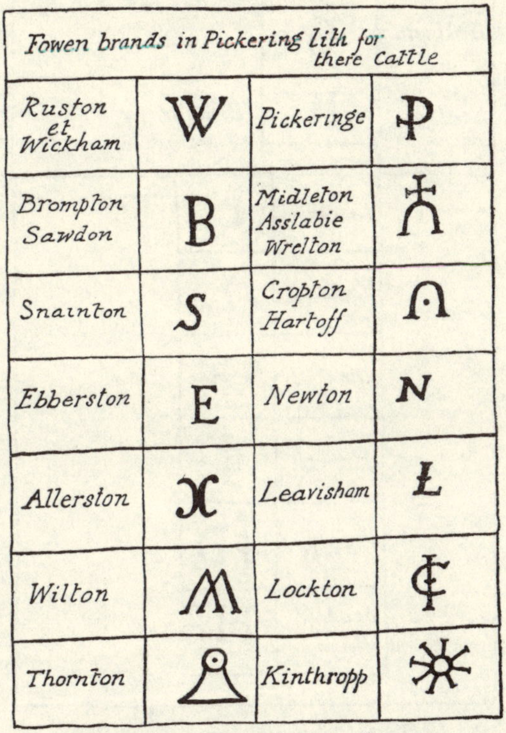

Cattle Marks of the Pickering District.

Copied from a MS. book dated at the close of the sixteenth century and in the possession of the Rev. A. Hill of Thornton-le-dale. The names are spelt as they are written, but are not given in facsimile. The book is a copy of an earlier one that is still in existence.

behalf, which we entend sharply to execute and punysshe in example of al othre like offenders, not failyng herof as ye wol avoide our grevous displeasure and answher unto us at their perell."

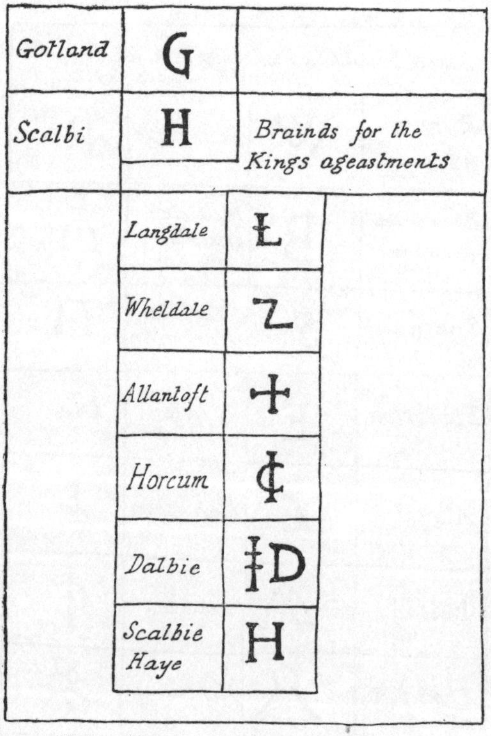

Cattle Marks in the Pickering District.

There are many other commissions of this character made out to "Sir Rauf Evers knight," "Sir Richard Cholmeley knight," "Sir John Huthem," "John Pykeryng knyght," "Leon Percy [Lionel Percehay] squyer," and many other influential men of the sixteenth century.

During the reign of Henry VII. there was a prolonged dispute between Sir Roger Hastings of Roxby and Sir Richard Cholmley concerning the alleged riotous and unlawful conduct with which each side accused the other. The pleadings on either side are by no means easy to follow, but the beginning of the trouble seems to date from Sir Roger Hastings' succession to the estate of Roxby. Mr Turton, who has transcribed all the documents relating to the quarrel, thinks that Sir Roger attempted to shift the death duties from himself to one of his tenants named Ralph Joyner, who refused to pay. "After an abortive attempt to recover the sum by distrain" says Mr Turton, it "resulted in an appeal to the Earl of Surrey, and Sir Roger was compelled to pay it himself." The records tell us that this Ralph Joyner was often "in Jeopardy of his liff; And how he was at diverse tymez chased by diverse of the menyall servantes of the said Sir Roger Hastynges, wheruppon the said Roger Cholmley sent to the said Sir Roger Hastynges in curteyse waise desyring hym to kepe the kynges peax, whiche he effectuelly promysed to doo, uppon truste wherof upon Christmas day now Laste paste the said Rauff Jenore cam to his parisshe chirche, called Elborne [Ellerburne] chirche, as belonged to a christenman to doo, in peassible maner, not fearing the said Sir Roger Hastynges, because of his said promyse, Howbeit soon after that comme thedir the said Sir Roger accompenyed with the numbre of xx [twenty] persons diffencible arrayed with bowes, billes and other weponz, And then as sone as the said Roger came nyghe unto the Chircheyerd of the foresaid Chirche, And had undirstandyng that the said Rauff was within the said chirche, he manassed [menaced] and threted the said Rauff and said that he wolde slee hym. And in a great fury wolde have entred the said chirche to have complisshed the same."

This bloodthirsty desire was checked for a time by the vicar, who "knellyng upon his knees before the said Sir Roger," and with other "well disspposed personez," induced him to delay his purpose.

"Theruppon the wif of the said Sir Roger Hastynges cam into the said chirche & said unto the said Rauff, 'Woo worthe man this day! the chirche wolbe susspended and thou slayn, withoute thou flee awey and gette the oute of his sighte' wheruppon the said Rauff Jenore flede oute of the said chirche by a bakke doore and cam to Pykeryng, and petyously desired of the said Roger Chalmley that in so muche as he was the Stewardes deputie there and hadde rewle of the Countre, that he myght be in suertie of his liff." The records then describe how Ralph Joyner induced Roger Cholmley, "beyng there Bailly," with "Sir Rauff Evers & other jointly & severally" to bind Sir Roger Hastings to "Maister Bray" for the sum of a hundred pounds to keep the king's peace within the liberty of Pickering. The aggrieved side did not dare to deliver the deed with only their usual personal servants, but had to call upon a number of others owing to the fact that Sir Roger was "a worshipfull man of the said libertie & of great myghte havyng many Riottous personez aboute hym" When the little cavalcade of mounted men and servants reached Roxby they found that Sir Roger Hastings had left for Scarborough. He describes the procedure of the Cholmley party in a most picturesque fashion, stating that within an hour after the delivery of the Privy Seal they "came Ryottously with the nowmbre of xii persons, with bowis arrowes longe sperys in maner and furme of warre." In another place he details their armour and arms saying that they were arrayed with "Cures (cuirass) Corsettes (armour for the body) Brygendyns, Jakkys, Salettis (a light helmet), Speris, Bowes, Arrowes, Sourdis, byllys and Launcegays, (a small lance) with other maner of wepyns defencive." As Sir Roger and his wife rode towards Scarborough they met "Sir Rauf Ivers, which in Curtes (courteous) maner then departed." When he was thought to be on the road homewards to Roxby, however, Sir Ralph Evers was accused of having laid "in a wayte to have murderyd" Sir Roger Hastings at Brompton, for at that place Evers and eight of his servants came upon Sir Roger's men who were being sent ahead to discover the ambush that they had reason to fear. When Sir Ralph found that the men who reached Brompton were only servants and messengers, he was accused of having said to them "ye false hurson Kaytyffes, I shall lerne you curtesy and to knowe a gentilman." Thereupon Sir Ralph "set his arowe in his bowe, seying these wordes, 'And your Master were here I wolde stoppe hym the wey.'" When they reached Snainton twenty persons issued from the house of "one Averey Shymney, servant to the seid Sir Rauf . . . arrayed with bowys bent, arrowis, billis and Gleyvis."

There is also a complaint against some of the servants of Sir Ralph Evers who were held responsible for "an assaute and Fraye made upon my lady Hastynges." Thomas Thirlwall, on being examined, said that "my lady came rydyng that ways with vi horses with hir, and oone of hir servantz thet rode afore, had a male [a portmanteau] behynd hym, and with a bowe in his hand bent, and that the said servant rode soo nygh hym th[at] the male touched hym and he bade hym ryde forther and asked, why his bow was bent, and he said that was mater to hym, and the sayd deponent with I[d] knyff [in another place it is called a dagger] which he had in his hand cut the bow string, bicause he rode soo nygh hym with horse that he had almost stroken hym downe; And forther he deposith that my lady light downe from hir horse hirself and said that, 'and she liffed, she would be avenged'; and thereupon Ric: Brampton came to hir and said, 'Madame be not afferd, for here shall noo man trouble you nee yours.'"

The accusations of attempts on the part of Sir Ralph Evers and the Cholmleys to stir up trouble between their servants and those of Sir Roger Hastings are very numerous and involved, but despite the elaborate details given by the owner of Roxby the case went against him at the court of the Duchy of Lancaster at Westminster Palace. Sir Roger seems to have been too high handed in his dealings with his neighbours, even for the unsettled times in which he lived. Some of the items against him throw a vivid light on his proceedings. "Itm the said Ser Roger Hastynges with hys household servants, daily goyng and rydyng trough the Countrey more like men of warr then men of peas, in ill example to other, thrught the Kinges markettz and townez of hys liberte of Pykeryng lith, with bowes bent and arrowes in ther handes, feryng [frightening] the Kinges people and inhabitauntes of the same, whereupon the Countrey diverse tymes hath compleyned thame to Roger Cholmeley, there being hys brother's depute and baylly etc."

"Itm the wyeff of the said Sir Roger Hastynges with here awn company of houshold servants as forcaid (?) come into Blandisby Park, and there found a Fat Stott [a young ox] of Rauff Bukton, and with dooges toke the said Stott and slowe hym and ete hym and no mends will make etc.

"Itm that the said Sir Roger Hastynges the xiii day of October last past [circa 1496] with Force and armz of the nyghtertall [night time] sent his houshold servantes to the Castell of Pykeryng, and abowt mydnyght with lothus [qu: ladders] clame ore the walles, and then and there brake the kinges prison, and toke owt with them oon John Harwod, the which was set there for diverse Riottes by hym made agayns the kinges peas, wherefore he was indited; and aftirward the same nyght when he for thought that he had done, prively sent hym in agayn; howbeit the kings prison and hys Castell was broken."

Such incidents as these enliven the pages of the Duchy of Lancaster Records, and if there were more space available it would be interesting to give many more of these graphic incidents that took place four hundred years ago. In many places one finds references

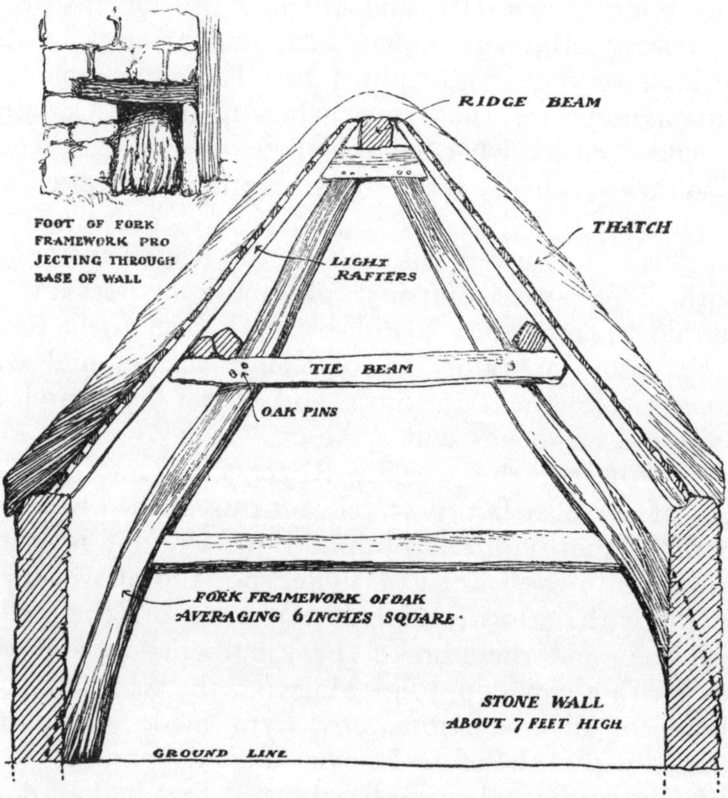

A Section of one of the Oldest Type of Cottage to be found near Pickering.

Some of these ancient buildings are still inhabited; several of the survivors are in ruins. The details given in this drawing are taken from a cottage at Thornton-le-dale; one end has already been demolished (*Oct.* 1905). The low walls appear to have been built after the framework, and the house may have been thatched to the ground at one time.

to the illegal taking of oaks from the forest for building houses. Big boughs or the stems of small trees

Doorway with hoary oaken framework on the garden side of the Post Office at Middleton.

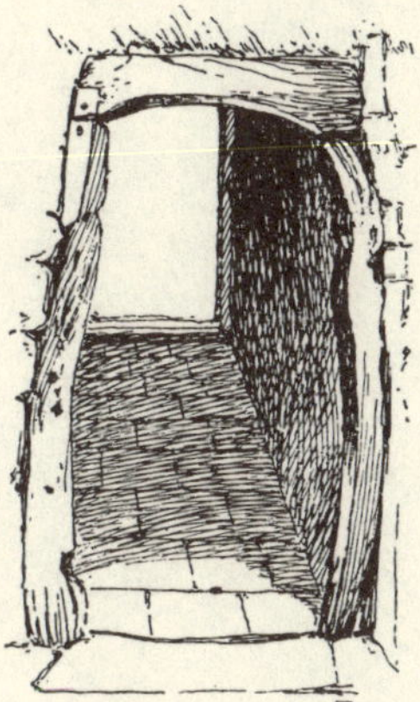

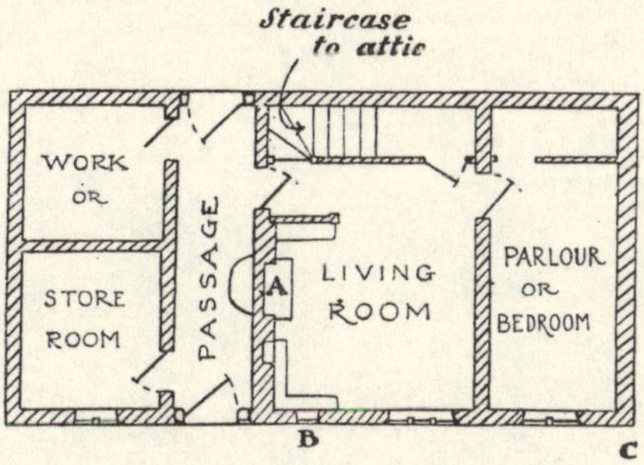

A. Fireplace in the ingle-nook.
B. Window lighting the ingle-nook.

THE USUAL PLAN OF THE FORK-FRAMED COTTAGES IN EXISTENCE NEAR PICKERING.

The exterior (viewed from C on the plan) is generally as shown. The small window by the door (B) lights the ingle-nook, and is never missing in the oldest type of cottage. It can be seen blocked up in those that have been remodelled.

K

were placed together in the form of an A with the ends resting on the ground. These beams, that formed the bays of a house, are locally called "forks," the name by which they are known in the records of the reign of Henry VII. In 1498 we find that "The abbot of Whitby had as many oakes taken in Godlande [Goathland] as made aftre the maner of the Coutrey iij pair of forkes, with other bemes and wall plaites as were mete for the repairalling of an hows of his in Godlande."

The great legal case between Sir Roger Hastings and the Cholmleys seems to have impoverished the turbulent owner of Roxby, for after the adverse decision Hastings seems to have had difficulty in raising the moneys to meet all the heavy expenses of the trial, and Mr Turton thinks that Roxby was at first mortgaged and afterwards sold to Roger Cholmley, brother of Sir Richard, who had received knighthood in 1509. Sir Richard Cholmley may be considered the founder of the Yorkshire families of Cholmley, and he was in his time a man of great power and influence, holding the four chief offices in the Honor of Pickering, and at the commencement of the reign of Henry VIII. he was appointed Lieutenant of the Tower of London. He had no legal offspring, and his illegitimate son, a Sir Roger, who must not be confused with his uncle, was successively Chief Baron and Lord Chief Justice, died without issue. Sir Hugh Cholmley [1] tells us many facts concerning his great-grandfather Sir Richard, who was a nephew of the former Sir Richard. "His chief place

[1] "Memoirs of Sir Hugh Cholmley," p. 7.

of residence," he says, "was at Roxby, lying between Pickering and Thornton (now almost demolished), where he lived in great port, having a very great family, at least fifty or sixty men-servants, about his house, and I have been told by some who knew the truth, that when there had been twenty-four pieces of beef put in a morning into the pot, sometimes not one of them would be left for his own dinner: for in those times, the idle-serving men were accustomed to have their breakfast, and with such liberty as they would go into the kitchen, and striking their daggers into the pot, take out the beef without the cook's leave or privacy; yet he would laugh at this rather than be displeased, saying, "Would not the knaves leave me one piece for my own dinner?' He never took a journey to London that he was not attended with less than thirty, sometimes forty men-servants, though he went without his lady. There was a great difference between him and his brother-in-law, the Earl of Westmoreland; and, as I have heard upon this cause: That, after the death of his sister, the Lady Anne, the Earl married the second sister, Gascoigne's widow, which occasioned continual fighting and scuffles between the Earl's men and Sir Richard's, when they met, whether in London streets or elsewhere, which might be done with less danger of life and bloodshed than in these succeeding ages; because they then fought only with buckler and short sword, and it was counted unmannerly to make a thrust. . . . This Sir Richard was possessed of a very great estate worth at this day to the value of about £10,000 a year; . . . He died in the sixty third year of his age, at Roxby, . . . and lies buried in the chancel of Thornton church [the monument there to-day bears the effigy of a lady and is nameless], of which he was patron, May 17th, 1599. He was tall of stature and withal big and strong-made, having in his youth a very active, able body, bold and stout; his hair and eyes black, and his complexion brown, insomuch as he was called the great black Knight of the North; though the word *great* attributed to him not so much for his stature, as power, and estate, and fortune. He was a wise man, and a great improver of his estate, which might have prospered better with his posterity, had he not been extra-ordinarily given to the love of women." There is unfortunately nothing left above the ground of the manor house of Roxby, the grass-covered site merely showing ridges and mounds where the buildings stood. It is therefore impossible to obtain any idea of the appearance of what must have been a very fine Tudor house. That a gallery was built there by Sir Richard Cholmley, the Great Black Knight of the North, in the reign of Elizabeth, appears from the record which says "that the saide Sr Rychard Cholmley did send Gyles Raunde and George Raude two masons to the Quenes Castell of Pyckeringe whenn he builded his gallerye at Roxbye to polle [pulle] downe the chefe stones of Masonn work owt of one howse in the same castell called the King's Haull, and took owte of the pryncypall and cheffest Towre of the same castle the stones of the stayres which they did and the said Sr Rychard caused xiiii wayne lodes of the same stones to be caryed by his Tenantes to his owne house at Roxbye."

Leland,[1] who wrote in the reign of Henry VIII., tells us that at Wilton there was "a Manor Place with a Tower longging to *Chomeley*" He also says "This *Chomeley* hath a Howse also at *Rollesley* (*Rottesby*): and *Chomeley's* Father that now is was as an Hedde officer at *Pykeringe*, and setter up of his name yn that Quarters." "Thens to *Pykering*: and moste of the Ground from *Scardeburg* to *Pykering* was by Hille and Dale meate (metely) plentifull of Corn and Grasse but litle Wood in sight.

"The Toune of *Pykering* is large but not welle compact togither. The greatest Part of it with the Paroch Chirch and the Castel is on the South Est Part of the Broke renning thorough the Toune, and standith on a great Slaty Hille. The other Part of the Toun is not so bigge as this: the Brook rennith bytwixt them that Sumtyme ragith, but it suagith shortely agayn: and a Mile beneth the Toun goith into Costey [the Costa].

"In *Pykering* Chirch I saw 2 or 3 Tumbes of the Bruses wherof one with his Wife lay yn a Chapel on the South syde of the Quirr, and he had a Garland about his Helmet. There was another of the Bruses biried in a Chapel under an Arch of the North side of the Body of the Quier: and there is a Cantuarie bering his Name.

[1] "The Itinerary of John Leland the Antiquary," Thomas Hearne, 1745. Vol. i. pp. 64 and 65.

Pickering Castle from the Keep, looking South-West.

The gate tower is just shown on the left. In the centre is the Mill or Miln Tower, with the circular stone staircase projecting like a turret at one corner, and in the foreground is one of the ruined towers that guarded the inner gateway. In the distance is the broad Vale of Pickering. The high ground is behind one's back to the north.

"The Deane of *York* hath by Impropriation the Personage of *Pykering*, to the which diverse Churches of Pykering Lith doith Homage.

"The Castelle Stondith in an End of the Town not far from the Paroch Chirch on the Brow of the Hille, under the which the Broke rennith. In the first Court of it be a 4 Toures, of the which one is Caullid Rosamunde's Toure.

"In the inner Court be also a 4 Toures, wherof the Kepe is one. The Castelle Waulles and the Toures be meatly welle. The Logginges yn the ynner Court that be of Timbre be in ruine, in this inner Court is a Chappelle and a cantuarie Prest.

"The Castelle hath of a good continuance with the Towne and Lordship longgid to the *Lancaster* Bloode: But who made the Castelle or who was the Owner of afore the *Lancasters* I could not lerne there. The Castelle Waulles now remaining seme to be of no very old Building.

"As I remembre I hard say that *Richard* the thirde lay sumtyme at this Castelle, and sumtyme at *Scardeburgh* Castelle.

"In the other Part of the Toune of *Pykering* passing over Brook by a Stone Bridg of v Arches I saw 2 thinges to be notid, the Ruines of a Manor Place, caullid *Bruses-Haul* and a Manor Place of the *Lascelles* at *Keld head*. The Circuite of the Paroch of *Pykering* goith up to the very Browes of Blackmore [Blackamoor was the old name for the moors north of Pickering], and is xx miles in Cumpace.

"The Park by the Castelle side is more then vii Miles in [qu: circuit], but it is not welle woodid."

The site of the Manor House of the Bruces appears to be in a field to the west of Potter Hill where hollows and uneven places in the grass indicate the positions of buildings. The fine old Tudor house of Wellburn near Kirby Moorside until recently was in a ruinous state, and might possibly have disappeared after the fashion of Roxby and this Hall of the Bruces, but it has lately been completely restored and enlarged, and although its picturesqueness has to some extent been impaired owing to the additions, they are in the same style of architecture as the original building, and in time will no doubt mellow down to a pleasanter companionship.

It was in the first year of the reign of Elizabeth that the registers of Pickering were commenced. The yellowish brown parchment book is in fairly good preservation, and commences in the usual manner with this carefully written inscription.

"The Register Boke of these ꝑsons whiche Haithe bene Babticed Maryed and Buried at Pickeringe sence the firste yere of O[r] Sou'ange Ladye Elizabeth by the grace of god Quene of England ffrance and Ireland defender of the ffaithe etc. Anno dñi 1559.

There are no entries of any particular interest belonging to this period; the unusual occurrences belong to the seventeenth century and are recorded in the next chapter. Kept with the registers of Pickering parish there is, however, a book containing the records of some Elizabethan visitations made between 1568 and 1602. The entries, which have been transcribed by Mr T. M. Fallow, are in a mixture of Latin and English and some of them are exceedingly interesting. The following describes a curious scene in Pickering Church.

"Item they saie that vpon Sondaie being the iij of November 1594 in tyme off evynnyng praie [*sic*] Richarde Haie being parishe clerk of Pickring and begynnyng to rede the first lesson of the saide evynnyng praier, Robert Leymyng did close and shutt the byble to geither whereupon he was to red at, and so disturbed him frome reding it, and therevpon John Harding redd the first lesson And so hindred and disturbed the saide Richard Haie parishe clerke who was readye and abowteward to rede the same / And the saide John Harding did likewise disturbe and hinder the saide Richarde Haie vpon All Saynts dais last when he was to haue helped the vicar to saie devyne service and so hindred him being commanded to the conrye[1] by the churche wardens, and having the admission of the saide Richard Haie openly redd with a revocation of the former granted to the saide Hardyng . wherebye he was commanded and enioyned to surcease frome execution of that office."

In 1602 when Edward Mylls was vicar of Pickering, complaints were made of him "that he for the most parte, but not alwaies dothe weare a surplesse in tyme of dyvyne service / they present there vicar for

[1] This word is doubtful, but is perhaps "conrye," for "contrary."

that they ar vncerteyne whether his wif was commended vnto him by justices of peace nor whether he

THE PRE-REFORMATION CHALICE THAT FORMERLY BELONGED TO PICKERING CHURCH.
It is now in use at Goathland Church, which was formerly included in Pickering Parish.
(*Reproduced by permission of the Society of Antiquaries.*)

was licenced to marrye hir according to hir Maiesties iniunctions / " This vicar was deprived of the living in 1615, for omitting to preach sermons and for not properly instructing the people and as will be seen in the next chapter he appears to have been a most reprehensible character.

At the same time as this " Richarde Nicoll, Widow Kitchin, Robert Skayles, John Flaworthe, and widow Shorpshier are presented for deteyning the clerkes wages / Elizabeth Dodds ffor having a childe in adultery withe one Anthonye Boyes, which Boyes is now fledd / William Steavenson ffor a slanderer. And also Frances Fetherston the wif of Robert Fetherston for a scowlde / Richard Hutchinson for harboring a woman which had a childe begotten in fornicacion They saie that [*blank*] Lavrock and [*blank*] Wilson did by the apoyntment of Richard Parkinson there master carrye turffes in to the house vpon the Sabboth daie The rest is all well."

The rigid observance of the Sabbath as a day of rest is vividly shown by this last complaint, and at Allerston we find that " Isabell Rea wiffe of William Raie " was reprimanded—" ffor workyng on the Sabbothe daie vizt for washing and dressing of hempe at the hemppe pitt vpon Sondaie was seavenyght / "

In 1592 appears the following / " The chancell of Pickering in decaie bothe the windowes and the leades and to be repaired as we suppose by Mr Deane / [The Dean of York] Mr Deane for want of the quarter sermons and for not geving the xl^{tie} part of his lyving of the parsonage of Pickering to the poore people of the said parishe Agnes Poskett wif of William Poskett of Pickering for a scold."

In the following year we find presented at Pickering "Elizabeth Johnson wif of Frances Johnson of Kinthorpe for an obstynate recusant in not comyng to the churche . to here dyvyne service by the space of ij° yeares last past and more / Anne Browne wiffe of William Browne of Pickering for an obstinate recusant in not commyng to the churche to here dyvyne service and so haithe done by the space of ij° yeares and more / Rauffe Hodgeson of Pickring for an obstinate recusant and haithe absented him self ffrome the churche by the space of ij° yeares and more. Anne Clerke being in John Wright his house of Blansbye and haithe meate and drinke there, ffor not commyng to the church to here dyvyne service by the space of half a yeare / Rychard Hutchinson sonne of William Hutchinson of Kinthorpp ffor absenting him self from the churche by the space of halff a yeare and more / . And he is excommunicate."

Elizabeth Dobson was presented in 1600 as "a slaunderer who saide to Thomas Gibson that he was a Mainesworne ladd /"

To call anyone "mansworn" was evidently a very serious offence, for in 1527 the Newcastle-on-Tyne corporation of weavers decreed that any member of the corporation who should call his brother "mansworn" should incur a forfeit of 6s. 8d. "without forgiveness." To *manswear* comes from the Anglo-Saxon *mánswerian* meaning to swear falsely or to perjure oneself. Among the men of note of this period mention must be made of Ralph Dodmer son of Henry Dodmer of

Pickering who was a mercer and Lord Mayor of London in 1521.[1]

The visitation book shows that it was no uncommon thing to accuse a woman of being a scold in these times and the following written in 1602[2] throws a lurid light on the methods for removing the effects of a witch's malice.

"To cure an ill caste by any Witch putt upon any childe be y^{t} ye evil eye, an overglent, spreeking, an ill birth touche or of a spittle boult but do as here given & alle shalle be overcome letting no evil rest upon y^{m} Take a childe so ill held & strike y^{t} seven times on ye face & like upon ye navel with ye heart of a blacke cat then roast ye heart & give of y^{t} to eat seven nights at bed meale & y^{t} shalle be well butt ye cat must be seven years olde & ye seventh dropped at birth otherwise y^{t} shalle faile to overcome any Witch spell soever ill worked ye blood from such an heart laid to any witches dorepost or thrown over nighte upon her dorestep will cause a sore & great paine in her belly."

In the period which includes the momentous defeat of the Spanish Armada (1588) it is fitting to describe the beacons of Pickering and the neighbourhood that must have helped to spread the news to the inhabitants of Yorkshire of the coming of that "Invincible" fleet. A contemporary manuscript book dated 1580 to 1590, and discovered by Mr J. G. Constable, tells us how Pickering beacon, which was presumably situated on

[1] Thomas Fuller's "Worthies."

[2] The original is stuck in Calvert's MS. Book of Folklore.

Beacon Hill opposite the castle, gave light to the neighbouring heights.

" Pickering Lythe 7 Beacons

Pickering beacon giveth light to Setrington beacon, in the East Riding, and to Ampleforth beacon, in Rydall. Seamer two beacons do give light to Pickering, Susfeld, in Whitby Strand, and Setterington beacon. Waipnesse beacon, within the liberties of Scarborough, do give light to Muston Beacon, in the East Riding, and to the west of the beacons before named

" Charnell, three beacons, within the town of Scarborough adjoining to the castle, do give light to Waipnesse and Muston beacon."

" Rydall 1 Beacon

There is a beacon in Rydall called Ampleforthe beacon well repaired. It taketh light from Pickering beacon. It giveth light to the Sumclife beacon, in the Wapentake of Birdforth, three miles distant from it westward "

In 1598 [1] the streets of Pickering are given as, Easte Gaite and Hallgarthe, Ungate, Birdgate, Borrowgate and Weste Gate.

Two interesting monuments of this period are to be found in Brompton and Kirby-Moorside Churches. The first is carved on stone in the north wall of the Church. It reads : —

" I.W. 1580. E.W. 1547. HEIR LIETH IAMES WESTROP WHO IN WARS TO HIS GREIT CHARGES SARVED

[1] MS. book of Pickering Records in possession of the Rev. Arthur Hill of Thornton-le-dale.

OIN KYNG AND TOW QVENES WITH DV$_{\circ}$BE$_{\circ}$IENS AND WITH OWT RECVMPENS."

The brass at Kirby-Moorside is to the memory of Lady Brooke and bears this verse as well as the inscription:—

"Prepare for death for if the fatall sheares
Covld have bene stayd by prayers, sighes or teares
They had bene stayd, and this tombe thov seest here
Had not erected beene yet many a yeare."

"Here lyeth the body of my Lady Brooke, who while she lyved was a good woman, a very good mother, and an exceeding good wife. Her sovle is at rest wth God, for she was svre y^{t} her Redemer lyved, and that thovgh wormes destroyed her body, yet shee shovld see God in her flesh. She died the 12th of Jvly 1600."

From the different aspects of life at Pickering in the Tudor Period that we have been able to give, something can be seen of the manner of living at this time; but to have done justice to the materials that may be drawn upon would have required a volume for what has of necessity been limited to a chapter.

CHAPTER X

The Forest and Vale in Stuart Times

A.D. 1603 to 1714

AS in the two preceding chapters the records belonging to the Stuart period are so numerous that one is almost embarrassed at the mass of detailed information that has been preserved, and it is only possible to select some of the most interesting facts. Commencing with the parish registers, however, we are confronted with a gap of about thirteen years. After having been kept with regularity since 1559, there appears on p. 48 of the earliest book this curious entry: "Edward Milnes Vicar of Pickering rent out all these following leaves." The missing pages contained the entries from 1602 to 1615, and this coincides with the years of Milnes's tenure of the living, for he appears to have come to Pickering in 1602, and he was deprived in 1615. The reasons for removing this vicar are recorded as follows in the last pages of the register, but the motives that prompted him to tear out these thirty-five parchment pages from the register do not appear:—

"A true copie of the Order of the Councel ther in Pickering Lith asserted? obtained by Mr Lawrence Trotter attornie at the Common law Año domi 1615.

[Much thumbed at the edge.]

"At the Court at Greenewich on Sunday the 21 of May 1615 in the afternoone: present L. Archbishop of Canterburie, L. Chancelor, L. Knolls, L. Treasurer Mr Secretarie Winwood, D. of Linnox, Mr Chanceler of the Excheq, E. of Worcester, L. Chiefe iusice, E. of Pembrooke, Mr of ye Rolles, L. Souch, Sir Thomas Lake.

"Complaint having bin made unto the boarde by the Inhabitants of the towne and parish of Pickering in the Countie of Yorke. That that personage now in possession of the bishop of Bristoll Deane of Yorke (it being an indowment of the said Deanerie) such slender care hath bene had by him for the preaching of the Gospell unto the said parishioners, and giving them that Christianlike and necessarie instruc̃on which is fitting, as for a long time they scarce had any sermon at all amongest them. Where upon their Lordships were pleased to direct their Letters unto the s^{d} Lord Bishop admonishing and requiring him to give speedie order for the redresse of so great an inconvenience and so scandalous to his ma^{ties} most Christian goverm^{t}. But receaving answer from his Lordship that in respect the said ꝑsonage being an impropriac̃on is indued wth a Vicarage and a Viccar presented thereunto he held him selfe freed in Law from any further charge, and that the said ꝑsnage was in Lease wth. such other like excuses but that notwithstanding he was contented to procure them 12 sermons every yeare, their Lordships thought fitting this day to call him to the boarde, and to let him sea in reason of State, besides the great obligacon they had as Christians it behoved them to presse his Lordship notwithstanding the former excuse to have yet a further care of the teaching so great a multitude (they being 4000 people) considering how busie the priestes and Jesuits are in these dayes (especially in these quarters) not only laboring to corrupt his ma^ties subiects in their religion but also infecting them with such damnable posiciones and Doctrine touching the valew . . . (?) unto his ma^ties sacred person where upon the said bishop made offer unto the boarde that he would forthwith (?) remove the vicar now there present and place in his roome some lerned and religious pastor who should as it was desired weekely preach unto the people and carefully instruct them in the points of faith and religion of which their Lordships were pleased to accept for the present, and accordingly inioyned him to the performance thereof and withall ordered the said preacher now to be presented should first be approved and allowed by the lorde Archbishop of Yorke in respect of abilitie and sufficiencie." This entry is thus attested :—

"Concordat cum registro
ffrancis Cottington
Laurence Trotter Attornie
Edward Bright vicarius de
Pickering Scriptor huius Exemplaris."

Edward Bright succeeded to the living in 1615. We may believe that he was selected as being a "lerned and religious pastor." He appears to have remained in possession until his death in 1659, though there is an entry of the baptism of a son of a certain Robert King in 1644, who is described as "minister." There must have been some exciting scenes in Pickering at this time, for in the year 1644, when many other churches suffered a similar fate, the registers record the breaking up of the font and the tearing to pieces of the church Prayer Book on the same day. The entries are in very small pale writing at the back of one of the books and read:—

THE FONT OF PICKERING CHURCH.

It dates in its present form from 1644, but the upper portion, which shows traces of painting, appears to be of very much earlier workmanship, and has been thought to be of Saxon origin.

"Baptisterii Pickerensis Demolitio, Septemb. 25, 1644."

And in another hand:—

"Liturgia ecclesie ibidem lacerata eodem die 1644."

Edward Bright had several children whose names

appear in the registers, and one of them, Joseph Bright, was on the 11th of July 1652 "elected and declared to be the parish clerk of Pickering." He was then twenty-five years old. On the night of August the 26th, 1634, there was a fire in the town which burnt down two houses and caused great fear among the inhabitants. Then among other entries on the back pages of register No. 2, 1615-53, appear recipes of this character:—

"A [cure?] for the dropsie in ye winter. Take a gallon of white wine and broome ashes to the quantitie [a few indecipherable words] sifted and drinke a pint thereof morning and [cause?] it [to?] be drunken also at meale times with ones meats and at other times when one is drie a little quantitie. Matthew Mitso . . e."

"For the same in Summer. Take a pecke of sage and bake it in a riddon (?) pastie, and when it is baked to a hard crust breake there crust and all in it . . . and . . . unne it up all into a barrell of drinke, and drinke it in the Sum̄er time especially in maye."

"*A remeadie for the stich.*

"Take a j^d. of treacle a j^d of aqua-vite and a j^d of sal . . . and apply them to the place."

"*A medicine for wormes.*

"Take lavander c . . . unset leekes an ox('or bull' *inserted above*) gall and cum̄in seed, fry these togither with . (?) . and lay them warme in a linnen clath to the childes belly."

Some other remedies that belong to this period were discovered by Mr Blakeborough[1] in this neighbourhood. I have taken them from the original seventeenth century writing:—

"Take for to clear the eyes 1 ounce of dried batts bloode groude to powder & white hens bloode & dung sift & when they be well mixed & quite dry then blowe a little in the ill eye & yt shall soon be well."

"*For a pinne or webbe in ye eye.*

"Take ye galle of an hare the gall of a mowerpate and of a wild cat and honey and hogs lard a like quantity mix all together and annoynt ye eye wth a feather dipped in yt and yt shalle be soon cured."

The details of a remedy "For a fallynge sickness" though possibly considered very efficacious are too repulsive for modern ears.

The following recipe, "For the making of Honey Cakes. Certayne to be acceptable to ye Fairy Folk," is from the same source and is dated 1605:—

"Taike of wilde honey thre ounce, of powder'd dill sede half ounce swete violet roote in fine powder 2 drachmes and six ounces of white wheaten meal which you will bringe to a light dowgh these thinges being all mixed together with faire water. This done with

[1] Calvert's MS. book in the possession of Mr Richard Blakeborough.

a silver spune helde in ye hand of a sure maid one be you sure who hath not as yet owther yielded her own or do then or ever hath worn a garter band there bound by her lover for such be not fitt and proper maids for the maykinge of Fairy Cakes. The Cakes thus mayde be they to the number of seven unbaked and mayde to the biggness of a marke. These cakes thus mayde may be used by any one wishfull to intercede with or begge a boon from the Fairy folk alwaie being mindfull of this matter be she passing as a maid lett her not dare to mayke use of the cakes." Then follows the story of the evils that befell "one Sarah Heugh who well knowing herself alacking her maidenhead" tried to pass herself off to the fairies as a "true" maid.

Coming back to the registers of Pickering we find that on the 13th August 1694 Archbishop Sharp held a confirmation in the church and confirmed about a thousand persons. The note is given in Latin as follows:—

"Memorandum. 13° die Augusti 1694 Johannes Divina providentia Eboracensis Archiepiscopus in ecclesîa parochiali de Pickeringe Mille (aut eò circita) Baptizatos Xti Relligioni Confirmavit.

"JOSHUA NEWTON.

"*Vicarius Ib.*"

The parcel gilt Chalice still in use at Pickering Church belongs to this period. It is dated 1613, and was made by Christopher Harrington, the goldsmith of York. The paten was made in 1712 by Seth Lofthouse of London.

During the Commonwealth Levisham and Pickering parishes seem to have been joined from 1653 to 1661. The Levisham burials and births appear in the Pickering registers. Among the regular entries of deaths at Pickering are recorded :--

"1619. Jane Greenwood a stranger buried March.
1631. Ellen Kirbye a poore Girle buried.
1634. A poor traveller buried here the 3 day of June.
1636. Gawen Pollard pauper Generosus 30th May."

It would be interesting to know how a pauper came to be a "generosus."

A bequest dated 1658 that seems to have been entirely forgotten appears in one of the registers. It says: "Be it Remembred that Robert Huggett of great Edston In the County of yourke Labourer did by his last will and Testamente bearinge date the Eleaventh day of January in the yeare of Grace one Thousande Sixe hundred fifty Eight give & bequeste unto Elizabeth Huggett his Mother in Law all that his Cottage or Tennemente att Pickeringe with all & singular the Appurtenances theirunto belongeing duringe hir life Naturall and No longer and then to Come unto James Coates of little Barugh Husbandman all the Right & Title of the above saide Tennemente in Pickeringe aforsaide after the death of my saide Mother in Law Hee payinge theirfor year by & every yeare for Ever the some of Twelve shilling of Lawfull money of Englande to be paide unto the Poore of Pickeringe att the feaste of Sainte Martin the bishopp in winter to begine the firste paymente at Martinmas after the death of my saide Mother in Law & not before which Twelve shilling shall be distributede at the discretion of the saide James Coats or his assignes Togeather with the advice of the Church wardins & overseers of the saide towne of Pickeringe for the time beinge."

THE JACOBEAN ALMS BOX IN THE PORCH OF PICKERING CHURCH.

The briefs collected at Pickering for various purposes were very numerous between 1661 and 1665; they are set out elaborately at the back of one of the registers, but they are given below in condensed form:—

BRIEFS COLLECTED IN PICKERING CHURCH.

1661.	July	28.	6s. 6d. for Condover Church, Shropshire.
	Sept.	8.	6s. Parish Church of Pontefract.
	Nov.	10.	4s. 2d. for the losses of Henry Harrison, mariner.
	Nov.	3.	13s. 7d. for the poor Protestants of Lithuania.

1661 Aug. 11. 5s. 10d. for the Parish Church of Scarborough.
Dec. 15. 5s. for the Parish Church, Dalby-Chalcombe, in the County of Leicester.
Dec. 29. 5s. for the reparation for the Collegiate Church of Rippon.
Jan. 29. 3s. 4d. for the loss of Christopher Greene of Beighton, in the County of Derby.
Feb. 23. 4s. 4d. Brief by his Majesty's special order for promoting the trade of fishing.
1662. April 6. 4s. for the loss of Thomas Welby in the County address.
,, 13. 4s. 4d. for the loss of William Copperthwaite.
No date. 5s. for the relief of John Wolrich of (erased) County of Staffords.
1665. April 16. 4s. 2d. for the repairing of the Parish Church of Tinmouth, in the County of Northumberland.

The system of briefs became subject to great abuses, and in 1828 it was abolished. Most of the Pickering collections were very small, but the people evidently had some sympathy for the poor Protestants of Lithuania, for they gave nearly three times as much as usual.

Despite the statement made by Clark in his valuable book on "Mediæval Military Architecture in England" that "Pickering was held for the king in the Parliamentary struggles," I can find no records to show that this was so or that any fighting took place there during the Civil War. I have searched many volumes of tracts relating to the period for any reference to Pickering, but although Scarborough on the east and Helmsley on the west are frequently mentioned, and details of the sieges and surrenders given, yet I have found no statement concerning

Pickering. I must, however, mention that at least two iron cannon balls have been discovered in recent times embedded in the ground beneath the western walls of the castle.

In a Cromwellian survey found by Mr R. B. Turton, among the records of the Duchy of Lancaster,[1] there is, however, a most valuable account of the castle dated July 15th, 1651. It mentions damage done by the soldiers "in the time of the late warrs," but it also tells us that much lead, wood and iron was taken to Scarborough Castle by Sir Hugh Cholmley, which seems to show conclusively that the place was not defended. The Cromwellian soldiers were probably quartered in the somewhat ruined castle and used what timber they could find for lighting their fires. The survey of 1651 is as follows:—

"The capital Messuage is scituate on the North side of Pickering Towne and knowne by the name of Pickering Castle; the Entrance whereof lyeth on the South through a Gatehouse which is somewhat (qu: decayed) in respect that all the covering is taken away. The outside gate you enter into a Spatious Court contayneing one Acre and three Roodes more or less; on which (on the East side) close adjoyning to the said Gate standeth a ruynous howse partly covered with Slate, in which were lately three severall Roomes below Staires, and as many above. But in the time of the late warrs, all the floares for the chambering have

[1] "North Riding Record Society's Publications," vol. 1, New Series, p. 65.

been pulled down by the Souldiers insomuch the whole howse is ready to fall, there being hardly any thing left to support the Roofe; The owt walles being partly built of Stone and part of Timber and the sparrs which are fastned to the mayne wall of the Castle do still remayne. Further eastward to the said howse along the wall standeth a Towre knowne by the Name of Dyet Towre, in which there hath beene three severall Roomes with other Conveniencyes thereunto belonging, which with litle Cost may bee made habitable, but the Lead Wood and Iron was by Sr Hugh Cholmley (as we are informed) carryed to Scarbrough Castle. Further along the said Wall standeth an other Tower North to the aforesaid howse and knowne by the Name of Rossimund Towre, the walls in good repaire, but the Wood Leade and Iron quite taken away. On the West side of the aforesaid Gate along the Wall standeth an other Tower knowne by the Name of Milne Tower, built within all of hewen stone with a staire Case of the same, conteyneing one Roome above lately used for a lodging chamber, but within these six or seven yeares all the Iron Lead and wood have been taken away and nothing left besides the out walles which are in very good repaire and one Rotten beame which lyeth cross the topp of the said Towre. On the North side of the said Court opposite to the Gate standeth an other Gate which is the Entrance over a decayed bridg into the midle Castle and leadeth into an other spatious Court conteyneing two Roodes more or less. On the North east of the said Gate standeth a fourth Tower knowne by the name of Coleman Towre contenyneing two Roomes, but the floars covering and all the wood is taken away. On the West side of the said Court standeth a Large Ruyned hall almost all fallen to the ground nothing of the Timber remayneing. At North end of which hall Eastward standeth one howse covered with slate and in indifferent good repaire conteyneing one Roome and knowne by the Name of the Chappell which is now used for keepeing of Courts for the Honor aforesaid. On the backside of which lyeth a third Court conteyneing two Roodes more or less in which hath been diverse buildings but now ruyned and fallen to the ground. In the midst of the whole Castle standeth a mount conteyneing one Acre on which there is a spatious, ruyned, and old decayed building being nothing but ruyned walls which in many places begin to fall downe. The said building is commonly knowne by the name of the Moate. The Materialles of the said Castle (which are there now remayneing), as the Timber hewen stone and slate, wee estimate to bee worth in ready money (besides the charge of takeing them downe)—CC^{li}. The Ground lying within the walls and Ditches of the Castle aforesaid conteyne in the whole three Acres and three Roodes which is worth upon Improvem^{t} p. Ann.—$C^{s.}$"

The story which has already been mentioned of the wanton destruction by the Parliamentary soldiers of ancient documents that had been preserved in the Castle may quite reasonably be true, but unfortunately Hinderwell, who seems to have been the first to record the tale,[1] does not give any authority for his statement. Another story which is sometimes mentioned among the people of Pickering states that Parliamentary soldiers were quartered in the church during the Civil War, but we can place no reliance upon the legend. Some details of the raising of train bands in the district are given in the memoirs of Sir Hugh Cholmley, the gallant defender of Scarborough Castle. Writing of the year 1636, he says, "I was at this time made Deputy-lieutenant and Colonel over the Train-bands within the hundred of Whitby Strand, Ryedale, Pickering, Lythe, and Scarborough Town." Three years later Sir Hugh tells us that in preparation for the king's march against the Scots, he had much business in mustering and training the soldiers of the Train-bands, and many journeys to York to consult with the Vice-President and other Deputy-Lieutenants. "About June the king sent down his army into Yorkshire, and himself came to it in August. The Earl of Northumberland was General from whom I had a commission. Divers of the colonels of the Train-bands, with their regiments, were called to march with the king into Northumberland; amongst which I had been one, but at that time I had caught cold and a dangerous sickness, in raising and training my whole regiment together on Paxton-Moor near Thornton, where one Hallden, a stubborn fellow of Pickering, not obeying his captain, and giving me some unhandsome language, I struck him with my cane, and felled him to the ground. The

[1] Thomas Hinderwell, "History of Scarborough," 1811, p. 350.

cane was tipped with silver, and hitting just under the ear, had greater operation than I intended. But either the man was ill or else counterfeited so, to be freed from service; which I willingly granted, and glad when he was well: but it was a good monition not to be hasty in the like or any other provocation, for passion doth not only blind the judgement but produceth other ill effects."

In 1640, when Sir Hugh (as a burgess for Scarborough) was attending the Short Parliament in London, his regiment was commanded to march to the Scottish Border. His brother Henry Cholmley, being Lieut.-Colonel, went with it, but at Durham they were ordered back.

In November 1641 Sir Hugh was again attending Parliament, and at that time he feared the advance of the Scots into Yorkshire, "which," he says, "did not a little disquiet my mind and thoughts for my dear wife and children; the snow being so great, I could not possibly remove them so soon as I desired"; "but at the latter end of February, as soon as the ways were passable, I had her and all my family in London." It must have been an unusually prolonged period of snow to keep Sir Hugh and his family apart for two or three months. Roxby Castle was his birthplace, and his account of his early years there includes an accident which might have had fatal results.

"I was," he says, "the first child of my dear mother, born upon the 22nd of July, being a Tuesday, and on the feast day commonly called Mary Mag-

John Cholmley of Cheshire.

Sir Richard,
Lt.-Gov. of the Tower in the time of King Henry VIII.; d. without issue; m. Elizabeth, one of the daus. of —— Nevill of Thornton Bridge; probably bought land there.

Sir Roger Cholmley,
First to settle in Yorkshire; m. Catherine, dau. of Sir Marmaduke Constable of Flamborough. Sir Roger knighted 5th of Henry VIII., when English had a great victory over the Scots; died April 28th, 1538; bought Roxby.

Sir Richard,
Called "The Great Black Knight of the North"; inherited property; knighted at battle of Mussleburv Hill, 5th of Edw. VI.; m. 1st Margaret, d. of Wm. Lord Conyers. Purchased many lands in Yorks, Manors of Whitby, Whitby lithe, and Stakesby purchased in 1555; lived at Roxby; m. 2nd Katherine (d. 1598), dau. of Henry, 1st Earl of Cumberland, widow of Lord John Scroope of Bolton.

John,
Slain in his youth.

Anne,
m. to the Earl of Westmoreland.

Margaret,
m. Henry Gascoigne of Ledbury, near Richmond.

Francis,
m. Mrs Joane Boulmer; died without issue.

Richard and Roger, m. 2 bastard daus. of Dallrivers. [Both set on one side.]

Marmaduke.

Margaret. Jane. Elizabeth.

Katherine.

Sir Henry, m. Margaret, dau. of Sir Wm. Babthorpe; succeeded Francis.

Sir Richard Cholmley,
Born 1580, succeeded 1617, died 1632.

Sir Hugh Cholmley,
the defender of Scarborough Castle.
Born 1600, succeeded 1632.

GENEALOGICAL TREE OF THE CHOLMLEYS OF ROXBY, NEAR PICKERING.
(Taken from the details given in the memoirs of Sir Hugh Cholmley.)

M

dalen's day, in the year of our Lord God 1600, at a place called Roxby, in the country of York, within the Hundred of Pickering lythe near to Thornton, now much demolished, but heretofore the chief seat of my great-grandfather, and where my grandfather, Sir Henry Cholmley, then lived, which place (since I was married was sold by my father and self, towards the payment of his debts)."

Sir Hugh then describes his weakness as a child due to the fault of his nurse. This gave him such "a cast back" that he was a weak and sickly child for many years.

"At three years old, the maid which attended me let me tumble out of the great chamber window at Roxby, which (by God's providence) a servant waiting upon my grandfather at dinner espying, leaped to the window, and caught hold of my coat, after I was out of the casement. Soon after I was carried to my father and mother, who then lived with her brother Mr John Legard, at his house at Ganton nine miles from Roxby, where I continued for the most part until I was seven years old; then my father and mother going to keep house at Whitby, went with them, and beginning to ride a little way by myself, as we passed over a common, called Paston moor [? Paxton, above Ellerburne] one of my father's servants riding beside me, I had a desire to put my horse into a gallop; but he running away, I cried out, and the servant taking hold of my arm, with an intention to lift me from my horse, let me fall between both, so that one of them, in his gallop, trod on my hat; yet, by God's protection, I caught no harm."

When his father was living at Whitby he had another narrow escape. "The next year," he writes, "being 1608 upon my very birth-day, being the feast of Mary Magdalen, and I just eight years old, by God's great Providence, I escaped as great, if not greater danger than this; which was, that, at my Father's house, at Whitby aforesaid, there was a great fierce sow, having two pigs near a quarter old, which were to be reared there, lying close together asleep, near to the kitchen door, I being alone, out of folly and waggery, began to kick one of them; in the interim another rising up, occasioned me to fall upon them all, and made them cry; and the sow hearing, lying close by, came and caught me by the leg, before I could get up, and dragged me half a score yards, under the window of the room now called the larder, and what in respect of the age and the amazement I was in, could not help myself; from the leg she fell to bite me in the groin with much fierceness; when the butler, carrying a glass of beer to my father (then in his chamber) hearing me cry, set down the beer on the hall table, and running out, found the sow passing from my groin to my throat."

Another famous name connected with this period is that of George Villiers, second Duke of Buckingham. After the death of Charles II. the royal favourite retired to his seat at Helmsley, his strength being very much impaired by the vicious life he had led at Court. He seems to have devoted himself to hunting and open-air sports. Certain stories connected with the Duke and mixed up with the usual superstitions were told to Calvert nearly a hundred years ago.

"Near the Checkers' Inn at Slapstean," he says, "there stood until a few years agone the cottage in which there lived many years sen one Isaac Haw, who in his day did hunt the fox with George Villiers, and many a queer story did he use to tell. Here be one. There lived on the moor not over an hour's ride from Kirkby Moorside, one Betty Scaife, who had a daughter Betty, a good like wench." George Villiers seeing this girl one day is said to have induced her to become his mistress either by force or with her mother's consent. After having a dream she told Villiers to come near her no more, foretelling at the same time the time and death he would die. He was so affected by this that he is said to have ridden away and never seen her again.

Haw also tells how he once rode on the moor with the spirit of the Duke of Buckingham, being not aware at the time that his Grace was dead. Villiers made an arrangement that when both were dead and the devil gave them a holiday they would both hunt together on a certain moor.

"There be those whose word has been handed down to us," continues Calvert, "who sware to having seen these two ahunting of a spirit fox with a spirit pack of a moonlight night. I know one who hath in memory a song of that day anent these two but it be so despert blasfemous that for the very fear of injuring the chance of my own soul's salvation I do forbear to give it, but if it be that you wish to copy on't, one Tom Cale a cobbler living in Eastgate Pickering hath to my knowledge a copy on't."

THE HOUSE AT KIRBY MOORSIDE IN WHICH THE 2ND DUKE OF BUCKINGHAM—THE FAVOURITE OF CHARLES II.—DIED.

The window of the bedroom is shown in the illustration. It is on the first floor at the right hand side of the house.

The Duke lived to the age of sixty in spite of his life of unbridled vice, and it seems that a sudden illness seized him after a hard day's hunting, and he died at the house in Kirby Moorside where he was taken instead of to Helmsley. The house is still standing, and one may even see the room in which the reckless

Duke expired. As may be seen from the illustration the house is a good one, and at that time must have been, with one exception, the best in the village. The lines by Pope descriptive of the favourite's death are, therefore, quite unwarranted:—

> "In the worst inn's worst room, with mat half hung,
> The floors of plaster and the walls of dung."

It never was an inn, and the Rev. R. V. Taylor[1] has discovered that the house was in the occupation of one of his tenants. I have carefully examined the house without finding anything to suggest that such squalor could have ever existed there. The staircase is very picturesque, and one of the brass drop handles on the bedroom doors shows that the building was a good one. The bedroom in which the Duke died has the fireplace blocked up; there is a recessed window containing a seat, and the walls, where they are panelled, are of fir, although the larger beams throughout the house seem to be of oak.

The sudden demise of this famous man must have created a sensation in the village, and although the body was not buried at Kirby Moorside, the parish register of that time has this illiterate entry[2]—

> "*buried in the yeare of our Lord* 1687
> *Marke Reame . . . . . Aprill y^e^* 12
> *Gorges viluas Lord dooke of bookingam etc.* 19"

A letter from Lord Arran to the Duke's late

[1] "Yorkshire Notes and Queries," May 1904, p. 68.
[2] The third volume of the registers at the top of page 4.

chaplain, dated April 17th, 1687, says, "I have ordered the corpse to be embalmed and carried to Helmsley Castle and there to remain till my Lady Duchess her pleasure shall be known. There must be speedy care taken; for there is nothing here but confusion, not to be expressed. Though his stewards have received vast sums, there is not so much as one farthing, as they tell me, for defraying the least expense." From this it appears that he died on or before the 17th of April, and that after the embalming process had been performed the intestines were buried at Kirby Moorside on the 19th and not on the 17th, as stated by Gill in his "Vallis Eboracensis."

One of the tattered registers[1] of Kirby Moorside also contains the following remarkable entry:—

"Dorythy Sowerbie of Bransdales (slayne with 6 bullett by theeves in the night) was buryed the 23th (sic) Day of May 1654." A few years before this in 1650 the burial is recorded of "a stranger y[t] sold stockins." On the first page of the register dated 1704, the vicar, "M. James Musgrave," gives a list of "things belonging to the church—a surplus, a Hud, a challis, a patton, tow-flaggons [these are of pewter and are kept in the church], a putter Dubler, a Tabill clorth, on napkin. A dubler for christening."

During this period the Duchy records show that Pickering Forest was still being robbed of its oaks, some of them being used to repair the defences of Scarborough Castle during the Civil War.

[1] Vol. ii. p. 2

" Wee are informed that there were xxxtie Trees or thereaboutes cut downe in Newton dale within the said fforest and carried to Scarbrough Castle by Order from Sir Hugh Cholmley then Gouernor of the same, to the value of	20	0	0"

Some of the other entries at the same time are given below.[1]

	lib.		
" Wee are informed that divers olde trees are cut downe within the fforest of Pickeringe in a place called Deepdale and Helley Greene by Robert Pate by the Appointment of Mathew ffranke Esquire to the value of	6	0	0
Likewise wee are informed that John Hassell gent hath cut downe diuers trees in Dalbye within the said fforest to the value of	19	0	0
Wee are likewise informed that Beatrice Hassell widdow hath cut downe diuers trees in Dalbye Hagges within the said fforest, to the value of	12	0	0
Wee are likewise informed That seuerall Tennantes of Goatland haue cut downe two hundred Trees and more within the fforest in the North part of Newton-dale and Gillwood to the value of	30	0	0
And that Robert ffranke gent did take Composicions and summes of money of seuerall of the said Tennants of Goatland for the same wood.			

	l.	*s.*	*d.*
And allso we are informed that there hath bene cut downe Two hundred Trees in Haughe Hagge within the said fforest, And that the said Trees were cut downe and Carried away by the poore people of Pickeringe in the yeares 1647 and 1648 to the value of	40	0	0

[1] From a thin foolscap book containing, *inter alia*, the findings of the Juries of the Courts Leet, etc., in the possession of the Rev. Arthur Hill of Thornton-le-dale.

From the same book we discover that

> "George Grayson holdes by Copie of Court Roll one Cottage in Pickeringe and one Garth thereunto belonging, dated the 11th of Aprill 1659 And was admitted . Tennant thereof by John Syms then Steward and paid ffine 0 0 4"

This is of considerable interest in view of the fact that the Grayson family are still tenants of the Duchy.

Tenants are mentioned as holding property in "Smiddiehill" and "Hungate Greene," and the entry given below is interesting on account of the mention of the market cross that has completely disappeared.

> "Jane Moone widdow holdes one Messuage and one parcell of waste ground in Pickering neare to the Market Crosse and was admitted Tennant thereof by John Sym, now deputie Steward, by Copie dated the 22d of November 1659: And paid ffine for per Admittance . . . 0 8 1"

Many of the small houses of Pickering must have been built at this time. One near the castle gateway has a stone in the gable end bearing the initials E. C. W., and the date 1646, another with a thatched roof on the south side of Eastgate, dated 1677, is now fast going to ruin. The roofs were no doubt at that time chiefly covered with thatch, and the whole town must have been extremely picturesque. The stocks, the shambles, and the market cross stood in the centre of the town, and there were none of the unpleasant features that modern ideas, unchecked by a sense of fitness and proportion, bring in their wake.

The castle, we have seen, was in a far more perfect state than at the present time, but the church must have appeared much as it does to-day. The circular wooden pulpit is Georgian, and thus the one that preceded it has disappeared. Two of the three bells that still hang in the tower bear the date 1638. The treble bell is inscribed "Praise the Lord," and sounds the note G sharp. The middle bell gives F sharp and the inscription is "Soli deo gloria." Hanging in the bell-cote of the schools adjoining the church is the small bell dated 1632 that was removed from the Bruce Chapel in 1857 when the schools were built. Before that date children were taught in the Bruce Chapel.

In Archbishop Sharp's manuscripts (page 106) preserved at Bishopthorpe there is a detailed account of the parish of Pickering. It is dated 1706, and is given under the heading of "Dean of York's Peculiars." There are numerous abbreviations, but the meaning is plain in most instances.

"*Pickering Vic. St Peter and St Paul.*

"1706. No Papist.

"A[nno] R[egni] Edw. I. 13. The Manor, Castle, Forest of Pickering were given to Edmund E. of Lancaster and so became thenceforward part of that Dutchy. The Church of Pickering was by Hen. I. given to the Deanery of York, wth the soke thereof and all the chappells and tithes belonging. It is let at the rent of 100 li.

"The Vicarage consists of a house &c. And the tithe

The Maypole on Sinnington Green.
The centre of many village festivities in the past centuries.

Hay of Garths wch may yield 7 or 8 Load in a year to the vicar, and all the small tithes of the Parish. Besides an augmentation of 20^{li} p an. made since the Restauration.

"This is a large parish in wch are 2 Chappells neither of them endowed as the minister Mr Newton tells me, but he allows 5th to a neighboring minister to serve the one and the other he goes to himself. This vicarage, of the D^{ns} Collation is val in my B at 28^{li}. It is I hope worth 60^{li} [not above 40 K. B. 8. 3. 9. T 16-40b.] *The Deans Tenant pays 20^{li} of it.*

"Within this Parish are the Towns of Newton upon Rocliff, Blansby Park, Kinthorp. Here also is Dereholm Grange and Loft Maress Grange. 1707. 41 (indistinct) John Pickering Vr.; 1715 Robert Hargreaves, Vicar; 1740 Saml Hill Vicar.

"1745. George Dodsworth.

"1706. Papists 9. £ s. d.

"The Chappell of Goteland. 1716 4 0 0

"Being distant above 8 miles from the Parish Church was by Dean Scot A. D. 1635 allowed the privilege of Sepulture for the inhab. Saveing to the Mother Church all its dues 1706 Certifyd by ye (indistinct) to the Dean to be worth 4 0 0 Arising out of Surplice Fees and Voluntary Contribution William Prowde, Curate 1722 Jonathan Robinson, Curate."

The country folk were in much the same state in regard to their morals and superstitions as in the Georgian Era described in the next chapter, but it is of great interest to know that efforts towards improvement were being made as early as the year 1708. The following account given by Calvert of an attempt to stop the May dance at Sinnington would show either that these picturesque amusements were not so harmless as they appear at this distance, or else that the "Broad Brims" were unduly severe on the innocent pleasures

An inverted stone coffin of much earlier date used as a seventeenth century gravestone at Wykeham Abbey.

of the time. The account is taken by Calvert "from one Nares book."

"In the year 1708 there did come a great company of Broad Brims for to stop the May Dance about the pole at Sinnington, and others acting by concert did the like at Helmsley, Kirby Moorside and Slingsby, singing and praying they gat them round about the garland pole whilst yet the may Queen was not yet come but when those with flute and drum and dancers came near to crown the Queen the Broad Brims did pray and sing psalms and would not give way while at the finish up there was like for to be a sad end to the day but some of the Sinnington Bucks did join hands in a long chain and thus swept them clean from the pole. At Slingsby there was a great dordum of a fight, but for a great while the Broad Brims have set their faces against all manner of our enjoyment."

Fine examples of the carved oak cabinets, chests, and other pieces of furniture of this period still survive in some of the houses of Pickering. The cabinets generally bear the date and the initials of the maker, and the I.B. to be seen on some of the finest pieces from this district are the initials of John Boyes of Pickering, whose work belongs chiefly to the time of William and Mary.

CHAPTER XI

The Forest and Vale in Georgian Times, 1714 to 1837

WITH the accession of King George the First in 1714 we commence a new section of the history of Pickering, a period notable in its latter years for the sweeping away to a very large extent of the superstitions and heathen practices which had survived until the first quarter of the nineteenth century.

The town had probably altered very little in its general appearance since the time of the Restoration. Most of the roofs were thatched; the castle was probably more dismantled within the outer walls, but the church of the Georgian period must have been almost identically the same as during the century that preceded it, and as it remained until the restoration in 1879.

At the top of the market-place stood the stocks at the side of the old stone-built shambles that disappeared in 1857, having for many generations formed a background to the groups of buyers and sellers in the steep and picturesque street. We can people the scene with the quaint costumes of the eighteenth century; knee-breeches and long waistcoats are to be seen in every direction, the three-cornered hat and the wig tied with a black ribbon are worn by the better classes. The wives and daughters of the squires and lesser gentry reflect in a modified form the fashions prevailing in London, and to be observed in actuality among the gay crowds that thronged the Spa at Scarborough, assuming and discarding the hooped-petticoat according to the mode of the moment. We can see the farmers of the Vale and those from the lonely dales discussing the news of the week and reading the scarce and expensive newspapers that found their way to Pickering. How much they understood of the reasons for the great European wars and alliances it is not easy to say, but when the reports came of victories to the British armies, assisted although they may have been by paid allies, the patriotic feelings of these Yorkshiremen did not fail to manifest themselves in a heavier consumption of beer than usual. We can hear the chink of glasses and the rattle of pewter tankards in the cosy parlours of the "White Swan," the "George," and the rest; we can hear as the years go by the loud cheers raised for Marlborough, for Wolfe, for Nelson, or for Wellington, while overhead the church bells are ringing loudly in the old grey tower. These were the days of the highwaymen, and even as late as 1830 a postman was robbed near the moorland village of Lockton, on his way to Whitby. The driver of the mailcart at that time used to carry a large brass-mounted cavalry pistol, which was handed to him when he had mounted his box by one of the two old ladies who acted as the post-mistresses of

Pickering. It is not much more than ten years since the death of Francis Gibson, a butcher of East Ayton, who was over a hundred years old and remembered the capture of the last highwayman who was known to carry on the old-time profession in the neighbourhood. He was tracked to an inn at East Ayton where he was found sleeping. Soon afterwards he found himself on the road to York, where he was hanged.

The road across Seamer Moor between Ayton and Scarborough was considered sufficiently dangerous for those who travelled late to carry firearms. Thus we can see Mr Thomas Chandler of the Low Hall at West Ayton—a Justice of the Peace—having dined with some relations in Scarborough, returning at a late hour. The lights of his big swinging barouche drawn by a pair of fat chestnuts shine out on the white road; the country on either side is unenclosed, and masked men may appear out of the shadows at any moment. But if they are about they may have heard that Mr Chandler carries a loaded pistol ready for emergencies, for they always let him reach his house in safety.

To the simple peasants highwaymen were probably considered of small account in comparison to the apparitions that haunted many parts of the lonely country. Nearly every part of the moor had its own wraith or boggle, and the fear of these ghosts was so widespread that in many cases the clergy were induced to publicly lay them, after which were seen no more.

To record the advent of these strange beliefs is impossible, for who can tell how or when they originated? We can only describe them at the time of their destruction. Chaucer, writing in the fourteenth century, seemed to imagine that belief in elves and fairies had received its death-blow in his own time, for in "The Wife of Bath's Tale," he says—

> "In tholdé dayés of the Kyng Arthour,
> Of which that Britons speken greet honour,
> All was this land fulfild of faïrye.
> The elf queene with hir joly compaignye
> Douncéd ful ofte in many a greené mede.
> This was the olde opinion as I rede,—
> I speke of manye hundred yeres ago,—
> But now kan no man se none elvés mo,
> For now the greté charitee and prayeres
> Of lymtours, and othere hooly freres,
> That serchen every lond and every streem,
> As thikke as motés in the sonné beem,—
> Bléssynge hallés, chambres, kichenes, boures,
> Citees, burghes, castels, hyé toures
> Thrópés, bernés, shipnes, dayeryes,—
> This maketh that ther been no faïryes."

Five hundred years, however, had to pass before the most implicit belief in hobs, wraiths, and boggles was to disappear, and even at the present day those who have intimate associations with the population of the North Yorkshire moors know that traces of the old superstitions still survive.

Several books have been written on the folklore of Yorkshire and from them it is possible to get a rough idea of the superstitions common to many parts of the county, but these do not particularly concern the district surrounding Pickering. We should probably have never heard of many curious facts specially belonging to this part of the county if a small manuscript book of closely written notes had not been discovered by Mr Richard Blakeborough of Stockton-on-Tees, who has kindly allowed me to quote from it. The stories were collected by one George Calvert, who writes in 1823, and frequently mentions that the customs he describes were rapidly dying out. Under the heading of "Witch Hags who have dwelt hereabouts" he writes—

"They be so great in number that mayhap it will shew the more wisdom if mention be made only of those who in their day wrought some wondrous deed or whose word cast fear upon all."

From this list I have picked out those that belong to the neighbourhood of Pickering, and by the letters placed after each name one can discover in the key given below the special arts practised by each "hag."

"Nancy Nares o' Pickering" [T V Z W Y].
"Nanny Pearson o' Goathland" [X].
"Nan Skaife o' Spaunton Moor,"
called also Mary or Jenny.
"Aud Mother Migg o' Cropton" [Z].
(Her real name was Sabina Moss).
"Sally Craggs o' Allerston" [V Z].
"Dina Sugget o' Levisham" [W Z].
"Hester Mudd o' Rosedale" [T V].
"And Emma Todd o' Ebberston [Y].

KEY TO LETTERS AGAINST THE WITCHE'S NAMES.

T Did also use the evil eye.
U Could turn thersels into a hare.
V Could turn thersels into a cat.
W Had a familiar.
X Could cripple a quickening bairn.
Y Well up in all matters of the black art.
Z Did use ye crystal.

"All these," says Calvert, "were at one time of great note and did in their day work great deed and cast many an evil spell and charm and were held in great fear by great many good and peaceful folk. It be not for me to here put an argument in the favour of what do now be doubted and scorned by some. I will but say that I have seen and know that which hath been wrought by these hags o' the broom and of their power which they held at their beck and wink the which is not to be set on one side at the flip and flout of our young masters and misses, fresh from some teaching drove into their brain pans by some idiotick and skeptick French teacher. I therefore say no more on this matter."

Nancy Skaife of Spaunton Moor had a wonderful receipt for making a magic cube, and as she was a famous witch of her time and was reputed to possess most remarkable powers of foretelling events to come, it will be interesting to learn the ingredients of her magic cubes.

"Get you of the skull the bone part of a gibbetted

man so much as one ounce which you will dry and grind to a powder until when searced it be as fine as wheatenmeal, this you will put away securely sealed in a glass vial for seven years. You will then about the coming of the end of that time (for your cube must be made on the eve of the day come seven years of his gibbetting) get you together these several matters,

Two ways of marking Magic Cubes. (*From Calvert's MS. Book of Folklore.*)

all well dried and powdered and finely searced so much as three barley corns weight of each

Bullock blood.
Moudy [mole] blood.
Great Flitter mouse blood.
Wild Dove blood.
Hag-worm head.
Toade heart.
Crab eyes.
Graveyard moss and worms.

These being all gotten together on the eve of that day make a stiff dough of wheaten meal to the which you will add all the other powders working them to a stiff mass and into cubes of one inch square, to be pressed to a hollow, then they are to be set away to dry in a warm place for seven months to the day when with a sharp screever you shall deeply screeve the like of these upon each side, but be you mindful to screeve in the order as here ordered always turning the cube over and towards the left hand, the fifth side by turning the cube towards you, the sixth from you and thus you make your magic cube."

"The proper way to draw the virtue from and read a forecast with such cubes," says Calvert, "as yet I know not, but I learn that one Jane Craggs, a mantu maker of Helmsley, not only owns a cube but does at times play the craft for the entertainment of her lady visitors who wish their fortunes casting. I learn from Betty [Ellis] that these cubes were tossed upon the table and then used by the consultation of a book like unto that of the witche's garter but this book Betty kens nothing of its whereabouts. She aims one of her grandchilder must have gone off with it."

In the chapter devoted to Tudor times I have given an Elizabethan cure for an "ill caste" by a witch, but Calvert also tells us of a method for removing the spell from a "witch-held" house. "Of one thing I hear," he says, "which be minded unto this present day the which be that a bunch of yarrow gathered from off a grave and be cast within a sheet that hath covered the dead and this be setten fire to and cast within the door of any house thought to be witch held or having gotten upon it a spell of ill-luck, it shall be at once cleansed from whatsoever ill there be come again it as I hear even fevers and the like are on the instant driven forth. And this," he quaintly adds, " be worth while of a trial."

Of the awesome sights to be seen at night time Calvert gives many details.

" There be over anenst Cropton towards Westwood seen now and again at times wide asunder a man rushing fra those happening to cross his road with flaming mouth and having empty eye sockets, a truly terrible apparition for to come across of a sudden.

" At Bog Hall at times there is seen a plain specter of a man in bright armour who doth show himself thus apparrelled both on the landing and in a certain room.

" At that point where the Hodge and Dove mix their waters there is to be seen on Hallow Een a lovely maiden robed in white and having long golden hair down about her waist there standing with her bare arm thrown about her companion's neck which is a most lovely white doe, but she allowed none to come near to her.

" To the west of Brown Howe and standing by a boulder there be seen of a summer's eve a maiden there seated a-combing out her jet black tresses so as to hide her bare breast and shoulders, she looking to be much shamed to there do her toilet.

" And at the high end of Carlton anenst Helmsley there be seen at times a lovely maiden much afrighted galopping for very life oft casting her een behind her."

A Scene in Newton Dale when the Coach Railway between Pickering and Whitby was in use in 1836.

(*From Belcher's book on the Pickering and Whitby Railway*, 1836.)

Concerning the existence of this lovely maiden we have indisputable evidence given us, for Calvert says that in the year 1762 " Jim Shepherd o' Reskelf seed the maiden galloping."

Then there was the figure of "Sarkless Kitty"; but this spectre, we are told, " having been public laid will now be seen never again and has the very mention of her name be now a thing forbid by all it must soon come to pass that the memory of this lewd hussey will be entire forgot and it of a truth be better so."

But this only rouses one's curiosity, for the spectre must have been surpassingly terrible to require the suppression of its very name.

It was in August in the year 1807 or 1809 (the manuscript is too much soiled to be sure of the last figure) that either the Vicar of Lastingham or his curate-in-charge publicly laid this spirit, which had for many years haunted the wath or ford crossing the river Dove where it runs at no great distance from Grouse Hall.

The ceremony was performed at the request of the whole countryside for there was a widespread outcry over the last victim. He was a farmer's son who, having spent the evening with his betrothed, was riding homewards somewhat late, but he never reached his house. On the next day his cob was found quietly grazing near the dead body of its master lying near the ford. There were no signs of a struggle having taken place, there were no wounds or marks upon the body, and his watch and money had not been touched, so every one concluded that he had seen Sarkless Kitty.

In the year 1770 the ford "had come to be of such ill repute that men feared to cross after dark and women refused to be taken that way," although as far as is known it was only men who came to harm from seeing Sarkless Kitty. The apparition was that of an exceedingly lovely girl who appeared "as a nude figure standing upon the opposite bank to that of the approaching wayfarer." Her beauty was so remarkable that those who had the ill-luck to come across the spectre could not refrain from gazing at it, and all who did so were believed to have died either at the same moment or soon afterwards.

Calvert, however, tells us that one Roland Burdon, who possessed a "Holy Seal," came face to face with Sarkless Kitty, but fortified by its virtues he survived the vision; then he adds: "This same Roland did slay in single combat the great worm or Dragon which at one time did infest Beck Hole to the loss of many young maidens the which it did at sundry times devour. He slew it after a fierce battle lasting over half a day throw the great power of the Holy Seal being about his person. This worm did also infest Sneaton Moor."

If we are to believe anything at all of this prodigious story we must place it among those which have been handed down from the time of the Danes and have become somewhat confused with later superstitions.

Coming back to the story of the beautiful spectre

we find that in 1782 a certain Thomas Botran wrote down all the information he could find out in his time concerning the story of Sarkless Kitty, and Mr Blakeborough has added to it everything else that he has discovered relating to it.

It seems that there lived near Lastingham towards the close of the seventeenth century a girl named Kitty Coglan whose beauty was so remarkable that "folk at divers times come much out of their way in the pleasant hope of a chance for to look upon the sweetness of her face." She was, however, extremely vain, and her mother seems to have heard stories of her bad conduct, for she began to worry herself over her daughter's behaviour. Having had a curious dream she asked Takky Burton, the wise man of Lastingham, to tell her what it meant. He told her that the wonderful gem of her dream was her daughter Kitty, who like the gem had blemishes beneath the surface. Soon after this Kitty married the only son of a small farmer, but after they had lived together about four months he disappeared, and then Kitty seems to have gone from bad to worse. How long after this it was that the tragedy occurred is not known, but one day Kitty's naked dead body was found by the wath that her spirit afterwards haunted.

Two other stories that were at one time well known in the neighbourhood of Pickering must be mentioned. One feature of these old time legends is very noticeable, that is, how each ends with a moral usually of virtue overcoming vice. This was probably in some instances a new touch of colour given to the stories during the time when a religious wave swept over the dales.

"The White Cow of Wardle Rigg" is a good example of an old time legend, that owing to a natural process of alteration became gradually fitted to the beliefs and superstitions of each age in which it was told. How the story came to be localised is not known, but in its last phase it had reached this form.

Once an old couple lived near to Wardle Rigg, and bad seasons and other misfortunes had brought the wolf very near to their door. One night there passed by the humble cottage a little old lady driving along a thin and hungry looking white cow, she craved a crust and a drink of water for herself and shelter for the poor beast, this was readily granted by the old couple, they gave the old lady the easy-chair by the fire, and gave her of the best from their poor larder. She learnt from them how poor they were, and sorrowed with them.

In the middle of the night she called to them, as she stole silently out of the house, that for their kindness she left them all the worldly possessions she had, namely her white cow. This they were in no wise grateful for, because they could scarcely afford to feed it and it was too poor to sell or to hope to draw a drop of milk from.

But in the morning what was their surprise to find not a poor three parts starved cow, but a plump well fed animal, and with a bag full of milk, it indeed gave more milk than any cow they had ever known or heard of, their hay had also during the night grown to be quite a huge stack.

It was soon found that their butter was the best in all the dales, and was sought after far and wide, so that the old people were gradually filling their stocking with money. Added to this it was presently discovered that all who drank of the white cow's milk were cured, almost instantly, of a dreadful plague, which in the dales at that time was sending many young folk to an early grave. The fame of this wonderful cow soon spread. The old couple had given the milk to all those who fell ill of the plague, and people came to them from far off places.

It was then that their landlord determined by wicked arts to gain possession of this wonderful white cow, and sell the milk at a great price. His own child, his youngest daughter, falling ill of the plague determined him to carry out his evil design, and it was with sorrow and tears that the old folk watched their landlord lead their cow away.

When half way over the moor he was met by an old dame, "Where drivest thou my cow?" she demanded. Getting but a surly reply, and a threat to drive over her, she cried, "Let me teach thee how to milk my cow." So saying she seized hold of the cow's udder, crying out, "There's death in thee, there's death in thee," and then ran away. The landlord on reaching home was taking a cupful of the magic milk to his daughter, but setting it down for a moment a cat unseen commenced to lap from the cup and died instantly. The landlord then saw that in his greed he had outwitted himself. The good dame was brought to milk it under a promise of restoration, and all ended well.

The other story is known as "The Legend of Elphi." Elphi the Farndale dwarf was doubtless at one time the central figure of many a fireside story and Elphi's mother was almost equally famous. The most tragic story in which they both play their leading parts is that of Golpha the bad Baron of Lastingham and his wicked wife. The mother helped in hiding some one Golpha wished to torture. In his rage he seized the mother, and sentenced her to be burnt upon the moor above Lastingham.

Elphi to save his mother, called to his aid thousands of dragon-flies, and bade them carry the news far and wide, and tell the fierce adders, the ants, the hornets, the wasps and the weasels, to hurry early next day to the scene of his mother's execution and rescue her. Next morning when the wicked Golpha, his wife, and their friends gathered about the stake and taunted the old dame, they were set upon and killed, suffering great agonies. But Elphi and his mother were also credited with all the power of those gifted with a full knowledge of white magic, and their lives seem to have been spent in succouring the weak. Mr Blakeborough tells me that the remembrance of these two is now practically forgotten, for after most careful enquiry during the last two years throughout the greater part of Farndale, only one individual has been met with who remembered hearing of this once widely known dwarf.

The hob-men who were to be found in various spots in Yorkshire were fairly numerous around Pickering. There seem to have been two types, the kindly ones, such as the hob of Hob Hole in Runswick Bay who used to cure children of whooping-cough, and also the malicious ones. Calvert gives a long list of hobs but does not give any idea of their disposition.

Lealholm Hob.
Hob o' Trush.
T'Hob o' Hobgarth.
Cross Hob o' Lastingham.
Farndale Hob o' High Farndale.
Some hold Elphi to have been a hob of Low Farndale.
T'Hob of Stockdale.
Scugdale Hob.
Hodge Hob o' Bransdale.
Woot Howe Hob.
T'Hob o' Brackken Howe.
T'Hob o' Stummer Howe.
T'Hob o' Tarn Hole.
Hob o' Ankness.
Dale Town Hob o' Hawnby.
T'Hob o' Orterley.
Crookelby Hob.
Hob o' Hasty Bank.

T'Hob o' Chop Gate.
Blea Hob.
T'Hob o' Broca.
T'Hob o' Rye Rigg.
Goathland Hob o' Howl Moor.
T'Hob o' Egton High Moor.

The Hob of Lastingham was presumably named after the cross above the village, and not on account of his disposition.

Elphi we have seen had an excellent reputation and some eulogistic verses on him, written in a "cook book" and signed J. L., 1699, give further evidence of his good character.

Elphi bandy legs,
Bent an wide apart,
Neea yan i, this deeal [dale],
Awns a kinder heart.
Elphi great heead
Greatest ivver seen.
Neea yan i' this deeal
Awns a breeter een.

Elphi little chap,
Thoff he war so small
War big wi deeds o' kindness,
Drink tiv him yan an all.
Him at fails ti drain dry,
Be it mug or glass
Binnot woth a pescod
Nor a buss fra onny lass.

About the middle of the eighteenth century the people of Cropton were sadly troubled by "a company of evil water elves having their abode in a certain deep spring at the high end of that village," and in order to rid themselves of the sprites, a most heathen ceremony was conducted at the spring, "three wenches" taking a prominent part in the proceedings which are quite unprintable.

Belief in the power of the witches and wise men

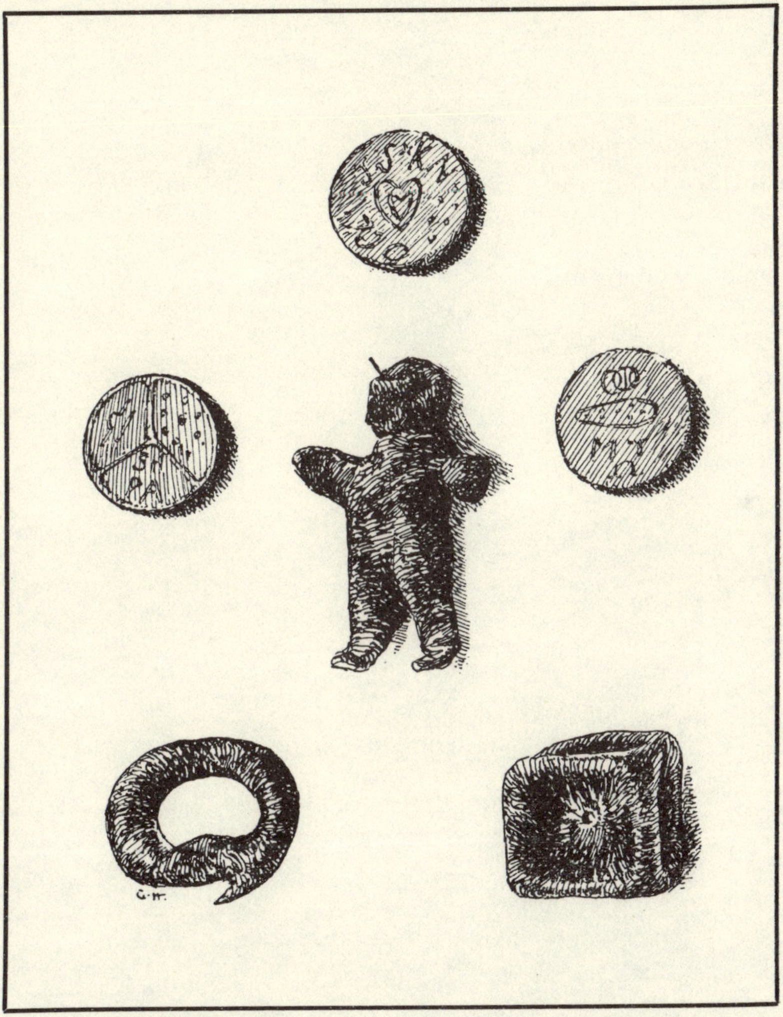

RELICS OF WITCHCRAFT FOUND IN THE NEIGHBOURHOOD OF PICKERING.

The little figure shown in the centre is made of pitch, beeswax, bullock's blood, hog's lard, and fat from a bullock's heart. It was used for casting spells on people, the pin being stuck in the figure wherever the "ill-cast" was required to fall. The magic cube and ring are made of similar ingredients to the figure. The sigils or charms are made of lead.

was universal, and youths and maidens applied to the nearest witch in all their love affairs. The magic cube, the witches' garter, leaden charms known as sigils, and the crystal were constantly in use to secure luck, to ward off evil and to read the future.

One of the witches was believed to have fallen out with the Devil for, says Calvert, "John Blades, ironmonger of Kirby Moorside, tells me he well minds hearing of a despert fierce fight which on a time did happen between ye Devil and an old witch over their dues, over anenst Yaud Wath (ford) and whilst they did so fight, one by stealth did slip himself over and in that wise did for ever break her spell."

I am able to give an illustration of one of the figures made by a witch of these parts for causing some bodily injury to happen to her client's enemy. The custom was a common one in the circles of witchcraft. A youth having a rival for the hand of some attractive maiden and wishing him every imaginary evil he would apply to "Aud Mother Migg" or one of the other hags of the neighbourhood and explaining his position the witch would prepare a small figure of the rival. The ingredients would be of the same class as the magic cube already fully described (generally pitch, beeswax, hog's lard, bullock's blood, and fat from a bullock's heart), and in order to cause his rival to lose an eye, or to go lame, or deaf, or to have any particular complaint in any particular part of his body the jealous lover had merely to stick a pin in that portion of the little brown figure. The ceremony was elaborate, especially in regard to the disposal of that part of the mixture not used to make the figure, for in every case the cunning old women worked on the imaginations of their dupes. There can be no doubt that the morals of the country folk during the eighteenth century were at an exceedingly low ebb. The practice of compelling girls who had misconducted themselves to stand in church for three Sundays was only given up at Pickering in the first quarter of the nineteenth century. Calvert describes how the miserable girl was first required to go before the parson or the squire or anyone of the "quality" to name the child's father, and "be otherwise questioned, and if it so happened that the squire was one of the hard-drinking class it was more than likely that he came well on in his cups. If so it would be more like than otherwise that he would put the lass and all present to shame by the coarse . . . questions he would ask the poor wench. I have heard shame cried aloud myself by those who then came together.

"On the Sunday when the poor lass had to do her first penance it was in this wise—She had to walk from her home to the church porch with a soiled white sheet cast over her head to her feet, and there stand from the ringing of the first bell calling to morning prayer, and as the good folk did so pass her to ask of them for to pray for her soul and forgiveness of her great sin and frailty; and thither did she have to stand until the parson, after the reading of the morning prayer, did go to her and bring her into the church with the psalm of *miserere mei* which he shall sing or say in English. Then shall he put her before all those present, but apart from them, when he shall publicly call upon her to confess her fault which, be she a single wench she did say aloud, 'wherefore I . . . putting aside my maiden duty to Almighty God have yielded unto the vile sin of fornication with . . . who is the true father of my child, may Almighty God forgive me my sin.' But be it a wedded woman then she shall stand bareheaded and barelegged, and instead of fornication she shall say the word adultery, she being nobbut covered with a sheet from the shoulders. At this day (1824) I cannot but say I am glad to say that there be a good feeling abroad for its abolishment, indeed, there be in many places so strong a feeling again this way of judging our daughters for a fault of this kind that they have bidden the clergy to set their faces against any lass ever being so judged, and though our clergy be in the main but a despert reckless lot, I hear that mostly they are of the same mind as those they do hold as their flock. Indeed, at one village not far from here a father set his back against his lass standing at the church, though she had been so judged to do, and the whole of thereabouts siding with the lass it was held by the parson and his fox-chasing, wine-bibbing crew for to pull in their tongues a piece which they most wisely did, or, for a truth, they would have found themselves astride of the wrong horse. It is now time this shameful practice was for ever laid on one side for it be not for the good of our own daughters that they witness such sights even in a place called God's house, but it oft be ought but that to our shame and the greater shame of all who hold its government of it. I could here give you a good list of curious cases of the which for the most part I did witness myself of both the hearing and of the standing of both many wed and single so browten to public shame, but as it would be to no good purpose I will hold from the putting pen to paper in this matter, letting what hath been wrote end this matter, for of a truth it is to a better purpose that both pen, ink, paunce box and paper, can be putten." Concerning the innumerable customs and superstitions associated with the dead and dying, Calvert collected a number of interesting facts. "It be held by many," he writes, "that a dying body cannot quit this life if they do be lying upon a bed which happen to have pigeon feathers gotten in by chance.

"A body cannot get their time over with ease to themselves if there be one in the room who will not give them up. It be better for all such who cannot bring themselves to part with those they love to withdraw from the room so that death may enter and claim his rights.

"It be held to be a sure sign that an ailing body will die if there be a downcome of soot.

"It be also a sure sign that death be awaiting for his own if an ullot [owlet] do thrice hoot so that the ailing one do hear it and remark thereon.

"It be an ill sign if a death glow be seen to settle upon the face of an ailing one or if such cry out they do see a shroud o' the quilt.

"If there be a death watch heard, then the ailing one need not longer hold on to hope, for it be for that time gone from that house and will not enter again until a corpse be hugged out.

"It be an ill sign to the dying if a dark winged moth make at the bed light and fall at it, but it be a good sign should a light winged one come thrice and go its way unharmed. Even if it do fall at it, it doth say nothing worse than the ailing one will soon die but that the death shall be the freeing of a happy soul.

"An ailing one shall surely die if a dog come and howl thrice under the window.

"It be a good sign of peace to a parting soul if there do come near to the window a white dove.

"It be the custom as soon as death doth enter the chamber for one present to immediate rake out the fire, turn the seeing glass to the wall and on the instant stop the clock, but this stopping of the clock in the death-room be not at all places a common practise. After the boddy hath been attended to in all its proper officies it be a good sign if the eyes do shut of themselves, if not then but a few years sen it was held to be the work of some evil spirits in some cases owing to a misspent life. In those days it was the common thing for to get or borrow a pair of leaden sigs (charms) from some wise dame or good neighbour, the like of those made by Betty Strother and others wise in such matters. They being magic made did ward off not only from about the bed but from the room itself all the deamons of every sort and kind and did hold the een fast shutten so that neither witch or hellspell could get aback of their power and cungel them open again.

"Many there be who yet do grace their dead with a salt platter putten upon the breast of the corpse, and all those friends who do view the dead and it be the common custom for all so to do, do first touch the corpse on the face or hands and then lay their own hands upon the platter first having full and free forgiven the dead any fault or ill-feeling they had in life held as a grudge again the dead.

"In some spots it is a common thing for the wake wail to be sung over the boddy each night it be in the house as also for a rushlight to be kept alight from sunset to sunrise and for the death watchers for to tend the dead throw the night owther in the same room or in one so held that those watching could see the corpse, and they due at this day deggle the quilt and floor with rue water.

"It be always most carefull seen to that no four-footed thing come nigh hand, for it would be a despert ill thing if such by any mishap did run just across or loup over the corpse.

"There be always a great arval feast after the funeral to which all friends are bidden."

The remedies of this period were not greatly superior to those of the seventeenth century if one may judge from the gruesome concoction the details of which were given to Calvert by William Ness of Kirby Moorside.

" For the certain cure of a cancer take a pound of brown honey when the bees be sad from a death in ye house, which you shall take from the hive just turned of midnight at the full of the moon. This you shall set by for seven days when on that day you shall add to it the following all being ready prepared afore. One ounce of powdered crabs clawes well searced, seven oyster shells well burnt in a covered stone or hard clay pot, using only the white part thereof. One dozen snails and shells dried while they do powder with gently rubbing and the powder of dried earth worms from the churchyard when the moon be on the increase but overcast, which you will gather by lanthorn which you must be sure not to let go out while you be yet within the gate or there virtue be gone from them. All these make into a fine powder and well searce, this been ready melt the honey till it simmer then add three ounces each of brown wax, rossin, and grease of a fat pigg, and when all be come at the boil divide your powders to seven heaps and add one at a time. Do not shake your paper on which the powder hath been put but fold it carefully and burry it at some grave as there be among what be left some dust of ye wormes which have fed upon ye dead. So boil it till all be well mixed and then let cool and if it be too stiff add swine grease till it work easy. When you would use it warm a little in a silver spoon and annoint the sore holding a hot iron over till it be nearly all soaked in, then sprinkle but a little finely doubled searced powder of viper where there be matter. This hath been tried many times and on different folk in these dales and hath done wonderous cures when all else failed them. "And these words wrate on lambs skin with lambs blood and hung above the ill one's head hath wrought a most magick wonders of healing and some I do find ready to take oath on it. I leave it so."

But Pickering was not very much behind the rest of England when we discover that in the second edition of "A collection of above 300 receipts in Cookery, Physick and Surgery" published in 1719, and printed and sold in London is given the following:—

"A *very good* snail-water *for a* consumption. Take half a peck of Shell-snails, wipe them and bruise them Shells and all in a Mortar; put to them a gallon of New Milk; as also Balm, Mint, Carduus, unset Hyssop, and Burrage, of each one handful; Raisons of the Sun stoned, Figs, and Dates, of each a quarter of a pound; two large Nutmegs: Slice all these, and put them to the Milk, and distil it with a quick fire in a cold Still; this will yield near four Wine-quarts of Water very good; you must put two ounces of White Sugar-candy into each Bottle, and let the Water drop on it; stir the Herbs sometimes while it distils, and keep it cover'd on the Head with wet Cloths. Take five spoonfuls at a time, first and last, and at Four in the Afternoon."

It was only about eighty years ago that the old

custom of racing for the bride's garter on wedding days was given up. In the early years of last century an improvement in public morals showed itself in a frequently expressed opinion that the custom was immodest, and gradually the practice was dropped the bride merely handing a ribbon to the winner of the race.

Immediately after the wedding-ring had been put on, the youths of the company would race from the church porch to the bride's house, and the first who arrived claimed the right of removing the garter from her left leg, the bride raising her skirts to allow him to do so. He would afterwards tie it round his own sweetheart's leg as a love charm against unfaithfulness. The bride-groom never took part in the race, but anyone else could enter, runners often coming from distant villages to take part.

At the time of the outcry against the custom it is interesting to find one, William Denis of Pickering, writing to a ſriend and stating that "this racing for the bride's garter and the taking of the same from the leg

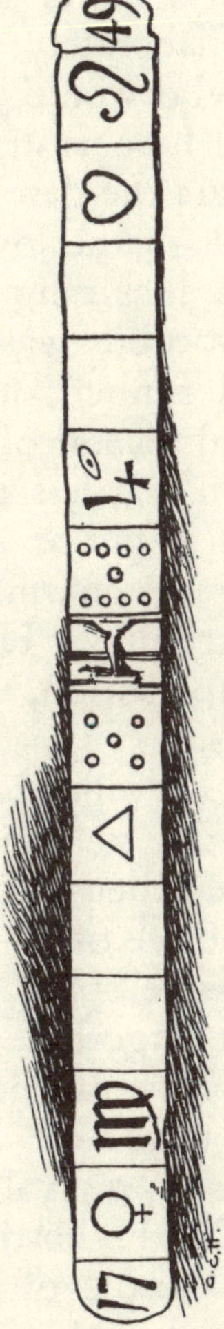

A LOVE GARTER, DATED 1749.

The spaces were for the initials of the wearer of the garter and her betrothed. These garters were raced for on wedding days, the winner of the race being allowed to take the bride's garter.

of the bride, is one of the properest public functions we have so far as modesty is concerned."

Elaborately worked garters were worn "by any lass who would be happy in her love." The one illustrated here is drawn from a sketch given by Calvert. It bears the date 1749 and the two spaces were for the initials of the lovers.

A Pickering man named Tom Reid who was living in 1800 but was an old man then, was in his day a noted runner and won many races. He must have owned several of these garters which are now so difficult to find. It is said that one of the vicars of Pickering did much to put an end to the belief in the powers of the garters as charms, collecting them whenever he had an opportunity. He also put his foot down on every form of superstition, forbidding the old folk to tell their stories.

The village maidens considered it a most binding vow to remain true to their sweethearts if they washed their garters in St Cedd's Well at Lastingham on the eve of St Agnes. Other practices performed at the same spot are, like the spectre of Sarkless Kitty, better forgotten.

There can be little doubt that the death blow to this mass of ignorant superstition came with the religious revival brought about by the Methodists. Despite the hostile reception they had in many places the example of their Christian behaviour made itself felt, and as the years went by parents became sufficiently ashamed of their old beliefs to give up telling them to their children. This change took place between about 1800 and 1840, but the influences that lay behind it date from the days of John Wesley.

The sports common in the early part of last century include:—

- Fox-hunting.
- Badger-drawing.
- Duck hunting with dogs and sometimes duck and owl diving.
- Cock-fighting.
- Cock-throwing at Eastertide.
- Bull baiting and sometimes ass baiting.
- Squirrel-hunting.
- Rat-worrying.

"To make it quite sure to you howe greatly cocking was in voge seventy years agone," says Calvert, "I have heard my own grandfather tell how he and others did match their cocks and fight em for secret sake in the crypt of Lastingham Church."

The entrance to the crypt was not at that time in the centre of the nave, and the fact that it could be reached from the north side without going into the church would make the desecration seem a far less scandalous proceeding than it sounds.

It has also been supposed that Mr Carter, curate-in-charge of Lastingham at a time prior to 1806, allowed his wife to keep a public-house in the crypt. There is only one authentic account[1] of this parson-publican

[1] Anonymous booklet entitled "Anecdotes and Manners of a few Ancient and Modern oddities, etc." Published at York, 1806.

as far as I have been able to discover and although it makes no mention of the crypt it states that Mr Carter used to take *down* his violin to play the people a few tunes. If this did not indicate the crypt it may have meant that he took his violin down from the vicarage to the inn, which may have been the "Blacksmith's Arms" that adjoins the churchyard on the east side. The parlour is certainly a much more cheerful place for refreshment than the dark and chilly crypt, and it is interesting to find that the benches in the inn are composed of panelling which I am told was formerly in the church.

As the whole idea of the parson's wife conducting a public-house is somewhat preposterous, although we have already been told that the clergy at that time were on the whole "a despert reckless lot," it is interesting to read the original account. "The Rev. Mr Carter, when curate of Lastingham," it says, "had a very large family, with only a small income to support them, and therefore often had recourse to many innocent alternatives to augment it; and as the best of men have their enemies—too often more than the worst, he was represented to the Archdeacon by an invidious neighbour, as a very disorderly character, particularly by keeping a public-house, with the consequences resulting from it. The Archdeacon was a very humane, worthy, good man who had imbibed the principles, not only of a parson, but of a Divine, and therefore treated such calumniating insinuations against his subordinate brethren, with that contempt which would ultimately accrue to the satisfaction and advantage to such as listen to a set of sycophantic tattlers. . . . therefore at the ensuing visitation, when the business of the day was over, he in a very delicate and candid manner, interrogated Mr C. as to his means of supporting so numerous a family . . . which was answered as related to me by one well acquainted with the parties, in nearly the following words:—

"'I have a wife and thirteen children, and with a stipend of £20 per annum, increased only by a few trifling surplice fees, I will not impose upon your understanding by attempting to advance any argument to show the impossibility of us all being supported from my church preferment: But I am fortunate enough to live in a neighbourhood where there are many rivulets which abound with fish, and being particularly partial to angling, I am frequently so successful as to catch more than my family can consume while good, of which I make presents to the neighbouring gentry, all of whom are so generously grateful as to requite me with something else of seldom less value than two or threefold.—This is not all: my wife keeps a Public-House, and as my parish is so wide that some of my parishioners have to come from ten to fifteen miles to church, you will readily allow that some refreshment before they return must occasionally be necessary, and where can they have it more properly than where their journey is half performed? Now, sir, from your general knowledge of the world, I make no doubt but you are well assured that the most general topicks, in conversation at Public-Houses, are Politics and Religion, with which, God knows, ninety-nine out of one hundred of those who participate in the general clamour are totally unacquainted; and that perpetually ringing in the ears of a Pastor, who has the welfare and happiness of his flock at heart, must be no small mortification. To divert their attention from those foibles over their cups, I take down my violin and play them a few tunes, which gives me an opportunity of seeing that they get no more liquor than necessary for refreshment; and if the young people propose a dance I seldom answer in the negative; nevertheless when I announce it time for their return they are ever ready to obey my commands, and generally with the donation of sixpence, they shake hands with my children, and bid God bless them.—Thus my parishioners derive a triple advantage, being instructed, fed and amused at the same time: moreover, this method of spending their Sundays being so congenial with their inclinations, that they are imperceptibly led along the path of piety and morality . . .'" with many other arguments Mr Carter supported his case so that "the Archdeacon very candidly acknowledged the propriety of Mr C.'s arguments in defence of his conduct, and complimented him on his discernment in using the most convenient vehicle for instruction."

Concerning a case of bear-baiting we have a most detailed account which Calvert heads with "The Baiting of a Bear at Pickering, Tuesday, Aug. 15th, 1809, which I did myself witness." Then he begins: " A week Wednesday senight there did with drum and pan pipes parade publickly the streets of this town two mountebanks leading by a chain a monster brown bruin which, as well as it being a good dancer and handing of its pole, its master did aclaim it to be the master of any dog of no odds what be its breed and which they would match for a crown to come off conqueror if given fair play and a fifteen-foot chain. Now it happening that in these parts there be living several sporting men some of which be owners of bull dogs of good courage and nowther dog nor master ever shirking a fight more than one dog was entered for to test its skill."

A day was fixed for the contests which were to take place in the castleyard, and soon the news was so handed from mouth to mouth that the demand for seats in the rough wooden stand, erected for those who chose to pay, was so great that another stand was built and the first one was enlarged.

On the appointed day a huge concourse including " farmers, butchers, hucksters, badgers, cadgers, horse-jobbers, drovers, loafers and scamps and raggels of all kinds " assembled in the castleyard.

There were " not a few young sparks and bespurred and beruffled bucks come thither from as far as Hull " who had brought with them certain over-dressed women.

The first dog matched against the bear was owned by one Castle Jack " a worthless waistrel." The bear received the rush of the dog standing on his hind legs and gripped him in his forepaws, biting and crushing him to death. After this no one seemed inclined to let their dogs go to such certain death and the assemblage gradually became disorderly and many quarrels and fights took place before the crowd finally dispersed.

Calvert says, "and so when I did withdraw myself, the whole crowd seemed to be owther cursing, fighting, or loudly proffering for to fight any one. As I took my steps back to my uncle I could not help but consider that those of the Methodist holding, who did as we went towards the green [at the west end of the market-place] beg and pray of us to be mindfull of our sinfull pleasures and of the wroth to come and who did pray us to then turn from our sinfull course, and though we who did pass them did so with scoffs and . . . gibes in some cases, yet I could not help but in my heart consider that they were fully in the right on't."

There is a remarkable story recorded of the fatal result of hunting a black-brushed fox found at Sinnington. It was on Thursday, January 13th, 1803, that "a black-brush'd fox was setten up at the high side of Sinnington. Some there were who left the hounds the instant they seed the colour of its brush for they minded that one who lived in those parts over a hundred years agone and who was held to be wise in dark things had owned a black-brushed reynard as a companion and which being on the moor on a time when hounds came that way they gave chace and presently killed, wch did so vex the wise dame that she was heard to cast a curse upon all those who should ever after give chace to one of its offspring and it hath being noted that by times when there be a black brush and it do be hunted that it is never catched and there be always some ill fall upon him who does first clap eyes on't and set the hounds on its scent. On this very day did some then present give chace and followed for ower three good hours while baith men, horses and hounds were all dead beat and just when they did aim for to claim its brush one Holliday fell from his horse and brake his neck, and he it was who had first set een on't. They were then close upon Chop Yatt ower forty mile by the course they had run. It was then brought to mind that one Blades a score years afore had been suddenly called to account on the same venture.

"One verse of an old hunting ditty which tells a tale of four bold riders who came by their death ower a cragg afollowing one of this same breed many years agone now, it tells in this wise:—

> "Draw rein and think, bold hunter halt,
> Sly Reynard let go free,
> To ride ahint yon full black brush
> Means death to you or me.
> No luck can come so get you home
> And there tie up your steed,
> Yon black brush is ye devil wand
> It scents ye grave to feed."

The Sinnington hounds have long been famous in the North Riding, and their history goes back to the earliest days of fox-hunting in these parts. The Bilsdale being the only pack that claims an earlier origin. William Marshall, the agricultural writer (mentioned a few pages further on), hunted with the Sinnington pack for many years, and Jack Parker, a

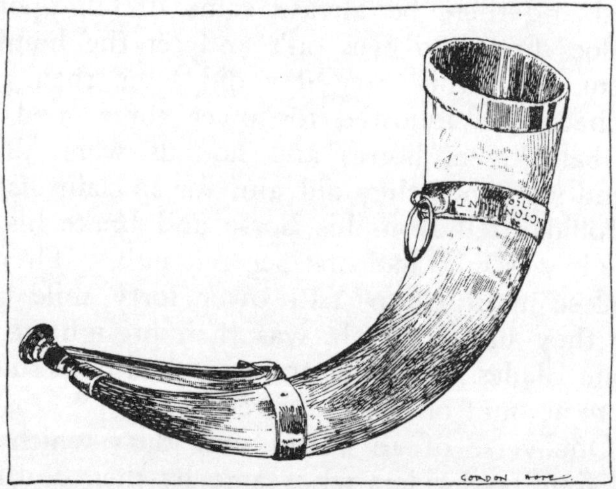

THE OLD HORN OF THE SINNINGTON HUNT.
It is dated 1750 on one of the silver bands.

huntsman of last century, was a very notable character whose witty anecdotes are still remembered. The silver-mounted horn illustrated here bearing the inscription "Sinnington Hunt 1750" is preserved at Pickering. Until about twenty-five years ago the pack was "trencher fed," the hounds being scattered about in twos and threes at the various farms and houses in the neighbourhood. The kennels are now at Kirby Moorside.

A curious "Dandy Horse" race was held at Pickering on June 22, 1813. Calvert describing it in his quaint way says: "On this day, Tuesday, June 22, 1813, Robert Kitching, Hungate, Pickering and S. Hutchinson of Helmsley, did bring off the wager they had laid of ten guineas apiece for their men to race from Pickering to Helmsley astride each of his master's dandy horse, which is a machine having two wheels in a line afixed with forks to a support beam upon which there resteth a saddle so high from the ground that the rider hath a grip on the ground, for it be by the pressure of the foot upon the ground that this new horse is shoved along, there be also a handle to hold by with a soft pad, this is for to rest the chest against as to gain a greater grip with the feet, the two Gladiators started fair away at ten of the clock, there been then come together from all parts upwards it was held of two thousand people, many on horseback arriving for to see this novel race from start to finish." However, when the opponents had covered about half the distance, one of them overstrained himself and gave up and the other admitted that "he was ommaist at the far end" so that the crowd assembled at Helmsley to see the finish waited in vain for the riders.

Although Pickering is several miles from the sea some of the more important people of the town were for many years closely interested in the whaling industry. It was about the year 1775, that Mr Nicholas Piper and some of his friends made a bold financial venture in the purchase of the *Henrietta* which became in time one of the most successful Greenland whalers sailing from the port of Whitby. Some of the ship's logs and also an account book are preserved by Mr Loy at Keld Head Hall, and from them I have been able to obtain some interesting facts. For a year or two the ship yielded no profits, but in 1777 there was a sum of £640 to be divided between the partners in the enterprise. Gradually the profits increased until they produced an annual total of about £2000.

Some of the entries in the account book are curious. These are some of the items in the preliminary expenses :—

" Jowsey's Bill for harpoon stocks and seal clubs, ...	£3	2	8
To ye master to get hands in Shetland, .	21	0	0
To ye sailors to drink as customary ye first voyage, ...	1	1	0
A crimp shipping seamen, . . .	0	6	0

Then in 1776 comes :—

" By ye crimp's bill Sept. ye 20th, . .	225	0	6

Each voyage meant an advantage to Pickering, for it supplied the salt pork for the sailors. These are some of the entries :—

" 1776.	Paid for piggs at Pickering, . .	£65	5	0
1777.	Do. do. . . .	59	19	6
	Tom Dobson for carriage of do., . .	1	11	0
	Window broke by firing a signal gun for sailing, ...	0	4	6

A TYPICAL COTTAGE OF THE OLDEST TYPE.

This is at Hutton Buscel. The small window lighting the ingle-nook is invariably in this position in the oldest cottages, and the recess and the carved oak cupboard door are usually to be found in the wall as in the illustration. In this, as in most of the cottages, a kitchen range has taken the place of the open hearth.

1778.	Cheeses at Pickering,	£2	10	9
	Paid for Piggs at Pickering,	55	14	5
	Tom Dobson for carriage of piggs,	1	3	0
1779.	James Gray's lodging ashore time of ye smallpox,	0	15	0
	Paid for piggs at Pickering,	51	2	0
	Paid at Saltergate for boys eating, etc.,	0	4	6

One imagines that these boys were in charge of the pigs. But they must have been pork by that time for the next entry is:—

"To Tom Dobson for carriage of pork, . £1 16 0

and another entry mentions that it was packed in barrels at Pickering.

" 1780. Grundall Saltergate for lads eating, etc., . £0 8 6

Then comes a gap of about eight years, several pages having been torn out.

" 1789.	Robt. Dobson for carriage of pork,	£1	4	0
1792.	Lads at Saltergate as they came home,	0	2	6
1793.	A man coming to Pickering to bring news of ship—be ashore,	0	8	0

This apparently means that a man was sent to Pickering to tell the owners that the *Henrietta* had arrived.

" 1799.	Piggs at Pickering,	£125	9	8
1801.	Do.,	181	8	8
1802.	Do.,	208	4	6
1815.	Old Tom's expenses, turnpikes at Pickering,	0	6	6

In 1785 when the *Henrietta* made her annual voyage to the northern seas she had on board William

Scoresby who in five years' time was to become captain of the vessel. He was the son of a small farmer at Cropton and was born on the 3rd of May 1760. His parents wished him to keep to agricultural pursuits and after a very brief education at the village school he commenced this arduous form of labour at the age of nine. He kept to this work until he was twenty when he could no longer resist his longings for a broader sphere of work. To obtain this he went to Whitby and apprenticed himself to a ship-owner. He acquired a thorough knowledge of seamanship with great rapidity and in his second year of service at sea detected an error in the reckoning which would otherwise have caused the loss of the ship. For this, his only reward was the ill-will of the mate whose mistake he had exposed. He therefore joined the *Speedwell* an ordnance ship carrying stores to Gibraltar but falling in with the Spanish fleet the *Speedwell* was captured. Her men having been taken to Cadiz they were sent inland to San Lucar de Mayor. From that place, through being somewhat carelessly guarded, Scoresby and one of his companions were successful in making their escape. They reached England after various adventures and Scoresby having endured many hardships at sea settled down again to farm work at Cropton for two years. Although having only the very smallest means he was married at this time to Lady Mary Smith (she was born on Lady-day), the eldest daughter of Mr John Smith, a landed proprietor in a small way and a native of Cropton.

Having reached the position of skipper of the famous *Henrietta*, in 1790, when only thirty years of age, Scoresby was saved from the financial extremes to which he was likely to have been reduced, owing to his small income and the increasing expenses of his family. Having successfully commanded the *Henrietta* for seven seasons and having augmented in this way the incomes of the half-dozen Pickeronians interested in the success of the ship, Captain Scoresby's reputation stood high in the Greenland trade. In 1798 he accepted the more advantageous offers of a London firm to command the *Dundee*. It was on his third voyage in that ship that, having called at Whitby as usual to say good-bye to his wife and children, Scoresby allowed his third child, William, to go on board the ship as she lay in the roads. When the time came for him to go ashore he was nowhere to be found, for having taken into his head the idea of going the voyage with his father the little fellow had hidden himself. The shouts for "Master William," however, brought him to the top of the companion at the last moment, but his father, understanding the boy's great desire to stay in the ship, decided to take him.

The voyage was notable on account of a very exciting incident on meeting with a foreign privateer. The *Dundee* was armed with twelve guns and was manned by a crew of between fifty and sixty men, so that if brought to extremities the ship could have made a good defence. Scoresby, however, had every reason for avoiding a conflict, so keeping his ship in an apparently defenceless state, with all the ports closed, he sent the men to their quarters to prepare the guns for immediate action. No sign of excitement or commotion was allowed to appear on deck so that when the privateer came within shouting distance Scoresby walking the quarter deck and the helmsmen steering were the only living beings visible to the stranger. Suddenly, however, the six gun ports on each side of the *Dundee* are raised and a row of untompioned cannon are seen pointing towards the enemy's broadside. The stratagem, according to the account given by the younger Scoresby,[1] was such a huge surprise for the enemy that he suddenly hauled off under full sail and not a shot was fired on either side.

After this voyage young Scoresby went back to school again until 1803 when he became an apprentice on board the *Resolution*, a new ship of Whitby, commanded and partly owned by his father. For several years he made the Greenland voyage in the *Resolution* and was chief officer when, in the year 1806, his father forced the ship through the pack ice, as far north as 81°30′. This was for long the highest point reached by any vessel and the ship's cargo was completed in thirty-two days with twenty-four whales, two seals, two walruses, two bears and a narwhal. The elder Scoresby who was about six feet in height was a man of extraordinary muscular power. His many successful voyages reveal his first-class

[1] Scoresby, the Rev. William, D.D., "My Father," p. 108.

qualities as a seaman and navigator and his good judgment in emergencies seems to have been almost instinctive. Although he is described[1] as an Arctic navigator, exploration was only incidental to whale-catching, but his inventions of the ice-drill and the crow's-nest did much to make Arctic voyages more feasible.

The versatility of his son William was remarkable, for he may be described as master mariner, author and divine and even then his varied scientific knowledge is overlooked. During his latter years he was particularly interested in magnetism and in 1856 made his last voyage in order to carry out a series of systematic observations.

His life, written by his nephew R. E. Scoresby-Jackson, is of great interest and Cropton may well be proud that it gave Dr Scoresby to the world.

The memory of the *Henrietta* is not likely to be forgotten so easily as that of the Scoresbys, for gate-posts made from whale jaws are common near the coast of north eastern Yorkshire, and one on the road from Pickering to Scarborough, between the villages of Hutton Buscel and East Ayton, bears the name of the famous ship.

A contemporary of the Scoresbys was John Jackson, R.A. He was the son of a tailor of Lastingham and was born at that very remote village on the 31st May 1778. As a boy he showed a predilection for portrait-painting in the sketches he made

[1] "Dictionary of National Biography."

of his companions, although his father discouraged his efforts in that direction, not wishing to lose his boy's services as an apprentice to the tailoring business. When he was about nineteen he had the good fortune to be introduced to Lord Mulgrave who brought him to the notice of the Earl of Carlisle and soon after we find him studying the great collection of pictures at Castle Howard.

Jackson's first attempt at a painting in oils was a copy of a portrait by Sir Joshua Reynolds lent to him by Sir George Beaumont. Lastingham was unable to supply him with proper materials, but he managed to obtain some very rough paints and brushes from the village house-painter and glazier, and with these crude materials made such an admirable copy that Sir George or Lord Mulgrave or both together advised him to go to London, promising him £50 a year during the time that he was working as a student. From this time his progress was rapid. In 1804 he exhibited at the Royal Academy for the first time, in 1815 he was elected an associate and in 1817 he received the full honours of the Academy. Although he was a Wesleyan Methodist, Jackson was broad-minded in his religious opinions, for he made a copy of Correggio's "Christ in the Garden of Gethsemane" (with the figures increased to life size) for Lastingham parish church. The picture is now on the north side of the apse but its original position was above the communion table and in order to give the picture sufficient space and light the apse of Transitional Norman date was very roughly treated. Jackson contributed £50 towards the alterations, but the restoration at a later date has fortunately wiped out these disfigurements.

Another boy destined to become a tailor was Francis Nicholson who was born at Pickering in 1753. His father, who was a weaver, gave young Francis a good education in Pickering, and wisely abandoning the tailoring idea the boy was sent to Scarborough for instruction from an artist. After three years he returned to Pickering and occupied himself in painting portraits and pictures of horses, dogs and game for local patrons. Then followed a period of study in London, where Nicholson made great progress and eventually began to devote himself to water colours, for which in his long life he was justly famous, well deserving the name generally given to him as the "Father of water colour painting."

William Marshall, the agricultural expert and writer to whom we owe the establishment of the Board of Agriculture was baptised at Sinnington on 28th July 1745. He was in his own words "born a farmer" and used to say that he could trace his blood through the veins of agriculturists for upwards of four hundred years. After fourteen years in the West Indies, he undertook, at the age of twenty-nine, the management of a farm near Croydon in Surrey. It was there, in 1778, that he wrote his first book. He showed the manuscript to Dr Johnson who objected to certain passages sanctioning work on Sundays in harvest time, so Marshall omitted them. His greatest work was "A General Survey, from personal experience, observation and enquiry, of the Rural Economy of England."

The country was divided into six agricultural divisions, the northern one being represented by Yorkshire in two volumes. In the first of these, the preface is dated from Pickering, December 21st, 1787, and the second chapter is devoted to an exceedingly interesting account of the broad valley to which Marshall gives the title "The Vale of Pickering." When he died in 1818 he was raising a building at Pickering for a College of Agriculture on the lines he had laid down in a book published in 1799.

His proposal for the establishment of a "Board of Agriculture, or more generally of Rural Affairs" was carried out by Parliament in 1793, and so valuable were his books considered that in 1803 most of them were translated into French and published in Paris under the title of "La Maison rustique anglaise." The inscription on Marshall's monument in the north aisle of Pickering church which states that "he was indefatigable in the study of rural economy" and that "he was an excellent mechanic, had a considerable knowledge of most branches of science, particularly of philology, botany and chemistry" is not an over statement of his merits.

In the year 1800 the little farm at Gallow Hill near Brompton was taken by one Thomas Hutchinson whose sister Mary kept house for him. She was almost the same age and had been a schoolfellow of the poet Wordsworth at Penrith and had kept up her friendship with his family since that time, having visited them at Racedown and Dove Cottage, while the Wordsworths had stayed at the Hutchinson's farm

The Ingle-Nook in Gallow Hill Farm near Brompton.
Where Wordsworth stayed just at the time of his marriage with Mary Hutchinson.

at Sockburn-on-Tees. There was nothing sudden or romantic therefore in the marriage which took place at Brompton in 1802. Wordsworth and his sister Dorothy went down from London to the pretty Yorkshire village in September, and stayed at the little farmhouse, whose parlour windows looked across the Vale of Pickering to the steep wolds on the southern side. The house, as far as I can discover, has not been altered in the century which has elapsed, and the cosy ingle-nook in the room on the right of the entrance remains full of memories of the poet and his betrothed—his "perfect woman, nobly planned." On the fourth of October the wedding took place in Brompton Church. The grey old steeple surrounded and overhung by masses of yellow and brown foliage in the centre of the picturesque, and in many respects, ideal little village, must have formed a perfect setting for the marriage of one who was afterwards to become the Poet Laureate of his country. The register for the years 1754-1810 contains the following entry:—

"*Banns of Marriage* . . .

William Wordsworth of Grasmere in Westmoreland, Gentleman, *and* Mary Hutchinson *of* Gallow Hill in the Parish of Brompton *were married in this* Church *by* Licence *this* fourth *Day of* October *in the year one thousand* eight *Hundred and* two *by me* John Ellis officiating min^{r}.

This marriage was solemnized between us."

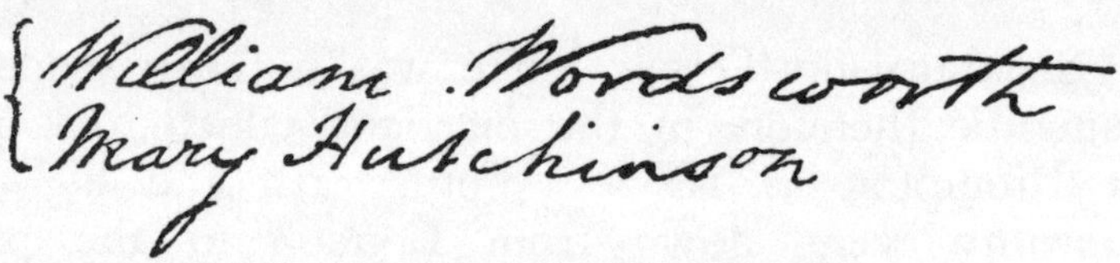

FACSIMILE OF THE SIGNATURES IN THE REGISTER.

"In the presence of THOMAS HUTCHINSON.
JOANNA HUTCHINSON.
JOHN HUTCHINSON."

The same day Wordsworth with his wife and sister drove to Thirsk and two days afterwards reached Grasmere, where they soon settled down to an uneventful life at Dove Cottage. Dorothy Wordsworth could not "describe what she felt," but we are told that she accepted her sister-in-law without a trace of jealousy.

There is still preserved in Pickering one of the parchments on which were enrolled the names of all those who were liable for service in the militia. It is headed

"Militia Enrollment 1807-8"

and begins:—

"An enrollment of the names of the several persons who have been chosen by ballot to serve in the Militia for five years for the west part of the subdivision of Pickering Lyth in the North Riding of the County of York and also of the several substitutes who have been produced and approved to serve for the like term and for such further term as the Militia shall remain embodied, if within the space of five years His Majesty shall order the Militia to be drawn out and embodied and are enrolled in the place of such principals whose names are set opposite thereto in pursuance of an act of the 47th of King George III., Cap. 71, entitled an act for the speedily completing the Militia of Great Britain and increasing the same under certain delimitations and restrictions (14th Aug. 1807)."

The thirty-six men were taken as follows:—

8 from Middleton.
5 „ Kirby Misperton.
16 „ Pickering.
1 „ Ellerburne.
1 „ Levisham.
3 „ Sinnington.
1 „ Thornton.

Jonathan Goodall, a farmer of Middleton, induced Geo. Thompson of Pickering, a farmer's servant, 30 years old, to stand for him, paying him £42.

Wm. Newton, a farmer of Middleton, had to pay Geo. Allen, a linen draper of Richmond, £47, 5s. as substitute.

The smallest amount paid was £20, and the largest sum was £47, 5s.

Substitutes seem to have been hard to find in the neighbourhood of Pickering, and those few whose names appear had to be heavily paid. George Barnfather, a farm servant of Kirby Misperton agreed to serve as a substitute on payment of £42, and a cartwright of Goathland agreed for the same sum, while men from Manchester or Leeds were ready to accept half that amount.

The extreme reluctance to serve of a certain Ben Wilson, a sweep of Middleton, is shown in a story told of him by a very old inhabitant of Pickering whose memory is in no way impaired by her years. She tells us that this Wilson on hearing of his ill-luck seized a carving-knife and going to the churchyard put his right hand on a gate-post and fiercely cut off the two fingers required for firing a rifle. He avoided active service in this way and often showed his mutilated hand to the countryfolk who may or may not have admired the deed.

In 1823 Pickering was kept in touch with Whitby, York and Scarborough by coaches that ran three times a week. On Monday, Wednesday and Friday a coach (Royal Mail) left the "Black Swan" in the market place for Whitby at the painfully early hour of four o'clock in the morning; another Royal Mail left Pickering for York at half-past three in the afternoon on Sunday, Tuesday and Thursday. The stages were from

Whitby to Saltergate.
Saltergate to Pickering.
Pickering to Malton.
Malton to Spital Beck.
Spital Beck to York.

There was also what was called the "Boat Coach" that ran between Pickering and Scarborough.

One of the last drivers of these coaches became a guard on the North Eastern Railway, and he still lives in Pickering at the time of writing.

The parish chest in the vestry of Pickering Church contains among other papers a number of apprenticeship deeds of a hundred to a hundred and fifty years ago, in which the master promises that he will educate the boy and "bring him up in some honest and lawful calling and in the fear of God," and in most cases to provide him with a suit of clothes at the completion of his term, generally at the age of twenty-one years.

The odd papers registering the arrival of new inhabitants in the district include one dated 1729, and in them we find a churchwarden possessing such a distinguished name as Hotham, signing that surname without a capital, and in 1809 we find an overseer of the poor only able to make his mark against the seal.

The largest bell in the church tower is dated 1755 and bears the inscription, "First I call you to God's word, and at last unto the Lord." It is said that this bell was cracked owing to the great strength of one of the ringers, and that the date 1755 is the year of the re-casting. The flagon is the only piece of the church plate belonging to this period. It was made in 1805 by Prince of York.

In the year 1837 the Rev. Joseph Kipling, grandfather of Mr Rudyard Kipling, was living at Pickering, and on the 6th of July of that year a son, John, was born. Mr Joseph Kipling was a Wesleyan minister, and his residence at Pickering was only a temporary one.

Another Wesleyan who was living at this time was John Castillo, the author of many quaint poems in the Yorkshire dialect, and an original local preacher as well. He died in 1845, and his grave is to be seen in the burial-ground of the Wesleyan Chapel. It bears a verse from "Awd Isaac," the poem by which he is best known—

"Bud noo his eens geean dim i' deeath,
Nera mare a pilgrim here on eeath,
His sowl flits fra' her shell beneeath,
Te reealms o' day,
Whoor carpin care an' pain an' deeath
Are deean away."

In 1720 a new chapel was built at Pickering for Protestant Dissenters, but before that time—as early as 1702—Edward Brignall's house was set apart for divine worship by Dissenters. An Independent Church was formed in 1715, the people probably meeting in private houses for several years. After this, little is known until 1788, when the Independent Church was again established, and in the following year a chapel was built, and it was enlarged in 1814.

It is an interesting fact that about 1862 the small manual organ in the Independent church was played by a Mr Clark, who was organist at the Parish church in the morning and at the chapel in the afternoon and evening. Before this time the Independents had contented themselves with violins and a bass viol, and for a time with a clarionette.

In 1801, the population of Pickering was 1994, and at the last census before the accession of Queen Victoria it had increased to 2555.

During the Georgian period Pickering's only external illumination at night was from that precarious "parish lantern," the moon. The drainage of the town was crude and far too obvious, and in all the departments for the supply of daily necessities, the individualistic system of wells, oil-lamps or candles and cesspools continued without interference from any municipal power.

The houses and cottages built at this time are of stone among the hills, and of a mixture of brick and stone in the vale. Examples of cottages can be seen in the village of Great Habton. They are dated 1741 and 1784, and are much less picturesque than those of the seventeenth century, though village architecture had not then reached the gaunt ugliness of the early Victorian Age.

The parish registers throughout the district were regularly kept, and as a rule contain nothing of interest beyond the bare records of births, deaths and marriages. The great proportion of villagers, however, who at this time signed their names with a mark, shows that the art of writing was still a rare thing among the peasantry. The church account books of the period reveal many curious items such as the frequent repairs of the *thatch* on the vestry at Middleton (thatched churches are still to be seen in Norfolk and Suffolk), and "£5, 19s. 6d. in all for the Violin or Base Musick" of the same church.

Churchwarden architecture of the deal boards and whitewash order made hideous many of the village churches that required repairs at this time, and if one discovers a ramshackle little porch such as that just removed at Ellerburne, or a big window with decayed wooden mullions cut in a wall, regardless of symmetry, one may be quite safe in attributing it to the early years of the nineteenth century. One of the staple industries of Pickering and the adjoining villages at this time was weaving, and a great number of the cottages had the room on the opposite side of the passage to the parlour fitted up with a loom.

We have now seen many aspects of the daily life in and near Pickering during the Georgian period. We know something of sports and amusements of the people, of their religious beliefs, their work, their customs at marriages and deaths, and we also have some idea of the dreadful beings that these country folk trembled at during the hours of darkness. We have discovered more than one remarkable man who was born and bred in these primitive surroundings, and we have learnt something of one of the trades that helped to make Pickering prosperous.

CHAPTER XII

The Forest and Vale from Early Victorian Times to the Present Day

A.D. 1837 to 1905

THIS most recent stage in the development of Pickering is marked by the extinction of the few remaining customs that had continued to exist since mediæval times. One of the most hardy of these survivals was the custom of "Riding t' fair," as it was generally called. It only died out about twenty years ago when the Pickering Local Board purchased the tolls from the Duchy of Lancaster, so that it has been possible to obtain a photographic record of two of the Duchy tenants who used to take part in the ceremony. On market mornings the Steward of the Duchy armed with a sword in a richly gilt scabbard would repair to the castle on horseback, where he would be joined by two freeholders of Duchy land, also mounted; one carrying the antique halbert and the other the spetum that are now preserved in a solicitor's office in Eastgate.[1] They would then ride down to the top of the market-place, where the steward would take out of

[1] Mr Arthur Kiching's office. The sword is kept by Mr Boulton.

THE OLD CUSTOM OF RIDING T' FAIR AT PICKERING.

Two of the Duchy tenants carrying the halbert and spetum as they used to appear when the market proclamation was read.

his pocket a well-worn piece of parchment and read the following proclamation.

"*O'yes! O'yes! O'yes!*

"Our Sovereign Lady the Queen and the Reverend John Richard Hill, Lord of this Manor, proclaim this fair by virtue of Her Majesty's writ of *ad quod Damnum*, for establishing the same for buying and selling of horses, geldings, cattle, sheep, swine, and all sorts of merchandise brought here to be sold, and do hereby order and direct a court of Pye Powder to be held at the house of Robert

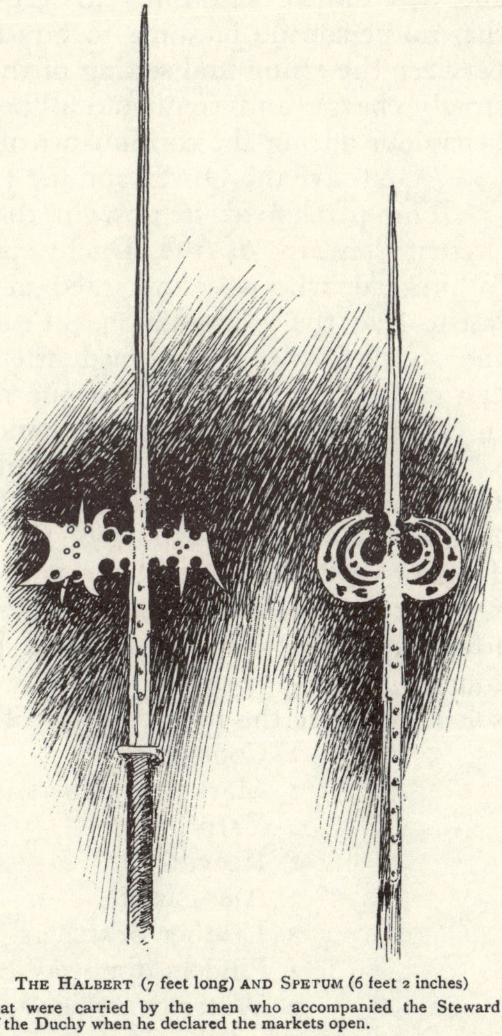

THE HALBERT (7 feet long) AND SPETUM (6 feet 2 inches) that were carried by the men who accompanied the Steward of the Duchy when he declared the markets open.

Simpson, where all matters in Difference will be heard and determined according to Law and Justice, and that no person do presume to buy or sell anything but between the rising and setting of the Sun, and they do strictly charge and command all persons to be of good behaviour during the continuance of this Fair.

"God save the Queen and the Lord of the Manor."

The parchment is now in the possession of the present steward of the Duchy property, Mr J. D. Whitehead, who was appointed in 1887 and was the last to read the proclamation. From the market-place the steward with his armed attendants rode to the east end of Hungate, and to one or two other points in the town, reading the proclamation at each place.

The Court Leet, or, as its full title appears, the Court Leet, View of Frank Pledge, Court Baron, Copyhall and Customary Court of the Castle Manor and Honour of Pickering, still meets every second year in October or November. Twenty-seven out of thirty-eight townships used to be represented by a constable and four men. Appointed annually and with much solemnity were the following list of officials:—

2 Constables.
2 Market Searchers.
2 Yarn Tellers.
2 Reeves.
2 Ale Tasters.
2 Leather Searchers.
2 Pinders (for stray cattle).
2 Water Searchers.

Of all these only the two pinders are now appointed to deal with stray cattle, and the sole use of the court at the present time is that of the enforcement of the clearing out of the drains and ditches on the Duchy property. The fines levied average from 6d. to 5s., but I have seen the record of as large an amount as 10s. imposed on a tenant who had allowed a tree to obstruct the flow of the water. The importance of keeping the level fields of the Vale properly drained is obvious, for a permanent obstruction might easily mean the flooding of a considerable area.

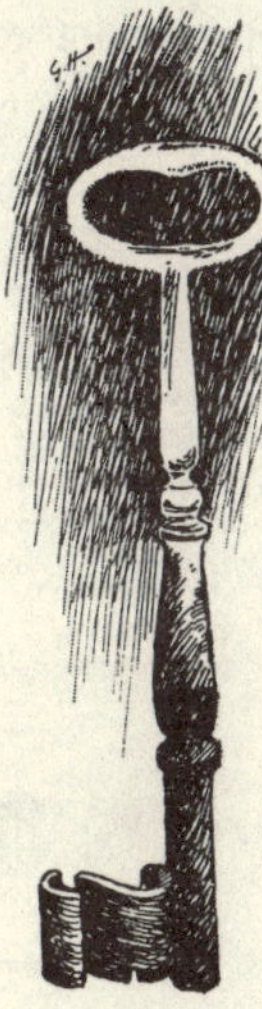
An old Key belonging to the Castle.
(Now kept by Mr John, Westmoreland, Bailiff.)

The jury dines at the expense of the Duchy of Lancaster at each meeting, and there is a "View Supper," as it is called, a week before the meeting, when the jury, having spent the whole day examining the ditches and drains between the fields, gather in the evening at one of the inns. The steward contributes a quarter of mutton, and the Lord of the Manor a couple of hares for soup.

The Court Leet still appoints the town's bellman in an informal manner; until lately he was reappointed and sworn in every year. At the present time the holder of the office is Levi Massheder, who has painted over the door of his house the curious inscription, "His Honourable Majesty's bellman."

In July 1857 the old shambles that stood at the

top of the market-place, and in which three bullocks a week were killed by the six butchers, came down to be replaced by the unsightly building that now disfigures the main street of the town. It is a matter for surprise that the townsfolk did not utilise a valuable opportunity and put up in its place something that would have added to the attractiveness of the place and at the same time have commemorated the reign of Queen Victoria. The building might have had an open space beneath that would have been useful in bad weather on market days. The disappearance of the shambles occurred about the same time as the sweeping away of the stocks that stood on the north side of them, for these were the years of a great municipal awakening in Pickering, an awakening that unfortunately could not distinguish between an insanitary sewer and the obsolete but historic and quite inoffensive stocks; both had to disappear before the indiscriminating wave of progress.

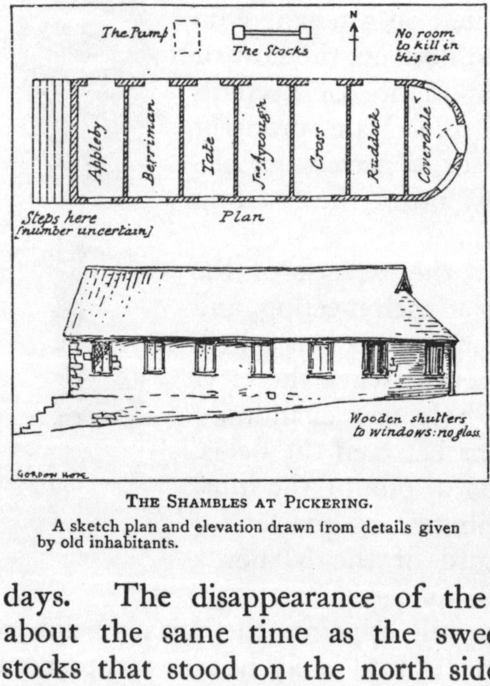

THE SHAMBLES AT PICKERING.

A sketch plan and elevation drawn from details given by old inhabitants.

In October 1846 the railway between Whitby and Pickering, that had been built ten years before for a horse-drawn coach, was opened for steam traction, and although this event is beyond the memories of most of the present-day Pickeronians, there is still living in the town a man named Will Wardell who is now seventy-seven, and as a boy of twelve acted as postillion to the horse railway. Postillions were only employed for a short time, the horse or horses being soon afterwards driven from the coach.

As a rule they employed one horse from Pickering to Raindale, where there was a public-house; then two to Fenbogs, and one to Bank Top above Goathland. If the wind were fair the coach would run to Grosmont by itself, after that one horse took the coach to Whitby. If more than one horse were used they were yoked tandem; five were kept at Raindale, where Wardell lived. There were two coaches, "The Lady Hilda" and the "Premier"; they were painted yellow and carried outside, four in front, four behind, and several others on the top, while inside there was room for six. Wardell helped to make the present railway, and has worked for fifty-five years as a platelayer on the line. He remembers Will Turnbull of Whitby who used to act as guard on the railway coach, and in the same capacity on the stage-coach from Pickering to York. He made the journey from Whitby to York and back daily, the coach running in conjunction with the railway coach; the two drivers were Mathew Groves and Joseph Sedman.

Gas, which must have been a perpetual wonder to the village folk when they came into Pickering, made its appearance in 1847; but even at the time of writing the town is only illuminated from the 10th of August until the end of April, and even in that period the streets are plunged in darkness at 11 P.M. The drainage of the town was taken in hand to some extent about fifty years ago, and the pestilential ditches and sewers that existed to within thirty years of the present time have gradually disappeared. Then between thirty and forty years ago the great spring in the limestone at Keld Head was utilised to give the town a water-supply, and thus the wells and pumps were superseded. Before the Local Board came into being about half a century ago, piles of timber were allowed to lie in Eastgate, and generally one may imagine the rather untidy quaintness so strongly characteristic of the engravings that illustrate country scenes in that period.

In 1841 or thereabouts there was a great gale that carried away the sails of the windmill which stood near the railway station, and a year or two afterwards the brick tower was demolished.

The early years of Queen Victoria's reign saw the destruction of several picturesque features, and they also witnessed the decease of some more of the old customs that were still fighting for their existence. Some of the old folks can just remember hearing their fathers tell of "the standing in church," described in the last chapter, and they quite well remember when the children used to receive prizes for saying poetry in front of the Communion-table in the parish church. Stang-riding continued up to twenty-five years ago in spite of the opposition of the police. Two figures to represent the individuals who had earned popular disfavour were placed in a cart and taken round the town for three successive nights, accompanied by a noisy crowd, who sang—

"Arang atang atang
Here do we ride the stang,
Not for my cause nor your cause
Do we ride the stang,
But for the sake of old . . ."

On the third night the effigies were burnt.

There was formerly a gallery at the west end of the church where the choir and organ were situated so that during the musical portions of the services the congregation turned towards the west to face the choir. About fifty years ago the leader who started the tune with a trumpet was James Ruddock "a bedstuffer." An old pitch-pipe used for starting the tunes was recently discovered by Mr J. Grant James, vicar of Marske-in-Cleveland.

Hungate Bridge, an iron structure, having made its appearance in 1864, is, as may be imagined, no ornament to the town.

In November 1851 the weathercock on the spire of the church was blown off, and in the following year it was replaced.

The restoration in 1878-79 included the very difficult work of renewing the Norman foundations of the tower, which were quite unable to continue to support the crushing weight of the spire. Sir Gilbert Scott, who inspected the tower and was pointed out several of the results of the unequal strains on the fabric, solemnly warned those concerned not to be stingy with cement if they wished to save the tower. The advice was taken, and after the removal of the crushed and rotten stones and many other repairs the tower and spire were left in a state of greatly increased security. The framework supporting the bells dated from about 1450, and as there were no louvres to the windows for a long time, rain and snow must have been blown in upon the woodwork, for it was found to be entirely rotten, and it was astonishing that the timbers had not given way under the great weight of the bells.

THE OLD FIRE-ENGINE AT PICKERING.

It is an old custom that is still preserved to ring the biggest, or the "pancake" bell, as it is often called, at eleven in the morning on Shrove Tuesday. At that welcome sound the children are allowed to leave school for the day, the shops are closed, and a general holiday is observed in the town. The work bell is rung every morning from 5.55 to 6.0, and from 6.0 to 6.5 every evening from March to November, and the bells are rung backwards to call out the fire brigade. The curious little fire-engine upon which the town used to rely is still preserved in a shed in Willowgate. It is one of. those primitive little contrivances standing on very small solid wheels, suggesting those of a child's toy horse.

Until the restoration of the church the pulpit was of the two-decker type, the clerk's desk being under the pulpit, with the reading-desk at the side. The inlaid sounding-board which was taken out of the church at the restoration is now preserved in the vicarage. It was in these days, namely about thirty years ago, that the sexton and his deputy used to visit the public-houses during church time in order to fetch out those who were wasting the precious hours. At Christmas time the waits still enliven the early hours with their welcomes to each individual member of every family. The two men, whose names are Beavers and Stockdale, carry a concertina and greet the household after this well-known fashion, "Drawing to —— o'clock and a fine frosty morning. Good morrow morning, Mr ——. Good morrow morning, Mrs ——," and so through the entire family. This process commences a week before Christmas and is continued until a week afterwards. In the villages the custom of "lucky birds" still survives. The boy who first reaches any house on Christmas morning is called a "lucky bird," and unless great misfortune is courted some small coin must be given to that boy. On New Year's Day the same process applies to girls, but they have no particular designation. Badger-baiting in the castle is still remembered, but at the present time lawn-tennis is the only game that is played there. This brings one to the everyday facts of Pickering life, which may sound almost too prosaic for any record, but taken in contrast with the conditions of life that have gone before they are the most recent page of that history which continues to be made day by day in the town.

The Pickeronian can no longer call himself remote in the sense of communication with the rest of the world, for the North-Eastern Railway takes him to York in little more than an hour, and from that great station he can choose his route to London and other centres by the Great Northern, the Great Central, or by the Midland Railway, and he can return from King's Cross to Pickering in about five hours. But this ease of communication seems to have made less impression upon the manners and customs of the town and neighbourhood than might have been imagined. It may perhaps show itself in the more rapid importation from London of a popular street tune or in the fashions of dress among the women-kind, but there are still great differences in the ways of living of the country folk and in the relations of squire and peasant.

Superstitions still linger among the moorland folk, and the custom of placing a plate of salt upon the breast of one who is dying is still continued here and there in a covert fashion. Clocks are still stopped, fires raked out, and looking-glasses turned to the wall at the moment of death, but such acts of deference to the world of fancy are naturally only seen by those who have intimate experience of the cottage life of these parts, and the casual visitor sees no traces of them.

The town at one time had a newspaper of its own. It was known as the *Pickering Mercury*, and was started in the summer of 1857; but it perhaps found Scarborough competition too much for it, for now it is almost forgotten, and an evening paper produced in the big watering-place is shouted round the streets of the town every night.

The changes that the present century may witness will possibly work greater transformations than any that have gone before, and not many years hence this book will no doubt be described as belonging to the rough and ready, almost primitive times of the early part of the twentieth century. The historian of a hundred years hence will sigh for the complete picture of daily life at Pickering at the present day, which we could so easily give, while he at that very moment may be failing to record the scenes of his own time that are to him so wofully commonplace.

CHAPTER XIII

Concerning the Villages and Scenery of the Forest and Vale of Pickering

"Wide horizons beckoning, far beyond the hill,
Little lazy villages, sleeping in the vale,
Greatness overhead
The flock's contented tread
An' trample o' the morning wind adown the open trail."

H. H. BASHFORD.

THE scenery of this part of Yorkshire is composed of two strikingly opposite types, that of perfectly wild, uncultivated moorlands broken here and there by wooded dales, and the rich level pasture lands that occupy the once marshy district of the Vale. The villages, some phases of whose history we have traced, are with a few exceptions scattered along the northern margin of the Vale. Lastingham, Rosedale Abbey, Levisham, Lockton, and Newton are villages of the moor. Edstone, Habton, Normanby, Kirby Misperton, and Great Barugh are villages of the Vale; but all the rest occupy an intermediate position on the slopes of the hills. In general appearance, many of the hamlets are rather similar, the grey stone walls and red tiles offering less opportunity for individual

THE MARKET CROSS AT THORNTON-LE-DALE.

The stocks are quite modern, replacing the old ones which were thrown away when the new ones were made.

taste than the building materials of the southern counties. Despite this difficulty, however, each village has a distinct character of its own, and in the cases of Thornton-le-Dale and Brompton, the natural surroundings of hill, sparkling stream, and tall masses of trees make those two villages unique. A remarkable effect can sometimes be seen by those who are abroad in the early morning from the hills overlooking the wide valley; one is at times able to see across the upper surface of a perfectly level mist through which the isolated hills rising from the low ground appear as islets in a lake, and it requires no effort of the imagination to conjure up the aspect of the valley when the waters of the Derwent were held up by ice in the remote centuries of the Ice Age. Sometimes in the evening, too, a pleasing impression may be obtained when the church bells of the villages are ringing for evening service. At the top of Wrelton Cliff, the sound of several peals of bells in the neighbouring villages floats upwards across the broad pastures, and it seems almost as though the whole plain beneath one's feet were joining in the evening song. Along the deep ravine of Newton Dale, in all weathers, some of the most varied and richly coloured pictures may be seen. If one climbs the rough paths that lead up from the woods and meadows by the railway, the most remarkable aspects of the precipitous sides are obtained. In a book published in 1836,[1] at the time of the opening

[1] Henry Belcher, "The Scenery of the Whitby and Pickering Railway," facing p. 51.

of the railway between Whitby and Pickering, a series of very delicate steel engravings of the wild scenery of Newton Dale were given. One of them shows the gorge under the deep gloom of a storm but relieved with the contrast of a rainbow springing from one side of the rocky walls. This effect may perhaps seem highly exaggerated, but on one occasion when I was exploring part of the Dale, between Levisham and Fen Bogs, I was astonished to see a brilliant rainbow backed by dense masses of indigo clouds and occupying precisely the position of the one shown in the old engraving. In such weather as this, when sudden rays of sunlight fall upon the steep slopes of bracken and heather and on the precipitous rocks above, the blazing colours seem almost unreal and the scenery suggests Scotland more than any other part of England. From the edges of the cañon, purple heather and ling stretch away on either side to the most distant horizons, and one can walk for miles in almost any direction without encountering a human being and rarely a house of any description. The few cottages that now stand in lonely isolation in different parts of the moors have only made their appearance since the Enclosures Act, so that before that time these moors must have been one of the most extensive stretches of uninhabited country in England. From the Saltersgate Inn, some of the most remarkable views that the moorlands present are all collected together in a comparatively small space. One looks towards the west across a remarkably deep ravine with precipitous sides that leads out of Newton Dale towards the old coach road upon which the lonely hostelry stands. At the foot of the steep rocks, a stream trickles into a basin and then falls downwards in a small cascade, finding its way into the Pickering Beck that flows along the bottom of Newton Dale. From the inn also, the great ravine we have been describing appears as an enormous trench cut through the heathery plateau, and we are led to wonder how it was that no legends as to its origin have survived until the present time. The Roman road, which is supposed to have been built by Wade and his wife when they were engaged on the construction of Mulgrave and Pickering Castles, seems uninspiring beside the majestic proportions of Newton Dale. To the south of the Saltersgate Inn lies the remarkable circular hollow among the hills known as the Hole of Horcum, and the bold bluff known as Saltersgate Brow rises like an enormous rampart from the smooth brown or purple heather. To the west lies the peculiarly isolated hill known as Blakey Topping, and, a little to the south, are the Bride Stones, those imposing masses of natural rock that project themselves above the moor. The Saltersgate Inn has lost the importance it once possessed as the stopping-place for the coaches between Whitby and Pickering, but is still the only place of refreshment for many miles across the moors, and its very isolation still gives it an importance for those who seek sport or exercise on these breezy wastes.

Levisham and Lockton, the twin villages that

stand upon the very edge of the heather, are separated by a tremendous valley, and although from above they may seem so close as to be almost continuous, in reality they are as remote from one another as though they were separated by five or six miles. To reach Levisham from Lockton means a break-neck descent of a very

LOCKTON VILLAGE.
The ash tree that grows on the church tower can be seen in the drawing.

dangerous character and a climb up from the mill and lonely church at the bottom of the valley that makes one marvel how the village ever came to be perched in a position of such inaccessibility. The older inhabitants of Levisham tell you that in their young days the village was more populous, and their statements are supported by the pathetic evidence of more than one cottage lying in ruins with the interior occupied by a jungle of nettles. The Vicarage is the only new building that breaks the mellowed grey tones of the wide, grass-bordered street.

Lockton is a larger and better preserved village. The little church with its grey tower is noticeable on account of the vigorous ash-tree that grows from the parapet. It has been there for many years, and I am told that the roots have penetrated for a very great distance among the stones, and may even be drawing their sustenance from the ground. In order to prevent the undue growth of the tree, it is periodically cut down to one branch, but even with this wholesale lopping the tree has forced many of the stones from their original positions.

The interior of the church is a melancholy spectacle of churchwarden methods, but probably Lockton will before many years receive that careful restoration that has taken place at Ellerburne and Sinnington. The font is one of those unadorned, circular basins which generally date from the thirteenth century. One of the village inns is known as "The Durham Ox," and bears a sign adorned with a huge beast whose pensive but intelligent eye looks down upon all passers-by. The village stocks that used to stand outside the churchyard wall on the east side, near the present schoolhouse, are remembered by the older inhabitants. They were taken away about forty years ago. The few thatched cottages that remain in the village are unfortunately being allowed to fall into disrepair, but this is the case in most of the villages.

Newton, or, as its full name should be given,

Newton-upon-Rawcliff, stands on the verge of Newton Dale. Its small modern church has no interest for the antiquary, but the broad roadway between the houses and the whitewashed cottages thrown up against the strip of grass on either side is picturesque enough.

Northwards from Newton lies the minute moorland hamlet of Stape, its houses and its inn, "The Hare and Hounds," being perched indiscriminately on the heather. Some miles beyond lies Goathland, that formerly belonged to the parish of Pickering. The present church was built in 1895, but it is here that the fine pre-Reformation chalice that originally belonged to Pickering is still in use. The village has a large green overlooked here and there by pretty cottages, and the proximity of the richly coloured moorland scenery that lies spread out in every direction makes the place particularly fascinating. The railway in the valley has brought a few new houses to the village, but there seems little chance of any great accretions of this nature, although the existence of the railway station is a permanent menace to the rural character of the place.

Middleton, the hamlet immediately to the west of Pickering, lies along the main road to Helmsley. Its interesting old church is surrounded by trees, and might almost be passed unnoticed. The post-office is in one of the oldest cottages. Its massive oak forks must have endured for many centuries, and the framework of the doorway leading into the garden behind must be of almost equal antiquity.

Between the years 1764 and 1766, John Wesley, on his northern circuit, visited this unassuming little village and preached in the pulpit of the parish church. A circular sun-dial bearing the motto "We stay not," and the date 1782, appears above the porch, and the church is entered by a fine old door of the Perpendicular period. A paddock on the west side of the graveyard is known as the nun's field, but I have no knowledge of any monastic institution having existed at Middleton. Aislaby, the next village to the west, is so close that one seems hardly to have left Middleton before one reaches the first cottage of the next hamlet. There is no church here, and the only conspicuous object as one passes westwards is the Hall, a large stone house standing close to the road on the south side. Wrelton is only half a mile from Aislaby. It stands at the cross-roads where the turning to Lastingham and Rosedale Abbey leaves the Helmsley Road. The cottages are not particularly ancient, and there are no striking features to impress themselves on the memory of the passer-by. At Sinnington, however, we reach a village of marked individuality. The broad green is ornamented with a bridge that spans the wide stony course of the river Seven; but more noticeable than this is the very tall maypole that stands on the green and appears in the distance as a tapering mast that has been sloped out of perpendicular by the most prevailing winds. It was around an earlier maypole that stood in the place of the existing one that the scene between the "Broad Brims" and the merrymaking villagers that has already been mentioned took place nearly two centuries ago. The present maypole was erected on May 29th 1882, replacing one which had come into existence on the same day twenty years before. The recently restored church of Sinnington stands slightly above the green, backed by the trees on the rising ground to the north of the village. The new roof of red tiles would almost lead one to imagine that the building was a modern one, and one would scarcely imagine that it dates chiefly from the twelfth century. A custom which is still remembered by some of the older villagers was the roasting of a sheep by the small bridge on the green on November 23rd in Martinmas week. The children used to go round a few days before, collecting money for the purchase of the sheep. Although these quaint customs are no longer continued at Sinnington the green has retained its picturesqueness, and towards evening, when the western sky is reflected in the rippling waters of the Seven, the scene is a particularly pleasing one.

Between Sinnington and Kirby Moorside about three miles to the west is the site of the priory of Keldholm, but there are no walls standing at the present time. Kirby Moorside is one of the largest villages in the neighbourhood of Pickering. It has been thought that it may possibly have been in Goldsmith's mind when he described the series of catastrophes that befell the unfortunate household of the Vicar of Wakefield; but although I have carefully read the story with a view to discovering any descriptions that may suggest the village of Kirby Moorside, I can find very little in support of the idea. Before the construction of the railway connecting Pickering and Helmsley, this part of Yorkshire was seldom visited by any one but those having business in the immediate neighbourhood; and even now as one walks along the wide main street one cannot help feeling that the village is still far removed from the influences of modern civilisation. The old shambles still stand in the shadow of the Tolbooth, the somewhat gaunt but not altogether unpleasing building that occupies a central position in the village. Adjoining the shambles is the broken stump of the market-cross raised upon its old steps, and close by also is the entrance to the churchyard. The church occupies a picturesque position, and contains, besides the Elizabethan brass to Lady Brooke, a *parvise* chamber over the old porch. This little room is approached by a flight of stone steps from the interior of the church and possesses a fireplace. It has been supposed that the chamber would have been used by the monk who served from Newburgh Priory when he had occasion to stay the night. The brick windmill, built about a hundred years ago, that stands on the west side of the village, is no longer in use, and has even been robbed of its sails. At the highest part of the village street there are some extremely old thatched cottages which give a very good idea of what must have been the appearance of the whole place a century ago. The "King's Head" Inn and the house adjoining it, in which the notorious Duke of

Buckingham died, are two of the oldest buildings of any size that now remain. An inn, a little lower down the street has a picturesque porch supported by carved posts, bearing the name "William Wood," and the date 1632. Kirby Moorside has preserved, in common with two or three other villages in the neighbourhood, its Christmastide mummers and waits. The mummers, who go their rounds in daytime, are men dressed as women. They carry a small doll in a box ornamented with pieces of evergreen and chant doggerel rhymes.

The beautiful scenery of Farndale and Kirkdale comes as a surprise to those who visit Kirby Moorside for the first time, for the approach by road in all directions, except from the north, does not lead one to suspect the presence of such impressive landscapes, and from some points Farndale has quite a mountainous aspect. The moors no longer reach the confines of Kirby Moorside, as its name would suggest, for cultivation has pushed back the waste lands for two or three miles to the north; but from that point northwards all the way to Guisborough the wild brown moorland is broken only in a few places by the fitful cultivation of the dales. The church of Kirkdale, and what quarrying has left of the famous cave, stand just at the point where the Hodge Beck leaves its confined course and flows out into the flat levels of the Vale of Pickering. It is only, however, after very heavy rains that the stony course of the stream at this point shows any sign of water, for in ordinary weather the stream finds its way

THE "BLACK HOLE" OF THORNTON-LE-DALE.
An underground cell beneath some cottages which was formerly the village prison.

through underground fissures in the limestone and does not appear above the ground for a considerable distance. The little church of Kirkdale, remarkable for its Saxon sun-dial and other pre-Norman remains, is surrounded by masses of foliage, and the walk up the dale from this point to the romantically situated Cauldron Mill is one of remarkable beauty. As one follows the course of the beck higher and higher towards it source north of Bransdale, the densely wooded sides become bare, and wide expanses and the invigorating moorland air are exchanged for the rich land scents and the limited views.

The village of Lastingham is surrounded by beautiful hills and is almost touched by the moors that lie immediately to the north. The Church has already been described, and we have heard something of the strange story of the ingenious methods for increasing his income of a former curate-in-charge. Cropton occupies a position somewhat similar to that of Newton, being on high ground with commanding views in all directions. The little church is modern, but it has the stump of an ancient cross in the graveyard, and commands a magnificent view towards the west and north. It is in connection with this cross that a curious old rhyme is mentioned in an old guide.

"On Cropton Cross there is a cup,
And in that cup there is a sup;
Take that cup and drink that sup,
And set that cup on Cropton Cross top."

There is a cottage on the east side of the street

bearing the date 1695, and the motto "Memento Mori," with the initials N. C., but more interesting than this is one on the same side but at the southern end of the village, and standing back more than the rest. This was used as a madhouse at a time well remembered by some of the villagers. People from Pickering and the surrounding district were sent here for treatment, and I am told that the proprietor possessed a prescription for a very remarkable medicine which was supposed to have a most beneficial effect upon his partially demented patients. I am also told that this prescription was given to one, Goodwill of Lastingham, who still possesses it. Cropton is only a short distance from the Roman camps that lie all surrounded and overgrown with dense plantations, so that it is impossible for a stranger to discover their position unless he be lucky enough to find some one close at hand to carefully describe the right track.

West of Pickering lies that long string of villages, generally less than two miles apart, that extends nearly all the way to Scarborough. The first point of interest as one goes towards Thornton-le-Dale from Pickering is the grass-grown site of Roxby Castle, the birthplace of Sir Hugh Cholmley, and the scene, as we know, of those conflicts between the retainers of Sir Roger Hastings and Sir Richard Cholmley. The position must have been a most perfect one for this ancient manor house, for standing a little higher than the level ings and carrs of the marshy land, it was protected from the cold northern winds by the higher ground above. From the top of the steep hill west of the village, Thornton-le-Dale has an almost idyllic aspect, its timeworn roofs of purple thatch and mellowed tiles nestling among the masses of tall trees that grow with much luxuriance in this sheltered spot at the foot of the hills. The village is musical with the pleasant sound of the waters of the beck that flows from Dalby Warren, and ripples along the margins of the roadways, necessitating a special footbridge for many of the cottages. The ancient stocks that stood by the cross-roads have unfortunately disappeared, and in their place may be seen the pathetic sight of a new pair that are not even a close copy of the old ones. The old stone cross that stands by the stocks has not been replaced by a modern one, and adds greatly to the interest of the central portion of the village. On the road that leads towards Ellerburne there stand some old cottages generally known as the Poorhouse. They are built on sloping ground, and on the lower side there is a small round-topped tunnel leading into a little cell dug out of the ground beneath the cottages. This little village prison was known as the "Black Hole," and was in frequent use about fifty years ago. An old resident in the village named Birdsall, who is now in the Almshouses, remembers that the last woman who was placed in the Black Hole was released by four men who forcibly broke their way in. The quaint little church of Ellerburne and the few antique cottages that make up the hamlet lie about a mile from Thornton up the steep valley to the north. The hills on either side are crowned with plantations, but farther up the dale appear the bare slopes of the edge of the moors. Allerston lies at right angles to the main road. It is full of quaint stone cottages, and is ornamented by the square tower of the church and the cheerful brook that flows along the road side. The church at Ebberston stands aloof from the village at the edge of the small park belonging to the Hall. The situation is a very pleasant one, and the building attracts one's attention on account of the wide blocked-up arch that is conspicuous in the south wall west of the porch.

The next village westwards is Snainton, a more compact and town-like hamlet than most of the others in the district. The church having been rebuilt in about 1835, the place is robbed of one of its chief attractions.

Brompton has already been mentioned in connection with Wordsworth's wedding. The view over the bright green pastures of the Vale when seen from the church porch is of conspicuous beauty, and the ponds that are numerous in the village help to make picturesque views from many points. The Hall is a large building possessing a ponderous bulk but little charm, and it is only by the kindly aid of the plentiful trees and an extensive growth of ivy that the squire's house does not destroy the rural sweetness of the village.

Wykeham has a new church with a massive spire, but the tower of the old building has fortunately been allowed to remain, and now answers the purpose of

Hutton Buscel Church.

The lower part of the tower is of Norman work. The head of the churchyard cross is modern.

a lich-gate. Only a few walls of the abbey now remain in close proximity to Lord Downe's recently enlarged house.

The church of Hutton Buscel is externally one of the most picturesque in the district, and the pretty churchyard on steeply falling ground is a charming feature of the village. The old Hall of the Osbaldestons is only represented by the massive gates that give access to the schools built on the site of the house that was burnt down about a century ago.

A curious story is told of Bishop Osbaldeston, whose monument is to be seen in the church. During his stay at Hutton Buscel he often amused himself with riding about the neighbourhood and conversing with any one he happened to meet upon the road. "One morning he saw a chimney-sweeper's boy laid on the roadside, whom he accosted as follows:—'Well, my lad, where hast thou been this morning?' 'Sweeping your chimnies,' replied the lad. 'And how much hast thou earned then?' said his lordship. 'Fifteen shillings, my lord.' After his lordship had observed that he thought it a very good business, the lad says, 'Yes, my lord, you see that *we black coats* get good livings for very little work.'"

The smaller villages of the Vale are without any particular interest in themselves, apart from the wide and expansive landscapes that stretch away in all directions to the enclosing hills that in distant times formed the boundaries of the lake.

Great Habton has a small chapel of ease of very recent erection.

Ryton is chiefly composed of two or three farms and a dilapidated little red brick building that scarcely deserves the name of church. The lane to this hamlet from Great Habton is remarkable for the series of about a dozen gates across the roadway.

Brawby and Butterwick have no particular features that impress themselves on the mind, and Great Barugh, though more picturesque than either of these, is chiefly interesting on account of its past.

Normanby lies on the dead level of the plain, and is watered by the Seven, that flows between high embankments throughout most of its course after leaving the high ground at Sinnington.

Salton lies a little to the west and is interesting on account of its beautiful little Norman church. The cottages are situated on a patch of green, and the whole place has a cheerful and tidy appearance.

At Kirby Misperton there is a very green pond by the church, and the remains of the stocks may still be seen by the pretty rose-covered cottage that contains the post-office. Many of the cottages were rebuilt between 1857 and 1877, the dates being conspicuous on their big gables.

CHAPTER XIV

Concerning the Zoology of the Forest and Vale

THE great expanses of wild moorland, the deep, heavily wooded valleys, and the rich and well-watered level country included in the scope of this book would lead one to expect much of the zoology of the Pickering district, and one is not disappointed. That the wild life is ample and interesting will be seen from the following notes on the rarer varieties which Mr Oxley Grabham of the York Museum has kindly put together.

ON THE MOORS *the Curlew*, *the Golden Plover*, and the *Merlin* nest regularly together with other more common species.

IN THE WOODS *the Woodcock*, *Pied Flycatcher*, and *Wood Wren*, together with *the Green* and *the Great Spotted Woodpeckers*, breed by no means uncommonly.

IN THE MARSHY AND LOW-LYING LANDS *the Snipe* and *the Redshank* find congenial breeding quarters.

Many rarities have been obtained in the district such as *the Kite*, *the Great Plover*, *the Smew*, and *the Golden Eagle*, and numerous varieties of wildfowl during the winter months. I have seen large flocks of *Crossbills* and *Bramblings* hunting for food in the severe weather, and occasionally a small flock of *Waxwings* appears in the district.

There is a well-protected *Heronry* in the neighbourhood, and these fine handsome birds may frequently be seen in the vicinity of the Costa, a stream famous for the size and quality of its *Trout* and *Grayling*.

From a sporting point of view there are few better districts in the north of Yorkshire. *Grouse* are abundant on the moors, and there is some most excellent *Partridge* ground at hand, whilst certain of the coverts are famous for *Woodcock* during the winter months.

Foxes are numerous, and three packs of regular hounds, Lord Middleton's, Sir Everard Cayley's, and the Sinnington, hunt the country, whilst the old established trencher-fed Goathland pack accounts for a goodly number every season.

Otters and *Badgers* are far more plentiful than most people have any idea of; but, unfortunately, they are generally killed whenever a chance of doing so presents itself, the trap and the gun being regularly employed against them.

The usual smaller mammals are present in goodly numbers, and present no special or peculiar features, with the exception of *the common Rat*, which has been of late a perfect pest in some parts of the country; the hedge bottoms have been riddled with rat holes. Gates and posts and rails have been gnawed to bits, and in one instance a litter of young pigs were worried during the night. On one farm alone, during the year 1904, over two thousand rats were killed.

OF REPTILES, *the common Adder or Viper*, locally known as the Hag-Worm, is numerous in the moorland districts. It seldom if ever attacks human beings, but occasionally dogs and sheep get bitten with fatal results. *The Slow or Blind Worm* is also to be found here, as are the other usual forms of reptiles.

OXLEY GRABHAM, M.A., M.B.O.U.

* * * * *

The famous breed of horses known as the Cleveland Bays come from this district of Yorkshire. They are bred all over the district between Pickering, Helmsley, Scarborough, and Middlesborough, and although efforts have been made to raise them in other parts of England and abroad, it has been found that they lose the hardness of bone which is such a characteristic feature of the Cleveland bred animals. The Cleveland bay coach horse is descended from the famous Darly Arabian, and preserves in a wonderful manner the thoroughbred outline.

Pickering 1905 to 2000
by John Rushton

In this final year of the twentieth century, there is much about Pickering that would have astounded Home and yet much that would have been perfectly familiar to him. The Churches and Meeting Houses stand in their usual places as do many of the houses described in the previous chapters. The post boxes are still red and the children tumble out of school at the appointed hours. But the children are healthier, as are their parents and the town is cleaner and freer from floods and diseases. The cars and lorries would probably have disturbed him but the sound of a steam train would have been familiar even if he could not board it and go to London. If he could have looked into a late twentieth century house he would have noted its warmth, cleanliness and amenities such as hot water, bathrooms, computers and televisions. The history of the last hundred or so years has been one of great events on the national scale and steady improvement at the local level.

Early Years of a New Century.

The Victorians spoke much of "progress" but the benefits had spread anything but evenly. The countryside and its market towns were not its focus. They seemed rather to be drawn along behind forces that were concentrated in
the growing urban and industrial areas. Villages and dales had long produced more people than farming could employ. A steady stream left over many decades to find employment in industrial towns, or migrated to populate distant Empire and the United States of America. Pickering had 3491 people in 1901 rising to 3674 by 1911 but the town was not as populous as it had been at its Victorian peak.

Some Were Poor.

Pickering had 881 families living in 784 houses. Two thirds of the people were said to be poor but poverty has many degrees. Most were working people, men, women and their families for whom life was a struggle. Sickness, unemployment or old age could easily lead to dire poverty. A councillor remarked that "the poorer classes" couldn't pay for the scavenger's tubs of their ashes to be carted away, but they would have to be carted anyway. Winter soup kitchens were run to feed what they called "the deserving poor", 26 gallons made at a time "for the most necessitous". Six lived in a single room at Newbridge. A Union workhouse held fifty of the poorest and received fifty more vagrants a week in the casual ward.

The Better Off.

The "better off" third included farmers, shopkeepers, craftsmen and some artisans in a good way of work. Many owned small freehold properties. There were a few professionals and about seventy families, whose members were listed as "private persons". Their big, named houses were scattered around the town, or in the genteel precinct of Hallgarth. A few aristocratic or prospering business families had large estates in the countryside but the King was lord of the Manor in right of his Duchy of Lancaster. The Mitchelson family at Pickering Hall and at the Mount on Potter Hill were almost but never quite squires. The freeholders had always formed an independent body, not given to allowing squires to do their thinking for them.

Insofar as it was "governed" at all, Pickering looked to the Urban District Council, which replaced an earlier Board of Health in 1894. The villages had a separate Rural District Council meeting at the town. Elections were every three years, sometimes fought with rancour, but tempered by witty pamphlets, which might portray a candidate as "Maltonian, by Church Clock, out of Asphalt", "foaming at the mouth and blowing out gas". Divisions were Conservative against Liberal, Church against Chapel, and "upper" against "not quite so upper". When a "people's candidate" did gain a seat, he had the temerity to question Chairman Mitchelson's impartiality. Like Robin Hood, a challenger to the mighty could win popularity. The council removed a wall built by corn merchant Sam Baker. He took them to court, won his case, received a returning hero's welcome at the rail station, and at the next election topped the poll. Mrs Coultman shocked the all-male Council by marching in to the Council chamber, shouting "Don't say that I am ONLY a women". It was not all serious. An elector complained about cocks crowing every morning. A dog walked into a Council meeting, listened for a time, curled up and went to sleep.

Services.

Councils had few functions. What a later age would see as "essential services" were not yet part of everyday life. Where they existed, they were privately provided for those who could afford them. The Pickering Gas and Water Company was slowly laying pipes around the town, though the water was turned off nightly at eleven, to the dismay of the Volunteer Fire Brigade. One result was the abolition of public pumps and the covering of private wells. A big cow fell deep down the White horse yard well but when hauled out, calved without evident dismay. Women who took in washing used the Eastgate Mangle. There were street gas lamps, toured daily by a lamp lighter with a long pole. The new Post Office brought emigrants letters, its postmen helped by new street nameplates and house numbers. A uniformed Town Crier with a bell proclaimed announcements, such as items lost and found. The Malton Messenger and Yorkshire Gazette newspapers weekly brought the news, often to confirm what word of mouth had already made known.

Farming.

Farming and dependant trades were the basis of the market town. Outer parts of the parish held thirty one farms and the villages many more but sixteen farmsteads were in Pickering itself. Cattle and sheep were familiar in the streets. Farmers gathered on Mondays for fortnightly pig sales and weekly cattle markets, with much dealing done at public houses. Among the horse breeders, Frank Sterricker for thirty three years exported fine Cleveland Bay horses to America. Notable sales went to the Kings of Italy and to King Edward in London. The station approaches came alive when scores of horses awaited despatch. There were nurserymen too and water cress growers. Much fruit went out by train to jam makers. Cottagers had back yard pigs and hens, while a "coo-tenter", daily herded their cows from seven in the morning till four, around lanes which had grass verges far broader than the narrow tracks of their roads.

Craft and Industry.

High Mill, Low Mill and Vivers Mill still ground corn, while the "Railway Mill", powered by a steam engine, crushed bones for meal. Craftsmen made besoms or witches broomsticks and Pickering was sometimes called "Besomshire". Stone was quarried extensively for building, road works and agricultural lime at Newbridge. Rosedale iron mining was on a far greater scale. Bricks and tiles were made at Upper Carr. Three timber merchants operated in a big way although the hills north of the town were very bare. Small producers made artificial teeth, baskets, and Pape's sauce. Here were the workshops of James Taylor, the Potter Hill wheelwright, of seven joiners and cabinet makers, six tailors, four dressmakers, three saddlers, two printers, and an asphalter. Three "watchmakers" and ten "shoemakers" were already repairers rather than makers. Besides two bakeries, there were six blacksmiths and small iron foundries at Market Place and Park Street, Digby Wrangham later recalled "there was nothing much they couldn't make on the spot".

Shops.

Pickering was a town of sixty six small shops and a weekly produce market attracting carriers carts from twenty five villages. Shops opened at eight and closed at seven, except Sundays and Wednesday afternoons. Many were in the town centre with new plate glass windows and blinds but there were a few corner shops. Food retailers were numerous with sixteen grocers, and seven general stores. Ten butchers, ten fruiterers, four bakers & confectioners, two wine and spirit stores, a fishmonger, and milk dealers made up the food trades. Five drapers, four dressmakers, seven tailors, ten shoemakers, the hosier and hatter provided clothing. Retail stores with workshops behind included Henry Coverdale's boot and shoe factory". Fowler & Srigleys" cash stores" on the north side of Market Place expanded into several retail departments. The new Pickering & District Co-operative Society found a ready appeal for its "mutual aid principle" among poor people. Five hundred members at their 1902 demonstration, processed to the Temperance hall for a knife and fork tea. The town also had two tobacconists, two chemists, ironmongers, pot and furniture dealers, and a range of service trades

Self Help and Charity.

Food, clothes and warmth were the main necessities of life and few wasted what they had of them. Typical cast iron coal grates held minuscule amounts of fuel. Yet many people made progress, when prices moved in their favour. One family marked 1907 by wallpapering a bedroom, even putting up a picture rail. A young lady might indulge the folly of fashion and buy a "pneumonia blouse". Seven hundred members of four Friendly Societies, called Druids and Oddfellows, paid regular subscriptions to provide half the people with a decent burial and modest insurance against illness and unemployment. Allotments were started and a Yorkshire Penny Bank encouraged saving. The first payment of Old Age Pensions was made in 1909, one of the first really useful things that national government did. Two decades later, a Pickering woman, who had missed six years pension through not asking, found it "a blessing to have ten shillings a week" but added that "she had never had any money but what she had worked for till now". She had worked all her days. Self help was supplemented by family help and informal charity. The Pickering District Nursing Association formed in 1911, raised over ú120 a year, to support a valued district nurse. Doctor Robertson was highly regarded since "he did a lot of doctoring for nowt".

Childhood.

Pickering School Board had been formed in 1896 to extend free but compulsory elementary education. A school was opened at Stape on the moor edge and town children were sent to a new Infants School near Kirkham Lane. A School Attendance Officer, the "Kid catcher" sought truants. After 1902 The North Riding County Council took over from the School Board. About 500 children attended the other Day Schools, founded fifty years earlier, the Wesleyan Day School in Westgate with over 300 pupils and the Church of England School in Hallgarth with 200 more. The small Pickering Grammar School, behind the master's house in Hallgarth, had merged with the younger Lady Lumley Grammar School of Thornton Dale. A fine new Lady Lumley School was built at Middleton Road in 1904 providing secondary education for about 70 boys and girls. The fees were beyond most pockets and of 14 free scholarships only 4 were for Pickering. Critics thought it wasn't a lot of use to the town, but it was a start. When Yorkshire College became Leeds University, two pupils went from the School, W. Randall to gain his M.Sc. in electrical engineering in 1906 and F. Newstead, later his wife, her M.A.

Horses and Carts.

Pickering was compact, in shape an inverted T, long from north west to south east, but pulled north towards the mediaeval castle. Newton was a distinct village. Stape, Keld Head, Upper Carr and Newbridge were small hamlets near the industries that sustained them. Most people walked everywhere but riding horses were numerous, sometimes bolting or throwing their riders. Others pulled carts, wagons and fancy carriages. Few roads were surfaced with anything more than Summer dust and Winter mud though the Council adopted tarmacadam in place of whinstone on the main town roads in 1918. Everyone talked horses. Farm lads judged their employers by how "she" fed them and how "he" looked after the horses. Joseph Watson aged 85 in 1901 could recall working horses that pulled railway carriages to Whitby. Now trains pulled by steam engines linked the town with London. Branch lines ran to Scarborough and around Ryedale to the Vale of York. Meanwhile Tim Garbutt hired out traction engines. That mechanically minded

Lloyd George addresses the crowd at Smiddy Hill, Pickering, 1st May 1931.

Market Day in Pickering Market Place in the early 1930's.

Soldiers from the territorial army leave Pickering in 1914 marching down the Market Place to embark from Pickering Station.

"Threshing Day". Threshing corn at Lister's Toft Barn Farm, near Black Bull Pickering.

man F.W. Skaife had designed his own bicycle and a Pickering Cycle Club employed a bugler to warn of their approach

The New Motor Car.

Blacksmith Robert Dobson obtained a licence to store 30 gallons of petrol at Kirkham Lane in 1902. Dr Kirk bought a Minerva motor cycle the next year. A Pickering letter of August 17, 1904 excitedly warned of motor cars coming through town the next day. Thomas Frank acquired the first local car and Kirk bought a De Dion Bouton. Two years later he was motor racing on Saltburn sands. Local traffic was limited to speeds of twelve miles an hour. W. Sleightholme, a pioneering Eastgate motor engineer who taught many later garage men their trade, advertised Shell motor spirit "every can sealed". The Ford Model T arrived in 1906 and a precipitous motor cyclist damaged himself and the Low Hall railings in 1909. Cars remained rare for decades, but Holliday's and Sleightholme's cabs awaited gentry and commercial travellers at the railway station.

Church and Chapel

"In Pickering Nonconformity is everything" said a contemporary urging the "different classes and creeds" to work together. The exaggeration was forgivable since the Primitive Methodist Society had the largest membership at their Potter Hill chapel and meeting houses at Black Bull & Stape. The Wesleyan Methodist Society was no less active with a renovated Hungate Chapel and another at Stape. Wesleyans and Primitives had numerous places of worship in their wider circuits. Methodism commonly had two chapels to a village. Vicar Lightfoot had done much for the poor in a twenty six year ministry at Pickering Parish

Church, amending its identification with the better-off. He had a Marishes church and a mission room for the Newbridge quarrymen. Vicar Drage came in 1902 and missioned Pickering itself four years later. Father Bryan for the Roman Catholics had missioned the town in 1901 with enough success to build St Joseph church and form a school. The old established Independent Church at Hungate had an active minister in Mr Goldsbrough. The Society of Friends gathered at their Castlegate Meeting House. A Salvation Army barracks moved to Goslip Lane and a Blue Ribbon Gospel Army used the Allelujah Hall in Westgate. The town had six full time clergymen and many lay preachers. Seven hundred children attended four denominational Sunday Schools.

The Round of Events.

A six day working week left Sunday as the day of rest. The year was framed traditionally. Holidays were short but some seasons were slacker than others, even on farms. Lent was widely kept as a time of abstinence. In the week before, there were special days for eating 'collops', pancakes and black puddings. The Pickering pancake bell rang at eleven, stopping work for the day. Women with frying pans raced down the Market Place. Children played with ball and shuttlecock. The Easter Horse Show filled the streets. Eggs were rolled at Rookers Hill. The Castle yard was thrown open on Easter Sunday. A cottager's pig killing, a Carling Sunday, or a farmers harvest celebration could bring a short flush of plenty. Children's conkers, marbles and hoops had each their seasons. Sunday School treat day regularly emptied the town for sports and picnics. Thirty-one July Galas took place in Avenue field till shocking goings-on upset the ministers. Sporadically circuses, fairs, booth theatres, sword dancers, concert parties, German bands and men with walking bears were seen. The 4th of November was mischief night - time to paint black treacle on a door handle. Martinmas gave a November holiday week for farm servants with money in their pockets. Christmas might stretch to twelve days when, the Fanciers Society show was in the Market Hall, when choirs sang and brass bands played in the streets, the Waits visited houses musically greeting inmates and "Lucky birds" called to beg. The workhouse inmates received a roast beef and plum pudding dinner.

At Ease.

A half circle chattering around a fire at night was leisure. The better off might sing around a piano or harmonium. Church and chapel provided meetings, not only for women. Pickering had "mutual improvement societies" and political reading rooms. Clubs supported interests in sports, in angling, rambling, charity, bibles, natural history and the prevention of cruelty. There were brass bands and string bands. Perhaps people have sung since the beginning of time but popular songs changed rapidly with the Victorian boom in sheet music sales Westgate Hall saw soprano Maggie Petch and her Glee Party. The Pickering Choral Society gained a fillip from the fine organ placed in the Parish church in 1905. About five years later, Arthur Frank Tate of Pickering was inspired to write the music of a best seller "Somewhere a Voice is Calling" while walking with a girl friend beckside towards Newbridge. There was one public house for every 153 people in the town and much social life was in them. Yet, the temperance cause was the one thing that could unite Nonconformists and many others. There were temperance halls, a temperance coffee house, and a temperance hotel. Children joined "Bands of Hope" and many adults signed the abstinence pledge to avoid "the demon drink", some on a regular basis. Lassies pondered whether "the lips that touch liquor shall never touch mine". The Liberal Club built on Smiddy Hill in 1906 remained dry. The Conservative Club was newly housed in 1913.

National Occasions.

When Queen Victoria died in 1901, the church was draped in black and its bells muffled. A general holiday of mourning was declared, leading the Railway company to dock a day's wages from their poorer employees. The monarch was lord of Pickering manor but the link faded when the market and castle were granted to the Urban Council. Decades later, the Duchy of Lancaster discovered that the Council still used the Imperial Crown and the Duchy coat of arms. They were abruptly told to desist. Nevertheless, Royal Coronations and Jubilees were loyally marked by general holidays, with celebrations paid for by the better off. In 1902, for the Edward VII Coronation and in 1911 for that of King George V, sport and feast ended with great torchlight processions to vast Beacon Hill bonfires, fuelled with railway sleepers and tar barrels. A stone cross was placed on Smiddy Hall in 1912 to mark these royal occasions.

The Pageant.

Gordon Home raised interest in the local heritage. The Pickering Historical Pageant of 1910 used this in a massive communal effort with players from both town and villages. Major Mitchelson chaired the main Committee and almost everyone with money was recruited to a Committee of Guarantors. There were jobs for everyone. Mrs S. Baker became "the secretary for knitting the chain armour". Mr J.M. Mitchelson played St Wilfrid, and his rural equivalent Colonel Scoby became the Roman Governor Agricola. If it seemed that acting roles were closely geared to social station, there was still immense pride in a communal occasion which ended the four days of August performances in the Castle with marches behind the band through Pickering.

War.

The Pickering Rifle Volunteer Company in the Second Battalion of the Yorkshire Regiment had a Drill Hall, employed a Drill Sergeant and shot at targets in Haugh Howl. Their best shots went to the South Africa War. Private John Myers of Brant Hill was cheered off at the rail station in 1900. From the Cape he had a 300 mile march up country. Pickering celebrated when news came of the relief of Mafeking. Edgar Chandler was taken prisoner by the Boers. The band was out again to give him and his brother a heroes welcome. Captain Loy of Kitcheners Fighting Scouts did not return. He has an early military memorial in the church. After the Peace in 1902, church bells rang, bands played and flags were flown. One enthusiast lacking flags hung out his shirt. A new Drill Hall was built at Muck Lane in 1906 and the Commander in Chief Lord Roberts visited Pickering to thank the volunteers for their contribution.

The Great War.

The scale and impact of the "Great War" with Germany was totally different. The Pickering Volunteers marched away on August 6th 1914. Each man carried a cape, bullet pouches, water bottle, shovel, helmet, and eating tin. A Pickering parent wrote of "such a weeping, mothers losing sons and husbands". The main British army equipped with rifles, machine guns and artillery dug into lines of trenches in north east France. Many men never returned. Dr J.F. Murphy of Pickering won the Military Cross in the retreat from Mons and lived to see the second gas attack at Ypres when the men had no gas masks. April 1915 brought the first wounded soldiers to the Hallgarth Red Cross Hospital run by Mrs Kirk. The Earl of Feversham raised a Volunteer Battalion at Helmsley that year. A

Pickering recruit wrote home from his Duncombe Park training camp of "bread, bacon and eggs for breakfast, beef for dinner and bread and jam for tea", adding "we are as happy as Kings". It was not for long. By 1916, 248 Pickering men were in the army. 11 in the Navy and 10 in the Royal Flying Corps. The pressure to enlist mounted. A woman wrote "It is either enlist or be disgraced. It is too bad". Then, the huge volunteer army, including many local men, was thrown in at the Somme and lives were wasted, as never before. Here was a war that destroyed and scarred generations.

The Home Front.

There were alarms at home. On 16th December 1914, Pickering people heard rumbling and thudding. An hour later a motor car brought a family to the Black Swan whose Scarborough home had been destroyed by bombardment from German battle-cruisers. The Winter of 1916-17 was grim as unrestricted German submarine attacks on shipping reduced the imports essential to national survival. Food was scarce, prices doubled and poor land was ploughed up, So many "lads" were out of the town it seemed deserted, but as the casualties mounted, the married men went as well. Women took on men's jobs and raised one parent families. Nothing seemed secure when great air ships - Zeppelins - flew over Pickering and dropped bombs at Rosedale. Men went to serve in Italy, the Dardanelles and in the fleets. Mark Ward was in the Dover patrol and submarines. Most went to the army on "the Western front" where the heavy casualties of the long trench war of attrition eventually brought conscription. Pickering letters speak of the Tribunal deciding which occupations were reserved and who had to go. Older folk sent parcels to the front, small comforts and flea powder. A Pickering father wrote with moving gratitude to his soldier son, "It is due to thousands of our young English lads that have gone out to fight for us, that we are able to have such a quiet and happy gathering. If you young chaps were not out there". Many received letters that began "It is with great sorrow that I have to inform you of the death of ....".

The Memorials.

Almost every household was affected by the deaths and maimings of the War. A whole segment of several generations died. War wounded and shell shocked men were legion. Gas lingered as fluid in lungs decades later. Father Bryan's sister opened a Catholic war orphanage at the town. Many women were widowed and others who might have wished to marry remained single. When 212 service men came back, they were entertained in the Drill Hall and on Peace Day the Beacon Hill bonfires flared again. There was wide awareness of the role that American entry to the War had played in bringing the Germans to sue for peace. Brass plaques were placed in the Parish church commemorating the American Alliance and Ambassador Walter Hines Page, widely regarded as responsible for the alliance. The Pickering War Memorial carries the names of 72 Pickering men who did not return. Thornton Dale by 1918 had lost 25 men and there are village memorials too. Another memorial to the war dead was made in 1922 by the conversion of a mill into a community centre for the town, ever since known as the Memorial Hall.

The Quiet Years.

Pickering showed no growth for twenty years, the population of 1931 little different from 1
911. Some gentry families vanished. Pickering High Hall survived till demolition in the sixties but Low Hall would become a Hotel. The

fewer local "private persons" were tradesmen or professionals who also bulked large on the Councils. Their political and religious divisions remained strong making for definite opinions but Pickering remained a stable, compact, even intimate community where many prominent, eccentrics and others were known to all. It was usual to stay for decades in the same role. Jack Middleton was all his working years an engine driver and James Bowling station master for twenty two years. Thirty to forty years service marked the lives of G.G. Skelton Wesleyan School headmaster, and Miss Teasdale the Infants mistress. There was pride in a Pickering man of horses, Frank Gains who served 49 years till 1939, in charge of the royal Windsor Grey horses as Coachman to Queen Victoria, King Edward the VIth and King George the Vth.

Struggles to Keep Going.

The country had spent its wealth in war. Industrial collapse came early at Rosedale where iron mining ceased in 1926. General trade depression followed, perhaps worst between 1929 and 1932. Local wages were low and there was unemployment. R.V. Rogers managed to keep married men on at the Nurseries for three days a week in the worst period. Pickering Council offered stone breaking at the quarry to unemployed men. The town Charity Organisation Society gave coal and tea packets to the elderly poor. Distant larger scale producers were also ending the life of some local workshops. Rural water mills closed, or lingered sawing wood, as corn milling moved to the ports but Harry Burgess redeveloped the Thornton Dale mill to produce the noted Gold Medal plain flour. There were innovations - new Yorkshire Fisheries Board hatcheries at Keld Head, tarmac making and the extraction of refractory sand in Chadwick's quarry and the Deardens making hurdy gurdys. When recovery came, Lez Lazenby was an agricultural engineer, builders began to flourish and two Czechoslovaks called Ketsenbaum started sawmills. Yet, as late as 1935 the Buffaloes Friendly Society could still entertain 200 Pickering children of the unemployed.

Farming.

There were bad years for farming. Without the wartime stimulus land went out of use or out of condition. The number of farmsteads within the town halved. New techniques were there but few to use them. Five motor tractors had come in 1917 and a few Fordsons were bought soon after but there it stopped. Combine harvester experiments on the Wolds were ahead of their time. Street hirings of farm servants ended with the coming of Agricultural Wages Boards but country farmers still came to the cattle market to talk and trade. They had hot dinners at Hugills, where a bed was available, or visited Simpsons Black Swan for the farmers "ordinary". William Grayson and Fred Lakin still sent out horses. Others found new specialisms. Bill Robinson pioneered large scale poultry farming at Kingthorpe. Market gardening expanded and nurseries lined the approach routes from Malton and Whitby. Those of R.V. Rogers displayed famous "Rogers Roses" alongside the railway line. A Forestry Commission had been formed to create national reserves of timber and bought great tracts of land for planting in the hills north of Pickering. The work was initially labour intensive and in 1933 army style camps were opened at Dalby for hundreds of unemployed men, long out of work, from industrial areas, to take twelve week "reconditioning" courses. The trains at Pickering station took crops, stock, hides and skins, flowers, eggs and watercress to the cities, wood pit props to mines and Fred Hebden's besoms to Teeside factories.

Shops stopped making the things they sold when "mass produced" goods came from distant manufacturers Tailors "clothes made to measure" retreated before the flood of "ready made" although John Wiley still made breeches at Market Place. Some grocers cured hams and made baking powder but Marfitts candle making works went to a Museum and the odours of rancid mutton fat vanished from the Market Place. The chemist stopped making sheep dip. Hugills made sweets but sold Hovis bread. Tate Smith's Malton aerated waters replaced the "pop" that Pape had produced with a gas bottle in his yard. The balance of shops changed little but their windows filled with stacked tins while the newspapers showed advertisements for the branded goods inside them. You could get a "permanent wave" or a photograph taken by Sidney Smith. More solid new luxuries could be found at George Cooper's Ironmongers shop: Alladin wick lamps, galvanised water cisterns, carpet sweepers, tiled hearth surrounds or corrugated iron sheet for an allotment shed. To get a sink was to get ahead. Some change was in a different direction. Miss Ashby would bag you up "a penn'orth of sweets", local milk was sent round by hand rullies and the handcart of a muffin man could still be seen, but William Clayworth's first fish and chip shop on Potter Hill was soon joined by three more in the town. Children played games to the jingle "a penn'orth of chips to grease your lips and out goes you". Take away meals had arrived.

Houses and Services.

Pickering lost its thatch to the famous red tiled roofs. Beneath them, all was not yet well. The Medical Officer of 1921 said that two thirds of the houses were working class dwellings, of which 266 were unfit for habitation and seven totally unfit. Annually, he argued for improvement, well aware that childhood was still a struggle through prevalent diseases, such as mumps, whooping cough, scarlet fever and chicken pox which most experienced and not all survived. Progress was slowly achieved and in the face of that strongest of local political sentiments, the antipathy towards rate paying. Old cottages were small and though smaller families were more usual, there was little extra room. Movement into the few new houses allowed modest reshuffling. A new Maudon Avenue estate had 2 bedroom houses for ú300, three bedrooms for ú395 all with bathrooms but these were sums few could afford. Larger scale change came with the first 32 council houses opened at Goslip Lane south of the town in 1933, and another 34 later. General improvement came by providing services to older houses. The Gas Works near the railway fed a piped network from huge cylindrical gasometers. Keld Head water was pumped via reservoirs above the town and the last public well was sealed in 1932. Electricity reached the Memorial Hall in 1924. Underground cables were run around the town streets in 1930 and next year the Conservative Club went electric. New houses built beyond Eastgate in 1933 had electricity, gas and water. New sewage mains reduced the role of the beck as an open sewer and fed new treatment works in Carr Lane though the town still had 479 earth closets. The Memorial Hall had hot and cold baths and a small swimming pool. Twenty years later a quarter of the houses still had no kitchen sink or piped water.

Getting About.

Cars were confined to a few enthusiasts and better off people but commercial vehicles spread rapidly. There were six garages in town. A wedding party left Horseshoe Garage in 1920 for York in what they called "a Tin Lizzie", Rigger Snowden following on a motorbike. Children long remembered seeing the road through the floor of the Pickering taxi. Abraham & Gibbins blue motor bus ran to Scarborough by 1924 and soon bus services linked Pickering with the villages. A timber yard fire persuaded a wealthy man to give the town a motor powered fire engine in 1926 and a motor ambulance five years after. Charabancs offered excursions to new destinations. The Market Place road had to be watered when six charabancs created a dust storm and they moved unwillingly to Eastgate. The United Automobile Company integrated regular services into regional routes. Speed fascinated everyone but most people only aspired to a bicycle. A relatives letter from South Dakota in the United States told Lil Dobson that a chap there was planning to fly to the moon in his aeroplane.

Church and Chapel.

The chapels offered activity every day in men's, women's and young people's groups, in Sunday schools, bible classes and sewing circles. Great occasions were the missionary services, with talk and lantern slides of distant lands. Open air "camp meetings" had stopped but there could be prayers outside a public house for "the sinners within". Wesley Days were marked in Willowgate where the great missioner John Wesley had once preached. The parish church had 200 men attending discussion groups where Vicar Drage brought such famous speakers as "Woodbine Willie". The entire Deanery staged a large religious pageant at the castle in 1930. Co-operation between churches remained rare, but the Sunday Schools combined their annual treats into one, with a special excursion train to Scarborough, where masses of children swept like black ants down Eastborough to sample the joys of the beach. The great Band of Hope Rally of 1935 was also a combined operation. It barely troubled the Public houses, still in the "spittoon and sawdust" era and rarely entered alone by a woman. They sold ale reduced somewhat in strength during the war, but of Malton brew and with a character, and effects now rarely found.

Busy Players.

Many active pursuits flourished. The five tennis clubs were a bit exclusive and so was golf, moving from the nine holes at Rookers in 1921 to an 18 hole course on Thornton Road. Angling Clubs managed the Costa and Pickering becks. Football won most support but cricket was played everywhere. Pride was taken in Robert Frank of Pickering who was for fourteen years captain of the Yorkshire Second Eleven. The Cricket Field was purchased in 1938. A small swimming pool was built in the Memorial Hall and was used by groups divided by sex, whose shouts punctuated Council meetings next door. Crowds walked to the Rosedale Hill Climbs where motor cyclists ran time trials up steep hill roads devoid of tarmac. A Pickering Dramatic Club began in 1926 and has produced plays ever since. The Women's Institute formed in 1924 by Mrs Taylor, Mrs Coverdale and Miss Blench was part of a national movement and was an effective pressure group, pushing for bus shelters, street paving, piped water and telephones. They staged a three day Pickering rural development exhibition in 1925 and their whist drive had half a ton of coals as the first prize for men and a ham for ladies. The Institute were just as active in drama and song, performing "Macbeth" and "Moggeridges Cow" in 1927, while sending their choir to sing at Whitby in the Eskdale Tournament.

Music and Dance.

Pickering was "strong on music and drama". The Pickering Choral Society and the Albion Singers gave way in 1919 to the Pickering Musical Society. They performed Handell's "Messiah" in the church and next year "Cupid and the Ogre". Their "Hiawatha" was performed in the open air theatre at Scarborough in 1933.

There were Pickering, Salvation Army, Skaife's and Stape brass and silver Bands. Arthur Smith's orchestra played for dances, now a craze, with foxtrots, quicksteps and tangos. A Pickering youth could write that the town was very quiet - "no dances or whist drives". He said with feeling, "Lent puts years on me". Soon there could be music at home. Robert Dodson sold Edison phonographs with recordings on cylinders of black wax that played for two minutes. On the better gramophones, you could play Richard Tauber's record of "Somewhere a Voice is Calling".

Wireless.

New entertainments transformed leisure. The radio or "wireless" started with enthusiasts' crystal sets and an "A.B.C. of Wireless" bought form Chris Phillpotts' shop. A "Northern Home Service" of the British Broadcasting Corporation soon offered such regular programmes as "The News" and "Children's Hour" and broadened the enjoyment of music, drama and humour. Austin Hyde, headmaster of Lady Lumley's School, gained fame through the broadcasting of his Yorkshire dialect plays. He sold more than 20,000 copies and they were widely performed. Twenty-four Stape Bandsmen journeyed to Leeds to perform on the BBC in 1935. They were overheard and won an immediate second booking in a nearby cinema. Some of the bandsmen had never seen a city before. Not everyone was overjoyed. Alfred Smith, the 78 year old Allerston blacksmith said in 1939 that he had no room for syncopated music and thought "all wireless sets should be hit with a hammer."

Cinema

Film shows were a novelty, better known as "pictures" or the "flicks" since they did just that. Harold Cooper in 1914 showed them at the Bridge Street Temperance Hall, then converted the Central Hall into a cinema. Silent movies were accompanied by vigorous piano playing, changed by Margaret Pennock and Norah Smith to shift the mood from romantic desert sheiks and maidens to galloping cowboys. By 1920 Pickering had two cinemas showing four different films. A young man wrote "I often go four times a week". The "talkies" of 1929 brought recorded sound with Al Jolson's song 'Sonny Boy' on everyone's lips. Within a year, the cartoon character Mickey Mouse had altered childhood forever. Soon a Norton stable lad was nationally known as ukelele-playing film star George Formby. A purpose built Castle cinema was opened at Pickering by Winnie Allison in 1937. The next year brought Snow White. A new world of romance, adventure and fantasy had invaded our imaginations.

A Modest Tourism.

Dr John Kirk had noticed the changing way of life. He began collecting ordinary people's ordinary things, not yet considered antiques, which were dropping out of use. For a time, many were shown in the Memorial Hall. The incredible collection would be rehoused in a new Folk Museum at York in 1938 with shops and workshops reconstructed in streets to give a proper setting. Pickering craftsmen W. Goodall and A. Wilson took pride in helping to make the first street, called Kirkgate. Pickering visitors came on 13s 4d third class and 31s 5d first class railway journeys from Kings Cross. The castle was "given to the nation" in 1925 and the Ministry of Works made the ruins worth visiting. Four years later forty-five lodgings were advertised at Pickering and as many more in the villages. The Black Swan Inn had telephone number 17 and sported Automobile Association and Cyclists Touring Club badges. Shops sold local pottery and maps for motorists, cyclists and walkers. The Council surfaced some footpaths, put rest seats along them and published a sixpenny guidebook recommending heroic hill walks. It spoke of bracing healthy air, pure water and a town full of "pretty bits", where "old age flourished and Autumnal faces long produced the glow of departing Summer".

The Second Great War.

The Territorial Army reserves were called for war against Germany in September 1939 and went to France and Belgium. In anticipation of air raids, Hull children were evacuated to live with Pickering families and attend junior schools. From Middlesbrough High School, 263 girls in navy gabardine raincoats and wide brimmed velour hats were distributed by the Women's Voluntary Service to new homes and the Lady Lumleys School. Many evacuees soon put on weight but five per cent were said to be difficult. One lad who was continually asked to wash his hands, remarked that "it isn't an evacuee she wants, it's a duck".

Would they Invade?

After a few quiet months, fast moving German armoured forces in a lightening campaign smashed through French and British lines. The army was evacuated from Dunkirk but equipment was lost and many men became prisoners. This was a national disaster and invasion was expected. Church bells stopped ringing, needed to sound alarms. Pickering Home Guards were formed and Air Raid Wardens who practised dealing with incendiary bombs using shovel, sand bucket and stirrup pump. Windows were "blacked out" and gummed with brown paper against blast. Gas masks and identity cards were carried. An army camp was made near the castle and tank barriers built on roads. From July to September 1940 heavy air attacks on British ports and airfields seemed to herald a channel crossing. The barrier presented by the Royal Navy and the fierce defence by fighter pilots in "Hurricane" and "Spitfire" aircraft prevented that invasion.

Air War.

Prolonged bombing brought suffering to Teeside and Hull, their searchlights and "ack ack" gunfire lighting the distant night sky. Two German aviators baled out over Staindale, met by Frank Stead and his double barrelled gun. A Wellington bomber crashed at Upper Carr in 1941 after a Spitfire hit its tail. A Hurricane crashed on Lockton Moor and another Spitfire in Rosedale. A German aircraft gunned the railway station and Undercliffe. Pickering men later served in Bomber Command which, with heavy losses, took the air war back into Europe. Canadian squadrons suffered heavily, flying Halifax and Lancaster bombers from Wombleton airfield.

Home Front.

Young men and women registered for "call up" in 1940 and served in the army, navy, air force and merchant fleet, against Germany, Italy and Japan or in war industries and home defence. There were casualties, a great many though not on the scale of the earlier war. German submarines again nearly stopped the country's essential food and other imports. Rationing allowed each person weekly a few ounces of bacon, sugar and butter. A War Agricultural Committee planned local farming with new areas ploughed up and farm output raised. Gardeners "dug for victory" and Scouts gathered rose hips. The Women's Institute obtained a jam making machine to produce in quantity. A "British Restaurant" was run in the Memorial Hall to provide cheap, nourishing lunches. Iron railings were collected to make tanks. Anything useful was gathered in "salvage drives". Events raised money to buy weapons, through a Spitfire Fund, War Weapons, Wings for Victory, Warship and Salute the Soldier Weeks.

An Army Town.

Local men served in the Middle East and captured Italians were brought to Eden Camp, built to house 1200 prisoners in 1942. The moors above Pickering became a "battle training area", that year. Camps were widespread, country houses commandeered and Pickering welcomed Northumberland Fusiliers, Sherwood Foresters, the 27th Lancers, the Welsh Guards and Polish regiments. A noted film star Richard Greene of the Lancers staged an entertainment in the Castle Cinema. A well known interior and stage design artist Rex Whistler, serving as a Welsh Guards officer, painted large cartoons in the Memorial Hall, for a 1943 children's Christmas party which can still be seen. He was killed in Normandy as the Second Army joined United States forces in landings that started the campaign for the recovery of Western Europe. Russian, British and American forces broke German resistance in 1945 and during August atomic bombs dropped on Hiroshima and Nagasaki led the Japanese to surrender. Tablets placed on the War Memorial record the names of 21 Pickering men killed in the armed services during the second World War.

Peace Again.

The nation returned to a peace time economy, shorn of its wealth spent on war. Pickering kept a military character with the Guards Training Battalion in fifty "Nissen huts" at Castle Camp until 1956. Food and clothes rationing continued but there was a feeling that people had helped each other more during the war and a mood to make more rapid social advances, building on fairer wartime experience. The National Health Service was launched with a broad system of Social Insurance. Houses were short in Pickering for returning service men so twenty families took over a disused Southgate army camp as "squatters", their action approved by the Chairwoman of the Council Housing Committee. A County Library branch was installed in the Memorial Hall which soon gained a reading room and public toilets. A Welfare Clinic was opened in 1955 at Train Lane.

The New Educational Opportunity.

The Lady Lumley Grammar School gave secondary education to fewer than 200 pupils. A 100 children sought entrance in a year but the mere handful of scholarships meant they had to have parents able to pay the fees. A new Education Act ended the fees and if you passed the examination you could go. Numbers rose swiftly and by 1951 there were 320 in a school built to hold 200. David Baxandall succeeded Austen Hyde as headmaster in 1950 and eight years later, he moved the scholars into a new Lady Lumley's School built at Swainsea Lane. It was made comprehensive for all children from eleven years and soon held over 600 pupils. For 20 years, his firm hand at the helm ensured that the school opened up undreamt of channels for local sons and daughters to "do well" and came to frame the young lives of the whole town and district.

Extension of the Lady Lumley new School enabled the County Junior School to open in the Middleton Road building in 1968. University Education became available to those able to qualify for it and a broadening stream went from Pickering.

Struggles for a Market Town.

Pickering had grown to a population of 4193 by 1951 but shrank a little in the next decade, even though a hundred houses were built. Farmland and forestry extended as moor was deep ploughed with new machinery. Farming changes continued after the war with horses and steam engines giving way to tractors. There were some buoyant years as new techniques raised yields though not employment. The town gained an Agricultural Education Centre but there were losses as well as gains. Markets were becoming regional and Pickering Cattle Market finally closed in 1965. Nurseries flourished and Robinson's egg packing station was joined by others. Thornton Dale Mill ceased milling flour and changed to animal feeds and pet foods. Early forest planting had proved of limited value but giant tractors combined with specialised ploughs from Russells of Kirkbymoorside had brought success in penetrating hard soils and suppressing heather. A forest workers village was built at Dalby in 1949. Hargreaves Quarries were active at Pickering and Arthur Slater developed Thornton Dale quarry into a major extraction plant, modified in 1955 to meet village complaints of dust pollution. Then the national government closed railway branch lines including those to Scarborough and Pilmoor in the fifties and the Malton-Pickering-Whitby railway line in 1965.

The Search for New Employments.

Everywhere in Britain now wanted light industries to provide employment. Pickering had an employment exchange and since 1951 a Youth Employment Bureau. Much of their task was inevitably to find local young people work elsewhere, the more so with reduced farm employment. Joseph May's clothing factory opened that year at converted stables in Eastgate bringing new jobs for women. The future lay with out-of-town sites for factories and for farmsteads. When a milk distributor bought a site at Westgate Carr it was the beginning of a small but early industrial park. Derwent Plastics opened a factory there in 1970 for the manufacture of plastic mouldings and brought many valuable jobs. The threat of attack by unmanned missiles from Soviet Russia led to an "Early Warning Station" becoming operational in 1963 at Lockton Highmoor providing new kinds of employment. It was already clear that as more numerous cars made journeying easier, jobs and homes were less often together and it was as important that Kirkbymoorside saw Micro Metalsmiths and Slingsby Sailplanes develop. Several industries prospered within reach at other towns and villages. Countryside tourism was not helped by railway closures but coastal resorts had buoyant seasons till cheap air travel brought the fatal allure of overseas sun. Wider car ownership began a change. A National Park declared in 1952 covered most of the North Yorkshire Moors and Dales, including Thornton but only the most rural northern parts of Pickering Parish. Its impact lay in the future. A bold development saw Pentland Hick in 1962 create a Flamingo Park Zoo at Kirkby Misperton. He saw a need for a day tripper attraction closer to the populated centres than Scarborough. As Flamingoland it became a major attraction and a source of employment.

Pickering blossomed with societies new and old. Many had social service and charitable aims; the Volunteer Fire Service, Red Cross, Toc H and W.R.V.S. Memberships were broader than the town for Ryedale Rotary and Ryedale Lions Clubs. Sports clubs ran angling, badminton, billiards, bridge, men and women's cricket, football, hockey, motoring, pistol and rifle shooting and tennis. Polly Marshall went to play cricket for the Yorkshire Ladies team in 1952, and for England 1954-1960, with tours of Australia, New Zealand and South Africa. Pickering societies supported allotments, brass bands, cage birds, drama, freemasonry, pigeons, music, temperance, trade unionism and the United Nations Wesleyan and Primitive Methodist circuits amalgamated in 1951, a merger made practical with a later union of chapels at Potter Hill. The Church of England gained an old school as a Parish Hall in Hallgarth. Business and Professional Women formed a club in 1954, the year when Thornton Dale Players staged their first play. There were active Women's Institutes, whose demonstrations had prepared the way for the craft classes of busy Evening Institutes. Playgroups started in 1965 for four year olds and vigorous Youth clubs ran at the School. Some clubs secured their own buildings including a new Working Men's Club and the British Legion. A new Bowling green and Club house opened at Mill Lane where the Recreation Ground gained a new pavilion. Alan Pickup started a Ryedale Sports Club as a cricket club for those unable to get a game, but it soon branched into other sports. Mrs Berry Heap led the voluntary effort that created an Over Sixties all day Club house in Hungate in 1967. These were the decades for volunteers, when regular old folks Christmas parties and meals on wheels services began. Other enthusiasts in 1967 formed the Beck Isle Museum and others started a Railway Preservation Society to undertake the colossal task of re-opening a North Yorkshire Moors Railway.

High Day and Holidays.

The "Holidays at Home" movement fostered annual town Carnival weeks from 1949 ending with processions of floats prepared by each street. A Pickering Sports Committee started Northern Traction Engine Derbies in 1953 when four great engines 53 years old, raced for 5000 people and Ernest Mortimer steamed to victory. The third Derby had 42 engines on show and a 1964 rally claimed a 30,000 crowd. Dialect was vanishing but a local observed "Ah cam ta see t'ractions and 'ave 'ad mi money's wo'th". Home entertainment was also changing. The first television reception from Holme Moss came in October 1951 and some sets were hired to watch the Coronation of 1953. Electricians Hill and Jackson and Television House were soon installing them all over. A Traction Engine rally was the first town event televised. Mrs Dorothy Sleightholme of Pickering, made her T.V. debut in 1959 and became a familiar face to millions as the Yorkshire T.V. presenter of the "Farmhouse Kitchen" programme.

Expanding Again.

Then came the expansion. The 4186 people of 1961 in 10 years rose to 4545. A confident Council with women among its members, and with powers to build houses, started Council estates at St Nicholas Way in 1956 that would spread and ease the housing shortage. The council removed bad old housing, bought a grass cutting machine for town verges and pioneered old peoples houses with a Warden Service. The widening of approach roads and a traffic roundabout altered the town's main road junction in 1960. A new fire station, court house and police station were built nearby and a larger library opened in Market Place. The old Eastgate cattle market was made into a large car park. Changing technology in the wider world had influence too. There was talk of birth control clinics. The telephone exchange became automatic. Banks put in accounting machines and a launderette made new washing machines familiar.

The Leap Forward.

Pickering changed with dramatic growth. Instead of 4545 in 1971 there were 6269 people in 1991. A builder's boom took housing estates into fields while older houses were improved until there were 2856 houses. Most of the old town was made into a conservation area in 1972. In the whole community, balance was altered between natives and new comers, youth and age. Retiring pensioners could sell a high price house elsewhere and buy cheaper at Pickering, with a useful sum left over. Young couples came to benefit from new employments, often not at Pickering itself.

Government at a Distance.

As change became dramatic, the power to influence it moved away. Local government re-organisation in 1974 removed decision making from councils at Pickering to the County Council and a new Ryedale District Council managing a vast area. Local involvement became modest. A Town Council with few powers survived to do what it could. Many services probably gained in professional expertise and improved. Certainly the roads did. The County Council steadily gave them surfaces suitable to a motorised age. Local democracy lost out and public interest waned.

A Place to Work.

The very widespread ownership of cars made for greater change. Distant employment, shopping and leisure were possible for the majority with cars. Inevitably this would alter community ties. It mattered less whether there was a job in Pickering than one somewhere in reach. The town centre still kept builders merchants and joinery works, the fringes kept hauliers, while out of town farming, nurseries and forestry remained important though employing fewer men. Pickering remained fortunate in its large local employer. The Derwent Plastics factory at Westgate Carr expanded over 30 years to become McKechnie Vehicle Components, its products widely demanded. A second industrial estate was opened at Thornton Road. These two clusters of small factories, workshops and warehouses added other employments to make up for the loss of town printers, clothing factory, sawmill and much local quarrying. Significant employers in the wider district in food processing, metal preparation and prefabrication and specialised engineering were joined in 1998 by the Central Science Laboratory at Sand Hutton.

A Place to Enjoy.

Reg Harvey realised that Pickering had a town scene worth caring for. He was given the BEM for annually planting daffodils on grass verges. When railway closure left a blighted goods yard, a road was cut through it in 1976 to link Market Place and Hungate, removing a signal box and a seat where distinguished Pickering men had once made their first serious essays into social life. John Paul refurbished some old railway buildings and led a voluntary group to make a riverside walk framing a new central car park. A medical centre and a new library were built alongside and a multi-angular toilet to complete the scene. When a supermarket was built behind the Market Place conveniently near the car park, the town centre was saved for another day and planning control was thought to have served the town well.

A Place to Shop.

Prosperity and better health care changed every life. Weight watching outnumbered malnutrition. Washing machines left launderettes and came home along with central heating and microwave ovens. The changes were legion and the rise in living standards dramatic though each generation took what it found for granted. Pickering saw these things like anywhere else. In the process it lost a little individuality. Refrigerators and freezers in shop and home, altered food preparation and storage while self service proved cheaper than service. Many small food shops of the seventies gave way to a large supermarket in the eighties. The variety of shops shrank more than the variety of goods. Several retail trades seemed unaffected but shopping also became a travelling matter and giant specialist shops beckoned on the fringes of York and Scarborough. If there were more things, there were also more second hand things. Jumble sales gave way to nearly new fairs, then huge car boot sales and finally charity shops. Pickering Market place changed to meet the trade that there was. Estate Agents, new video and computers stores, charity shops and tourist gift shops filled the gaps. The cafes and fish and chip shops of the sixties were joined by large new cafes and Chinese and Indian restaurants answered shifting national food fashions to make a Yorkshire ham tea a rarity.

A Place to Visit.

Voluntary effort played a great part in fostering a tourist boom. The Railway Preservation Society made Pickering the southern terminus of the North York Moors Railway. People came in growing numbers to travel in steam trains as nostalgia gripped the nation. The town centre was often "throng" with visitors. Moorland Trout Farms offered angling experiences. Public houses, gave up best ends and rough ends and offered meals. The Castle attracted more, as "English Heritage" improved what it offered. Much of the trade was day trippers adding modestly to the local economy but country holidays expanded too. Caravan camps were joined by forest cabins, farm holidays, a holiday village, Luxury Holiday Cottage precincts, upgraded Inns and the whole variety of private accommodation. Tourists with good cars on better roads used Pickering or a village as a base to explore the coast and a wider country. A Tourist Information Office and new Holiday Cottage agencies helped. Stan Johnson opened a War Museum at Eden Camp in 1987, another instant attraction. Flamingoland could attract a million in a year and rate among the nations top attractions. A TV. series "Heartbeat" made Goathland a major destination. Tourism also has its good and bad seasons and recessions eased off traffic below boom year peaks. The National Park and the Councils retained responsibility for ensuring that tourism didn't destroy what it came to seek.

A Place for Leisure.

Pickering continued to add assets to its stock. New societies supported art, horticulture, judo, netball, Scottish dancing, single parent families and twinning with Corbie in France or worked for national charities. The Ryedale Swimming Pool opened at Mill Lane in 1974 was a major gain for local people and visitors alike. So was the founding of the Kirk Theatre by the members of the Pickering Musical Society and the opening by Yorkshire Olympic athlete Peter Elliot of a fine Sports Centre. The Workings Mens Club secured a new Club house. The Cinema added a play area called a fun factory. The Isabella Court, Day and Residential Centre opened at Keld Head by the Wilf Ward family foundation provided a respite for people with handicapped family members. In 1995 six doctors developed a new Health Centre in Southgate. Volunteers produced a first Community letter in 1998.

And a Few Good Do's.

It is a measure of community life if a place comes together for a good do. Don Chapman revived Pickering Carnivals in 1972 with decorated float processions continued in later years by Ryedale Lions Club. Queen Elizabeth II visited Pickering Castle to meet her tenants and was warmly received at a Castle Road walkabout. A new Ryedale Round Table ran street pram races till no prams were left and annual Pickering Market Place Feasts, one year famously converting their all male membership into female Majorettes. It was probably their finest hour. James Herriots story "All Creatures Great and Small" was filmed in the town. John Pearson directed historical Pageants at Smiddy Hill and the Castle. The 1981 Royal Wedding celebrations included a Teddy Bear Rally. Joe Passey started the successful annual Pickering Jazz Festivals and young townsman Simon Boak has through recent years staged traction engine rallies, trucking spectaculars and feasts. After celebration of the Queen's Jubilee ended with the customary torch lit march to Beacon Hill to light the great bonfire, George Blakeley, who had first come to Pickering as a war time evacuee, wrote - "It was above all a community do. Pickering is perhaps unique in the way it can get together".

BOOKS OF REFERENCE

Akerman, J. Yonge, Remains of Pagan Saxondom, 1852-55.
Allen, J. R., Monumental History of the Early British Church, 1889.
Anecdotes and Manners of a few Ancient and Modern Oddities, 1806.
Anthropological Institute of Great Britain and Ireland, Journal of.
Associated Architectural Societies' Reports, vol. xii.
Atkinson, John C., A Glossary of the Cleveland Dialect, 1876; Forty Years in a Moorland Parish, 1891.
Bateman, Thomas, Ten Years' Diggings, 1861.
Bawdwen, Rev. W., Domesday Book, 1809.
Belcher, Henry, The Pickering and Whitby Railway, 1836.
Blakeborough, Richard, Wit, Character, etc., of the North Riding of Yorkshire, 1898.
Brooke, John C., Illustration of a Saxon Inscription at Kirkdale, 1777.
Brown, Gerard Baldwin, The Arts in Early Britain, 1903.
Browne, G. F., Bishop of Bristol, Theodore and Wilfrith, 1897; The Conversion of the Heptarchy, 1896.
Buckland, Wm., Dean of Westminster, Account of Fossil Bones at Kirkdale, 1822.
Chaucer, Geoffrey, Canterbury Tales, 1902.
Cholmley, Sir Hugh, Bart., Memoirs of, 1787.
Clark, George Thos., Mediæval Military Architecture in England, 1884.
Codrington, Thos., C.E., Roman Roads in Britain, 1903.
Collection of above 300 Receipts in Cookery, Physick, and Surgery, 1719.
Corlass, R. W., Yorkshire Rhymes and Sayings, 1878.
Croll, James, Climate and Time in their Geological Relations, 1885.
Dawkins, Boyd, Early Man in Britain.

Books of Reference

Domesday Book, Facsimile of the Survey by Col. Sir H. James, 1861-63.

Drake, Francis, Eboracum, 1736.

Eastmead, William, Historia Rievallensis, 1824.

England, Annals of, 1876.

Fawcett, Rev. Joshua, Church Rides in the Neighbourhood of Scarborough, 1848.

Frank, George, Ryedale, North Yorkshire Antiquities, 1888.

Fuller, Thomas, The History of the Worthies of England, 1840.

Gidley, Lewis, Bede's Ecclesiastical History of the English Church, 1870.

Giles, J. A., Bede's Ecclesiastical History of the English Church, 1840.

Gould, S. Baring, Yorkshire Oddities, 1874.

Hailstone, Edward the Elder, Portraits of Yorkshire Worthies, 1869.

Hatton, W. H., and Fox, W. E., The Churches of Yorkshire, 1879.

Henderson, William, Notes on the Folklore of the North Counties, 1879.

Hinderwell, Thomas, History of Scarborough, 1798.

Holinshed, Raphael, Chronicles of England, 1807-8.

Jackson, R. E. Scoresby, The Life of William Scoresby, 1861.

Jewitt, Llewellyn, The Ceramic Art in Early Britain, 1883; Grave Mounds and their Contents, 1870.

Leland, John, The Itinerary of.

Marshall, William, The Rural Economy of Yorkshire, 1788.

Morris, Joseph E., The North Riding of Yorkshire, 1904.

Morris, M. C. F., Yorkshire Folk Talk, 1892.

Murray's Handbook for Yorkshire, 1904.

North Riding Records, 1894 and after. Edited by R. B. Turton.

Park, G. R., The Parliamentary Representation of Yorkshire, 1886.

Parkinson, Rev. Thos., Yorkshire Legends and Traditions, 1888.

Roy, Major-General Wm., The Military Antiquities of the Romans in Britain, 1793.

Scoresby, Wm., the Elder, Memorials of the Sea, 1851.

Smith, William, Old Yorkshire, 1881.

Stow, John, A Summarie of Englyshe Chronicles, etc., 1565

Books of Reference

Strangways, C. E. Fox, Geology of Oolitic and Liassic Rocks North of Malton, 1881; Geology of Country between Whitby and Scarborough, 1846; The Jurassic Rocks of Britain, 1846.

Tacitus, P. C., The Works of, Oxford Translation, 1848.

Windle, B. C. A., Remains of the pre-Historic Age in England, 1904; Life in Early Britain, 1897.

Yorkshire Archæological and Topographical Association, Record Series, 1894 and after.

Yorkshire Archæological Journal, Vol. V., 1879.

Young, George, A History of Whitby, 1817.

APPENDIX

A LIST OF THE VICARS OF PICKERING

THE living itself, at the time of the Norman Conquest, came into the possession of the Crown, and remained at the king's gift till Henry I. annexed it to the Deanery of York. It thus became one of the Dean's peculiars, until in the last century his property was vested in the Ecclesiastical Commissioners, and the patronage transferred to the Archbishop.

1150	Hugh	
13—?	Midelton, Thos de. Resigned for the Church of Scalton	
1341	Acaster, Hen de.	Dismissed
1349	Queldriks, Robert de	
	Pokelington, Robert de. Resigned for the Church at Holtby	
1388	Laytingby, Will de	
1568-1570	Coleman, William	
1581-1600	Owrome, William	
1602-1615	Mylls or Milnes, Edward. Deprived 1615	
1615-1659	Bright, Edward.	Died 1659

Appendix

1661-1690	Staveley, Robert.		Died 1690
1691-1712	Newton, Joshua, A.M.		Died 1712
1713-1740	Hargreaves, Robert.		Died 1740
1740	Hill, Samuel		
1745	Dodsworth, George		
1764-1784	Harding, Samuel.	(Blind.)	Died 1784
1784-1786	Robinson, John		
1786-1804	Harding, Samuel J.		Died 1804
1804-1809	Laye, W. T.		Died 1809
1809-1814	Graham, C. R.		
1814-1857	Ponsonby, F.		
1858-1863	Cockburn, G. A., M.A.		
1863-1875	Bennett, Edward	(Curate-in-charge)	
1875-1881	Lightfoot, G. H.	(Curate-in-charge)	
1881-1902	,, ,,	(Vicar)	
1902	Drage, E. W.		

"*Here taketh the Makere of this Book his Leve.*"

"*Now preye I to hem alle that herkne this litel tretys or rede, that . . . if ther be any thyng that displese hem, I preye hem also that they arrette it to the defaute of myn unkonnynge, and not to my wyl, that wolde ful fayn have seyd bettre if I hadde had konnynge.*"

Chaucer's Canterbury Tales.

INDEX

Index

Index

Index